ADAK

ADAK
The Rescue of
Alfa Foxtrot 586

Andrew C. A. Jampoler

NAVAL INSTITUTE PRESS
ANNAPOLIS, MARYLAND

Naval Institute Press
291 Wood Road
Annapolis, MD 21402

Library of Congress Cataloging-in-Publication Data
Jampoler, Andrew C. A., 1942–
Adak: the rescue of Alfa Foxtrot 586 / Andrew C. A.
Jampoler.
p. cm.
Includes bibliographical references.
ISBN 1-59114-412-4 (alk. paper)
1. Aircraft accidents—Alaska—Aleutian Islands Region.
2. Search and rescue operations—Alaska—Aleutian
Islands Region. 3. Aeronautics, Military—Accidents—
Alaska—Aleutian Islands Region. 4. Aircraft accidents—
Investigation—United States. 5. Survival after airplane
accidents, shipwrecks, etc.
I. Title.
TL553 .525 .A4J35 2003
363 .12'481'097983—dc21
2002013560

Printed in the United States of America on acid-free paper ∞
10 09 08 07 06 05 04   9 8 7 6 5 4

Illustrations courtesy of Rob Ebersol

This is the flight crew's story.
It is dedicated to them,
to those who survived and
to the memory of those
who did not.

Contents

Acknowledgments

The "Findings of Fact" in each chapter are quoted from the Judge Advocate General (JAG) investigation conducted by then–Lt. Cdr. James A. Dvorak, U.S. Navy, of Patrol Squadron 9, in November and December 1978 immediately after the ditching. His cooperation is gratefully acknowledged, as is the generous assistance of Ed Caylor, Ed Flow, Bruce Forshay, Matt Gibbons, Howard Moore, Garland Shepard, and John Wagner, whose story this is.

Other welcome help came from interviews of or correspondence with Aleksandr Arbuzov (former master of the *Mys Sinyavin*), Bruce Barth, Cynthia Beck, Chris Behrens, Geoff Birchard, John Branchflower (DF 704), L. Anthony Bracken (naval attaché, Moscow), Jim Burk, Jim Carman, Cliff Carter (Scone 92), Mary Casto, Pat Conway (XF 675), Pete Cressy (Patrol Squadron 9), Dave DeVarney, Mitchell Dukovitch, Allen Efraimson, Alan Feldkamp (Scone 92), Jon Feller, Rory Fisher (Patrol Squadron 9), Carol Flow, Randall Flynn, Nevins Frankel, John Frost, Robert Hay Jr., Jerry Holland, Lorren Jackson, Rick Kirkland, Dick Klass, Phillip Kolczynski, Kathleen Kujawa, Rachel Lewis, Perry Martini (aide and flag lieutenant, commander, Patrol Wings Pacific Fleet), Ralph McClintock (USS *Pueblo*), Mark Mergard, Denny Mette (XF 675) and Cindy Mette, Skip Miner, Larry Mitchell (24th SRS), Bob Myer (JB 022), Rod O'Connor (USCGC *Ironwood*), Joanne Petrie, Bill Porter (CG 1500), Bud Powers (Patrol Squadron 9), John Powers (CG 1600), Ron Price (XF 675), Al Ross, Chris Schroeder, John Shackleton (public affairs, NAS Moffett Field), Vladimir Shevlyakov, Philip Silvestri, Brenda Hemmer Smith, Sharon Snyder, Louis Tavares, Tony Tuliano (USCGC *Jarvis*), Dave Vonderheide, Shelly Wagner, Scott Wilson, and John Yackus. Any errors are, of course, my responsibility.

My thanks also to Al and Jo Hart, my agents, for their encouragement, assistance, and counsel, and especially to Suzy, my wife of thirty-seven years, who worked while I imagined myself an author.

Introduction

A line of bright, red triangles, dramatically annotated "Ring of Fire," lies immediately above the Aleutian Islands in one of the National Geographic Society's maps of the Pacific Ocean. The symbols announce that the earth is restless along this seam where the North American and Pacific tectonic plates meet, a work in progress. The eternal, grinding collision of these plates ensures that the Aleutians experience frequent earthquakes, hundreds in an average month. Most are barely detectable, but several temblors in the last century were rated on the Richter scale as 8 and above, each as powerful as the 1906 quake that devastated San Francisco.

Even the earth's magnetic field seems to be still under construction here. Aeronautical charts of the area are sprinkled with cautions about large magnetic disturbances over short distances, making conventional "wet" compasses unreliable guides to direction. The caution for Kagalaska in the central Aleutians, one mile east of Adak Island across a narrow strait, is typical of these warnings. "Magnetic disturbance of as much as 11° exists at ground level near the northwest end of Kagalaska Island," it announces in bold magenta type.

Extremes of topography and weather assemble naturally in this region, too. The eponymous Aleutian Trench lies just south of the islands. At its deepest point, the waters of the trench go down 4,200 fathoms, almost 4.8 miles, putting it among the great submarine canyons of the world. The shallow Bering Sea, north of the archipelago, with its notorious rogue waves and dense ice fogs as opaque as milk, has been a famous killing ground for fishing ships for three centuries.

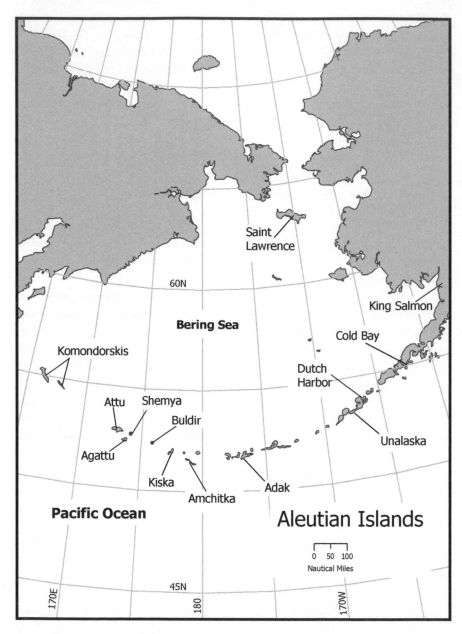

The Aleutian Islands and the Bering Sea

Two circular ocean currents bracket the islands north and south, slowly churning unimaginable quantities of cold salt water past the Aleutians in counterclockwise loops, or "gyres." On an oceanic scale, these gyres on both sides of the Aleutian chain are relatively small; nevertheless, they influence the rich marine life of the region and help shape its dramatic weather.

The Aleutians appear to have been first settled by native peoples moving to the islands from east to west, backfilled about eight thousand years ago, perhaps three millennia after the Bering land bridge that once connected Asia to North America was submerged beneath rising waters. ("Land bridge" erroneously suggests a fragile connection. In reality, the "bridge" was one thousand miles across.) The retrograde pattern of settlement suggests that the inhospitable, treeless islands—the peaks of submarine volcanoes once the ice cap withdrew and the ocean rose—were no one's first choice as a domicile, judged inferior even to the bleak Arctic Ocean shore that still sustains the Eskimo of mainland Alaska and the Inuit of Canada.[1]

The second Kamchatka Expedition of Discovery, led by Vitus Bering, a Danish-born, Russian navy officer, opened the Aleutians after 1740 to Russian hunters and trappers. It also brought catastrophe to the islands' native peoples, whom the Russians named "Aleuts."

There were not many Aleuts (they called themselves "Unangan") when the Russians came, perhaps never more than twenty-five thousand, wresting a difficult life in small dug-out hovels, hunting the mammals of the sea and fishing its waters from high-prowed *baidarkas,* rugged oceangoing canoes. Mean conditions on the islands for their human residents were offset by the Aleutians' generosity to their other fauna. The region once teemed with seals and sea otters, but these animals unwittingly committed the error of being worth more dead than alive. The sea otters' beautiful coats (the sleek beasts had no layer of fat to keep them warm and relied entirely on their thick fur for insulation in cold water) made them especially precious.

Lured to the islands by the descriptions of Bering's naturalist, Georg Steller, the first of the *promysloviki* (Russian trappers and skinners), reached Attu, westernmost of the Aleutians, in late 1745. Thousands of valuable skins were taken from the islands each year after that (more than 350,000 sealskins alone in one record season; the annual average was perhaps one-fifth of that) until the populations of these animals nearly collapsed under the weight of predation. By 1820, even the sea otters offshore the small Russian settlement on the central California coast were almost gone.[2]

Under somewhat similar pressures, the Aleut population crashed, too. In 1845, one Russian missionary estimated there were fewer than twenty-five hundred Aleuts alive; one hundred years later, a new estimate put the number at about fourteen hundred. Battles against Russians, slavery, servitude, disease (smallpox, tuberculosis, and the flu epidemic of 1808–9), famine, and alcoholism had taken away the rest. In two short centuries of contact with outsiders, the Aleuts had been very nearly driven to extinction.[3]

The Russian thrust across the North Pacific behind Vitus Bering (and Alexi Chirikov, his principal subordinate) was slender, but it had a long reach. Southbound Russians would eventually brush up—gently, their occasional meetings appear to have been wary but cordial—near today's San Francisco against northbound Spaniards, who were busily planting missions up the California coast to strengthen their own territorial claims and control over natives. But in time there would be little evidence left of the Russian presence on the Pacific Coast of North America: the occasional exotic structure (the onion-domed, Russian Orthodox Church at Ninilchik, Alaska, for example, or the restored Fort Ross on the California coast north of Bodega Bay); a few place names (the Russian River and Sebastopol, named after the Crimean seaport, in Sonoma County, California); and the gene pool of Alaska's native peoples.

The purchase of Alaska by the United States in 1867 substituted neglect for abuse, a condition which persisted until mid-1942. That is when the islanders were hastily relocated to the Alaskan mainland after the Japanese attacked Dutch Harbor on Unalaska Island as part of their Operation MI, a powerful, two-pronged trans-Pacific thrust.[4] In the north, the bombing of Dutch Harbor and Japanese amphibious landings on Attu and Kiska triggered a harsh and meaningless campaign in the Aleutians remembered as the "thousand mile war," one that cost many lives but had no influence on the larger conflict.

Operation MI's much more important southern offensive, on cornflower-blue seas in the mid-Pacific, ended in flaming disaster for the Imperial Japanese Navy (IJN). On 4 June 1942, in the most decisive battle involving Americans since Gettysburg, two U.S. Navy task forces sent four Japanese aircraft carriers and their air wings to the bottom northwest of tiny Midway Island. The successful ambush was possible only because cryptanalysts squirreled away at Station Hypo, in the basement of Pacific Fleet headquarters, knew Admiral Yamamoto's plans. They had been reading the IJN's encrypted radio transmissions. The lopsided loss—it cost the Americans only two ships, the carrier USS *Yorktown* and the destroyer USS *Hammann*—sank Japan's offensive ambitions at sea. For the rest of the war, the IJN played defense with growing desperation.

Three years later, immediately after World War II, the last of the Aleutian expatriates were allowed to return to their barren home islands. The returnees were resettled in half a dozen sites. No one settled on Adak Island, near the center of the chain. Instead, during the next forty years the U.S. Navy developed the northeast corner of Adak as an important base for cold war submarine surveillance and radio signals intelligence collection. The rest of the island remained uninhabited.

Chapter 1

Crew Six

In late October 1978, Patrol Squadron 9's Crew 6, Lt. Cdr. Jerry Grigsby's crew, flew from Naval Air Station Moffett Field, California, to Naval Station Adak, Alaska, for what everyone aboard the aircraft assumed would be the second and last six-week deployment to their parent squadron's detachment in the Aleutian Islands. Their route of flight was north up the jet airways along the Pacific Coast, then across the Gulf of Alaska, passing abeam distant Anchorage, and, finally, generally west out along the long, drooping arc of islands that formed the Aleutian archipelago to Adak. With the usual headwinds en route and at the cruising speed of their P-3 Orion turboprop, Moffett to Adak was an eight-hour flight.

Eight hours were enough to transport them to a different world. In those few hours, Grigsby's crew would be exchanging a mild autumn in California's Santa Clara Valley (dubbed Silicon Valley; during the next twenty years it would become the technology capital of the world) and the benign San Francisco Bay for early winter at a rocky and spare outpost, little changed since the end of World War II, on the stormy Bering Sea: Adak Island, "the birthplace of the winds."[1]

Adak, about 280 inhospitable square miles shaped like a Rorschach blot, is one of the larger Andreanof Islands of the Aleutian Islands chain. It lies roughly halfway between Seattle and Japan, at approximately 51°45' north latitude, 176°40' west longitude, close to the great circle navigation routes between the American Pacific Northwest and East Asia. The island is very near to the mid-point of the track from one continent to the other. From Adak it is thirteen hundred miles to Anchorage, fourteen hundred miles to Sakhalin Island, and closer still to the Kamchatka Peninsula and the infamous gateway to the Siberian Gulag, Magadan.

In an earlier era, a full squadron of twelve crews and nine aircraft would have deployed to Adak from its home station in California or Hawaii and hunted submarines from this base in the Aleutians for five or six months until relieved by another squadron. The cycle took squadrons away from their home stations for one-third of the time, leaving to the other two-thirds a heavy load of training and local area operations. This wearying peacetime operational tempo, months away from family and friends followed by long hours at work while at home, was one of the reasons that Navy junior officer and enlisted personnel retention was at near-permanent crisis levels.

At its peak, Naval Station Adak supported six thousand Navy people and their families, including civilian employees of the station and its tenant organizations. Also included in that number were the 350 or so officers and enlisted men of the rotating patrol squadron, who would deploy to the island while their families remained behind. Adak's maximum population gave it the status of a very large town in Alaska. By the late 1970s, down to just over three thousand residents, Adak was still the eleventh largest community in the state.

At the end of the 1970s, the level of Soviet Navy activity in the North Pacific was such that a full squadron at Misawa Air Base on northern Honshu, Japan, and a three-plane detachment at Adak were sufficient to meet U.S. Seventh and Third Fleet requirements in the region. The days when huge Soviet submarines would come speeding submerged out of Petropavlovsk or from the Bering Sea through the Amukta Pass to take up missile patrol stations in the Pacific had not yet passed, but Soviet naval activity in the Indian Ocean, where the U.S. Navy had no fleet permanently assigned, had compelled the Americans to redistribute assets to those remote and unfamiliar waters.

Under the 1978 deployment schedule, Grigsby's Crew 6 would miss Thanksgiving at home but would be back in California in time for Christmas. Another squadron would relieve Patrol Squadron 9, the Golden Eagles, at Adak early in December. Five months later, the process would repeat itself. The exchange of one squadron for another would keep the Adak detachment's complement at the prescribed four crews and three aircraft indefinitely, until strength reductions and more urgent operational requirements eventually siphoned the small force off into other waters.

Once back from Adak, Patrol Squadron 9 would be at home until early summer, when it would leave California with all its crews and aircraft for six months in Japan. In 1979, the wing's deployment schedule would make up for its generosity in 1978. The squadron would spend a lonely Christmas at Misawa Air Base on Japan's big island, Honshu.

In the few days immediately following Crew 6's arrival on Adak, the pilots and flight engineer flew the obligatory airspace familiarization flights and the standard instrument departures and approaches they would follow to get away from and back to the field during Adak's famously bad weather, when pilots said the clouds were stuffed with granite. From overhead, they could see again how the naval station's two short runways were shoehorned in between Kuluk Bay, Mount Moffett, and Tacan Hill on the island's northeast corner, five miles south of the abandoned World War II airfield on Clam Lagoon.

Together on the ground, everyone on the crew had trekked from the detachment's hangar to the adjacent Tactical Support Center (TSC) and listened to the required area familiarization brief. With that briefing, their reindoctrination to U.S. Third Fleet maritime patrol operations in the North Pacific was complete, and Crew 6 found itself once again in the hopper, eligible to be put into the crew rotation by the detachment schedules officer.

During the next six weeks, the crew's officers and enlisted sensor operators could expect to go into the Tactical Support Center, a complex of interconnected, windowless vans that resembled a small and claustrophobic trailer park, thirty or forty times, perhaps even more often. The vans contained several compact briefing theaters, rooms full of mission replay and acoustic analysis equipment, and what amounted to a large closet crammed with powerful communications transceivers with near-hemispheric reach. Yet another room was filled with tall computers standing shoulder to shoulder next to drives mutely spinning large rolls of half-inch magnetic tape from reel to reel behind glass doors, like men twiddling their thumbs.

All operational flights would begin and end at the TSC, as would every fourth day, when the crew stood one-hour alert duty. At Adak, the days of the week had no particular meaning. Saturdays, Sundays, and holidays were just like any other working day, and time off was snatched in packets of a few hours at a time, but each triangular trip between sleeping quarters, the TSC, and their assigned aircraft would become part of the rhythm of a crew's deployment by marking a step closer to California and home.

The first step would be today, 26 October. Crew 6 was scheduled to meet at the TSC a few hours before sunrise, to be briefed on Event Alfa Kilo 262, their first operational flight since returning to Adak.[2]

Adak is at about the latitude of London. At the end of October, the sun rises late over the island and sets early. The days are short and cold, and the weather is often violent. Thursday, 26 October, would not be especially bad by the standards of the Aleutians. The island would spend the day under decks of clouds layered almost five miles high, in and out of snow showers, and with up to thirty-three knots (nearly forty miles per hour) of wind blowing fitfully out of the southwest. Not balmy, but not bad. The next few days were expected to be much worse, thanks to a weather system sweeping in from the Bering Sea and headed for the Gulf of Alaska down a familiar storm track over the Aleutians.

AK 262 was a special mission, a PARPRO flight. The acronym stood for Peacetime Airborne Reconnaissance Program, a collective term for carefully coordinated reconnaissance events around the periphery of the Soviet Union.[3] Every month an elaborate politico-military planning process in Washington, D.C., ground out the PARPRO schedule, codifying a balance between what the intelligence officers said they needed to stay abreast of the Soviets' electronic warfare order of battle, what operators said the available ships, submarines, and aircraft could do, and what diplomats said the international political situation would tolerate. Event AK 262—a round trip, Adak to Adak in nine hours—was a single line on the October schedule, where it was identified as Beggar Heritage mission 50V3J8, flying on track 5J2571.

Later, in public statements to the news media after the plane went down, the flight would be described blandly as a "routine ocean surveillance air patrol." That is the phrase White House Press Secretary Jody Powell used in early November to characterize it. But it was not routine.

Grigsby's mission was to take his aircraft and crew west from their base in the Aleutian Islands, past Attu and nearly to the Kamchatka coast of Siberia, home to some of the Soviet Union's most sensitive military installations in the Far East. Once there, specialists in the Pentagon and at the National Security Agency hoped the flight would excite the Soviet air defense system into energizing its search radars and exercising its tactical communications. American intelligence collection units in the air and on the ground, focused intently on the aircraft and on the response its flight was expected to stimulate, would record everything the Russians radiated for later analysis. The whole process was watched over from afar by a command entity called Sky King. The call sign of Sky King's radio voice, Burning Bush, suggested an origin more divine than regal.

Maritime patrol aircrews disliked PARPRO missions. The flights were boring, long, and elaborate communications and navigation drills, with no upside but plenty of opportunity for conspicuous and embarrassing procedural errors, nothing like the airborne chess games pitting aircraft against submarine that crews relished. Patrol Squadron 9 crews had committed some of these comm errors in the past, most recently in mid-August, when Crew 5 had reported an incorrect position—one just inside of the standoff boundary to the Soviet landmass—during a PARPRO event. The crew's new tactical coordinator, or tacco, Lt. (jg) Matt Gibbons, had been admonished in writing for his uncharacteristic error—failing to supervise outgoing radio transmissions. Lt. Rory Fisher, the pilot flying in command of his first tactical mission, had been embarrassed, too. Now the squadron's policy was to have an extra navigator/communicator aboard, a "PARPRO rider," to assist the crew nav/comm as necessary.

Event AK 262 was not exactly chum—the Russians were not expected to bite; they had not in many years of watching PARPRO flights troll provocatively past— but it clearly was a lure with a special purpose.[4] And who could really tell what the Soviets might do?

Five years later, in September 1983, Lt. Col. Gennadi Osipovich would take his SU-15 fighter up from Dolinsk-Sokol Air Base, on Sakhalin Island, and obediently put two missiles into Korean Air Lines flight 007. He would do that despite the certain knowledge that the big Boeing transport in front of him was not a U.S. Air Force RC-135 intelligence collection aircraft. The shoot down would kill 269 innocent people, en route from Anchorage to Seoul in a B-747 and miles off course. (Retired years earlier, Osipovich would still be defiantly unrepentant during a 1996 interview, happy that his act had moved him to the head of the waiting list for a telephone in his quarters on base but bitter that his cash performance bonus for the attack had been only two hundred rubles. He had expected four hundred, about one month's pay.)

Five men, taking turns in the three flight station seats, two pilots' and one flight engineer's, would take the aircraft out and bring it home. Ten others would be riding in the "tube," the tactical compartment, crammed with sub-hunting electronics equipment. Most of that equipment would lie fallow during this flight.

Finding of Fact. Lieutenant Commander Jerry Carson Grigsby, USN, 445-38-4123/1310, was a designated Naval Aviator fully qualified to act as Patrol Plane Commander/Mission Commander aboard aircraft Buno 159892 on 26 October 1978.

It must have been 3:45 A.M. or so, and very dark outside, when Jerry Grigsby got up from his bed in the squadron's wing of the two-story Bachelor Officers' Quarters at Naval Station Adak, Alaska. He had agreed to meet some members of his crew at 4:15, and half an hour would have been more than enough time for him to clean up, get into flight gear and walk to the lobby of the BOQ. In daylight, the view from the officers' quarters took in the airfield and many of the naval station's buildings. At this early hour, the lights of the airfield would have been lit: white outlining the active runway and cobalt blue marking the taxiways; a bright green slash signaled the runway threshold. Almost everything else beneath the station's distinguishing rotating beacon would have been dark under the first deck of overhanging clouds.

Like most members of the crew, today Grigsby would be wearing the Navy's standard summer-weight flight suit, a shapeless pair of dark green, fire-retardant coveralls festooned with twelve zippers and eight pockets, a pair of laced, high-top leather boots, and the Navy's glamorous brown goatskin flight jacket with knit cuffs and fur collar.

The lightweight leather jacket evoked the famous naval aces of World War II, gimlet-eyed gunfighters flying bent-winged Corsairs or pudgy Hellcats. These heroes wore their jackets with a white silk scarf, while carving flaming reputations through the skies over the Pacific. Their bright, embroidered squadron patches—cheap knockoffs would become a civilian fashion favorite "look" years later—lent some style to what otherwise was drab and utilitarian garb, but Jerry Grigsby was not flashy by nature. If he were in civilian clothes, it would have been difficult to guess that this soft-spoken man with a dark red moustache (the detritus of last deployment's full beard) was heir to the legendary Black Cat, PBY Catalina flying boat patrol squadrons of that colossal conflict.

Lieutenant Commander Grigsby, thirty-six, was the senior officer and by far the most experienced member of the crew that would be flying with him today. All of the other air crewmembers but one—PO 2d Class Ed Flow, a flight engineer from the mill town of Monroe, North Carolina—were on their first tours of duty in a maritime patrol squadron. Only Grigsby and Flow were on their second.

Grigsby's first squadron tour had been in Patrol Squadron 50 in the late 1960s, where at first he flew the ponderous, boat-hulled Martin P-5M2 Marlin seaplane. The Marlins managed to look elephantine everywhere—ashore on temporary beaching gear, afloat on the water, and in the air on patrol—even with a maximum gross weight of only eighty-five thousand pounds, twenty-five tons less than a P-3.

The Marlin's big, turbo- *and* supercharged Wright 3350 Cyclone radial engines each sprouted eighteen cylinders, like kernels on a stubby corncob. "Balls to the wall" (prop, fuel mixture, and throttle controls full forward for maximum power), the 1960s version of the Cyclone engine, could produce more than 3,200 horsepower for takeoff. Hundreds of parts reciprocating furiously to make all that power. The original, and fragile, 1930s version (the 3350 first saw service in the B-29 bomber) could muster only 2,200 and required overhaul every one hundred hours.

Accretions over time, however, had increased the Marlin's weight to the point that sometimes its two engines were no longer enough to get it into the air safely. Takeoffs above sixty thousand pounds required a brief assist from four JATO (jet assisted takeoff) rockets clipped in pairs to the waist hatches of the aircraft. When the firing switches in the cockpit were closed, four thousand pounds of JATO thrust for fifteen seconds overwhelmed the P-5's seemingly innate reluctance to leave the water and fly, and catapulted the aircraft into the air.[5]

Approaching the end of the 1960s, the lumbering Marlin was a flying fossil, an airborne souvenir of World War II technology (the PBM Mariner) updated scarcely one decade. The P-5's replacement, a modern flying boat, the sleek P-6 Seamaster, had been scuttled, caught in a bitter roles and missions crossfire between the Navy and the Air Force. (To the Air Force, the Navy's jet-powered and swept-winged P-6, with a thirty-thousand-pound payload, a fifteen-hundred-mile combat radius, and a big, rotating bomb bay, looked a lot like a strategic bomber, and strategic bombing was its business, not its rival's. Under political pressure, the Seamaster program's funding evaporated in August 1959, and eventually so did Martin. The P-6 was the company's last major aircraft design.)[6]

Midway through Grigsby's thirty-three months as one of the Blue Dragons of Patrol Squadron 50, the squadron moved from North Island up the California coast to Naval Air Station Moffett Field, and transitioned from the hoary P-5 to the P-3B. His squadron was one of the last two in the Navy to put the old flying boats aside.

Nearly eight years after this first squadron tour, in October 1976, Jerry Grigsby left the Naval Post-Graduate School at Monterey, moving with his wife, Loreen, and their two young daughters north to San José, California, where they again would be close to Moffett Field, their new home port. Grigsby had studied operations research at Monterey, and in the back of his mind he thought that there eventually might be a second career for him in this math-heavy, new discipline. He was heading for Patrol Squadron 9 and another operational flying tour. On arrival, he would be joining four other second-tour pilots, contemporaries and competitors. Grigsby's new assignment was the next step in a typical career pattern, although the interval between squadrons was somewhat longer than usual.

Historic Moffett Field (it was built in the early 1930s by the New Deal's Works Progress Administration to be the home of the ill-fated dirigible, USS *Macon*) lay wedged between the salt marshes at the bottom end of San Francisco Bay, U.S. Route 101, and the small city of Mountain View.[7] Its huge Hangar 1 dominated the skyline along the southern end of the Bay, dwarfing even the paired World War II–era blimp hangars on the other side of the twin runways.

The Navy is gone from Moffett now, but then Moffett was the largest maritime patrol aircraft base in the Navy, home to seven fleet squadrons, including Grigsby's new command. While at home, Moffett-based squadrons were assigned to the Third Fleet, located at Ford Island, in Pearl Harbor. When deployed throughout the Pacific and Indian Oceans, they worked for the Seventh Fleet, headquartered at Yokosuka, Japan.

In October 1978, better than halfway through his second squadron tour, the U.S. Navy would have rightly counted Grigsby as an experienced patrol plane pilot. He had amassed just over twenty-five hundred flight hours since he started flight training at Pensacola, Florida, in 1964 and been designated a patrol plane commander in two fleet squadrons and a post-overhaul test pilot at the Naval Air Rework Facility in Alameda, California. Two months earlier, he had successfully completed the instructor pilot syllabus. More than sixteen hundred of Grigsby's hours were in the Lockheed P-3 Orion, the aircraft he would be flying nearly to the Soviet coast and back to the Aleutians that day.

Although an airline pilot with a like fourteen years of line flying experience could have ten thousand more hours in his logbook, Navy aviators usually alternated tours in aircraft squadrons or as ship's company ("sea duty") with other assignments ("shore duty"), and so three to four thousand hours in the cockpit could represent a full and successful career.

By late 1978, Jerry Grigsby's Navy career, however, could not be counted successful, as most naval aviators would traditionally describe success. The tour of duty at the Alameda aircraft rework facility—an unusual assignment for a young aviator rotating ashore after his first squadron tour, not "career enhancing"—hinted at as much. A shipboard tour in the USS *Hancock,* in charge of the elderly carrier's catapults and arresting gear, had not helped him break out from the pack either. These early omens were confirmed a few years later. After seventeen months in the squadron and enough time in grade for promotion, Grigsby was the squadron's safety officer, not one of his command's three key department heads. The assignment was evidence that he was not competing successfully on the ground against his contemporaries.

Professional competition aside, Grigsby was fully qualified to fly the aircraft and command the crew for Event AK 262. He was four weeks away from completing one year as a patrol plane commander (PPC) in Patrol Squadron 9. (The PPC was the senior pilot aboard an aircraft, the aviator personally responsible for the safety of the crew.) In three months he would be passing the anniversary of designation as mission commander, the officer on board the aircraft responsible for the tactical performance of the crew and the success of its mission. Not all PPCs held this distinction.

Less formally, Grigsby was widely regarded as a "good stick," a natural pilot with sound instincts and smooth moves on the controls. Lt. Ed Caylor, who would be flying with Grigsby today, years later would describe Grigsby as the "consensus best pilot in the squadron," but that was almost certainly generous overstatement. Still, Lt. Pat Conway, a tactical coordinator, remembered Grigsby as one of the pilots the guys in the back of the aircraft did not ever worry about. Cdr. Byron Powers, the squadron's commanding officer at the time (and a pilot himself), rated Grigsby as "good" but no better than the middle of the pack of second-tour aviators. Grigsby was not a charismatic leader, either. In fact, he had been paired with his tactical coordinator, Lt. (jg) Matt Gibbons, twenty-five, intentionally by Bud Powers in an effort to lend the crew more dynamic leadership.

The Navy's officer corps naturally divided itself into unequal thirds, "young studs, old fudds, and lieutenant commanders." The break point, at lieutenant commander, marked the division between the junior officer studs and commanders and captains, whose gilt-encrusted cap visors signaled that these old fudds were in the Navy for life. (Flag officers, admirals, enjoyed special status, a tiny and largely separate fourth estate, apart from the rest of the officer corps. More gold braid on their caps, too.)

Career pressures on lieutenant commanders facing promotion and then squadron command selection boards were intense, and occasionally brought out the worst in the competitors. Not so in the case of Jerry Grigsby, whose approachable and easygoing manner made him a favorite of Patrol Squadron 9's junior officers. Not charismatic, perhaps, but well liked.

Grigsby had passed his two annual flight checks on time. He had flown an instrument check at Adak in July and been evaluated then as a "very smooth pilot who demonstrated excellent knowledge of instrument procedures." "Smooth" was the word his flight engineer, Ed Flow, used to characterize Grigsby's airmanship, too. After his flight procedures standardization check in August, Grigsby was assessed as "qualified," the highest possible grade. The postflight evaluation report bore only one explicit, positive observation: "Expeditious, controlled ditching evolution." By every Navy measure of training and performance, Grigsby was fully qualified to command his mission. There was, however, a fleeting and insubstantial question raised after the mishap about his psychological readiness to make sound decisions in the cockpit that late October afternoon.

Grigsby was commissioned an ensign in the U.S. Naval Reserve during flight training, in October 1964, and had been promoted in due course three times during the next fourteen years. In the fall of 1978, very shortly before this flight, he had failed selection to the next higher rank, commander. The pass-over by the selection board should not have been a surprise. By late 1978, he knew the Alameda assignment had been a mistake, regardless what it had taught him about the aircraft, and that his graduate school tour had come too late. Reportedly, Grigsby had expected to be passed over.

Jerry Grigsby's career in the Navy had just become victim to a patrol squadron's peculiar geometry, shaped by the requirement for at least sixty flying officers, five to man each of twelve crews. The resulting personnel pyramid exhibited a broad base of junior officers—forty to fifty lieutenants (junior grade) and lieutenants—and then tapered sharply to six to ten lieutenant commanders and only two commanders at the apex. Among the typical squadron's seven, eight, or more lieutenant commanders, perhaps half would be promoted, and half or fewer among those would later be chosen to hold squadron command. Grigsby's first and best chance for promotion was now behind him. In the next twenty-four months, two other pass-overs would almost certainly follow the first.

In the early years of the nineteenth century, Royal Navy officers toasted each other with a macabre wish for "a bloody war and a sickly season." The expectation was that deaths from combat or disease would speed the promotion process, by accelerating vacancies in the senior ranks. In a personnel system that worked strictly by seniority and studiously ignored merit, anything—even war or pestilence—that thinned the field while it carried away your seniors was welcome.[8]

The twentieth-century U.S. Navy had another approach to making room at the top. Like a baseball batter at the plate, every eligible officer had three swings, a year apart, at promotion to the next grade. If the officer did not connect on one of them, meaning if the selection board passed over the aspirant, he or she was out, retired at the end of a period of years defined by applicable statute. Under the Navy's unyielding up-or-out promotion policy, Jerry Grigsby could now expect to retire in the grade of lieutenant commander in 1984, with twenty years of service, consoled by a monthly Navy retirement check equal to half his base pay, around a third of his total compensation. Not nearly enough for a family of four to live on.

Although it was theoretically possible that promotion would materialize unexpectedly in a year or two, it was most unlikely that Grigsby would be selected to hold squadron command, meaning that he might conceivably make commander, the next rank up the chain, but certainly not captain, the rank after that. And so, in another nine months, Grigsby would probably be out of Navy cockpits forever. A third squadron assignment, in command, was not in the cards.

But in October 1978 that farewell was still months away.

Finding of Fact. Lieutenant Commander J. Grigsby, Lieutenant E. Caylor, Ensign J. Wagner, Lieutenant (junior grade) M. Gibbons, Lieutenant (junior grade) B. Forshay, Lieutenant (junior grade) J. Ball, Petty Officer Second Class E. Flow, Petty Officer Second Class H. Miller, Petty Officer Third Class J. Brooner, Airman R. Rodriguez, Airman R. Garcia, Petty Officer Third Class H. Moore, Airman D. Reynolds, Master Chief G. Shepard, and Petty Officer First Class G. Hemmer were scheduled to fly a tactical mission on 26 October 1978. The flight was scheduled to originate and terminate at Naval Station Adak, Alaska, and was scheduled by Commander Task Group 32.3.

Lt. Ed Caylor, twenty-six, was the duty operations officer on 25 October, and so he prepared the detachment's flight schedule for the twenty-sixth and presented it to the detachment officer in charge, Lt. Cdr. Michael Harris. "Iron Mike" Harris's approval and signature made the draft schedule into a written order, to be executed the next day. On the twenty-sixth, Patrol Squadron 9's Adak detachment would fly two flights, with a third crew standing a one-hour alert. The first to take off would be Crew 6 at 9:00 A.M. with Caylor aboard as the copilot. He had called his own number.

By rights, Caylor should have been going home with the other flight on the detachment's schedule. Caylor was Crew 7's copilot. His crew's second (and supposedly last) rotation with the squadron's Adak detachment had just ended, and Crew 7 was to fly home on the twenty-sixth. However, Crew 6's regular copilot, Lt. (jg) Steve Anderson, had contrived to miss the obligatory island orientation flight. Unqualified to fly in the Aleutians with his own crew, Anderson was turned around and sent home with Caylor's crew, whose copilot had to stay on and take the slacker's place. The extra, back-to-back rotation meant that Ed Caylor quite unexpectedly would spend another six weeks, and Thanksgiving, away from home. He was pissed.

Hours later, afloat in a raft watching the aircraft he had just abandoned bobbing on the surface a short distance away, Caylor's anger at Anderson would be renewed by the thought that, once again, he was filling the other man's seat.

Anger, not fear, is the emotion Caylor recalls most clearly as their Orion sank out of sight.

Jerry Grigsby and his new copilot would meet in the cockpit that morning having arrived there along very different trajectories. Grigsby came from Miami, Oklahoma, population twelve thousand, and until he was twenty spent most of his life within a short drive from home. It is possible to be farther from an ocean in the United States than Miami, wedged in the lake country of the state's northeast corner, near where Oklahoma, Kansas, Missouri, and Arkansas almost come together. Possible—Lt. (jg) Dennis Mette, who joins the story later, was from tiny Madison, South Dakota—but not easy. Grigsby's undergraduate degree came from Northeastern State College in Tahlequah, Oklahoma, where he went after two years at Northeastern A&M. He probably inherited his woodworking hobby from his dad, George, who worked as a lumberyard clerk back home in Miami.

Another, more distant trip away from home, to Seattle, Washington, in 1962, resulted in his marriage in mid-December the next year. A few months before the wedding, while Ed Caylor was starting fifth grade in Atlanta, Jerry Grigsby had entered the Navy's Aviation Officer Candidate program. Grigsby's new wife, Loreen, joined him in West Florida, where he was now a student in the Naval Air Basic Training Command. He would get his wings on 19 November 1965.

Ed Caylor was a Navy junior, born in Key West, Florida, in 1952; his father was a lieutenant stationed aboard a submarine at the Navy's base in the Keys. The family's roots on both sides, however, were in rural north Georgia. Like many others of that generation, Ed's father enlisted in the Navy in the summer of 1942, right out of high school. Caylor senior left a home that included an alcoholic father and an angry, bitter mother. It must have included more, too: he was a junior radioman in the heavy cruiser, USS *Toledo,* when the commanding officer recommended him for the Naval Academy's prep school, an unusual distinction for one enlisted man among the hundreds on board. He graduated from the Naval Academy in the spring of 1948, one of the small sprinkling of Georgians who leavened the Navy's junior officer corps each year.

Another Georgia boy, one year ahead of Caylor at Annapolis, Ens. Jimmy Carter, from Plains, would become especially well known later in life. Like Carter, Caylor senior would also marry a local Georgia girl and then go to submarine school. Unlike the Caylors, the Carters were country gentry, with social status in the community. Carter would leave the Navy to tend his family's interests; Caylor senior would retire on medical disability as a lieutenant in 1955, seriously injured. The injury would prove to be fatal.

Ed Caylor's father died just before Christmas 1956, leaving a widow with a two-year-old daughter, and four-year-old son. She took her children home to north Georgia but relocated in 1958 to Atlanta, where jobs and schools were better. In 1970, Ed chose the Naval Academy and a free education over Furman University and four years of tuition, room, and board payments that his mother would have been hard-pressed to afford. Despite the fact that his late father was an Annapolis graduate, the selection was not a natural one. Furman had been his first choice.

Thirty years later, Ed would still remember hating several days underwater during a short summer indoctrination cruise aboard an attack submarine. The miserable experience quickly ended a vague plan to follow in his father's footsteps. A much more successful indoctrination to naval aviation at Pensacola, Florida, led the new Ensign Caylor to flight training in late summer 1974.

In early December 1976, Caylor reported to Patrol Squadron 9 for his first tour of sea duty. His goal throughout flight training had been the Hurricane Hunters of Weather Reconnaissance Squadron 4, in Jacksonville, Florida, but in a spasm of economizing, the Navy decommissioned the squadron weeks before he got his wings. Ed made the best of it. His second choice also kept him off aircraft carriers, something else he had tried as a Naval Academy midshipman and did not like.

In August 1978, with the experience of five months operational flying in the western Pacific from Okinawa, Japan, and pretty much on schedule, Ed Caylor flew his plane commander flight check at Moffett Field. The next month, he went back to Adak for his second and last assignment with the detachment. Six weeks later, at the end of October, Crew 6 flew up to replace Lt. (jg) John Healy's Crew 7, and Ed thought, wrongly as it developed, that he was heading for home with Healy to inherit Crew 7 from his departing plane commander.

Ens. John Wagner, twenty-five, would be the third and junior pilot in the cockpit. He was also, almost certainly, the junior pilot in the squadron. John Wagner was ten months out of Navy flight training. Most of those ten months had been spent as a student in the Replacement Air Group (RAG), the squadron that conducted initial and refresher type training for crewmembers going to the P-3 for the first time or returning to it from other assignments.

Wagner was from Colorado. He had been raised in Brighton, just north of Denver off U.S. 85, and gone to school with an Air Force ROTC scholarship not far from home, at the University of Colorado's Boulder campus. Air Force pilot training slots dried up in the years immediately following the end of the war in Vietnam while junior officer requirements shrank, so after graduation Wagner worked his way over to the Navy, first as a student naval flight officer and then into its pilot training program. Married and with two young sons, he had been aboard Patrol Squadron 9 for only one month and had just over 110 hours total pilot time in the P-3 when he showed up at planeside that Thursday morning, ready to go flying.

The plane commanders of maritime patrol flight crews customarily rotated junior pilots through the seats in an effort to equalize time and experience, and to ensure their steady progress through the designations—"no-P," third pilot, copilot, plane commander—leading to qualification to command a crew. Typically takeoffs and landings were rotated too, unless conditions interfered, so that at the end of the month each pilot would be able to log both his fair share of hours and of these more interesting exercises of airmanship.

With two aircraft commanders on board, Wagner could reasonably expect a lot of time in the seat on this flight, because he would always be paired with one of them. If one of the other pilots had been only a "2P," a copilot and not qualified to command the aircraft himself, the PPC might have elected to stay in the seat for the whole flight. Even then, Grigsby was known to be generous sharing flight time.

Flight time in your logbook was more than a dry statistic. Flight time, like rank, was one measure of your status, your worth to the squadron. The accumulation of flight time—pilot time, copilot time, nighttime, instrument time—paced a pilot's progress through the chairs toward the goal of his own crew. Only "special crew" time meant nothing; that was the hours aloft when you were not in the seat.

In the late 1970s, most of the P-3's "housekeeping" systems (for example, air conditioning and pressurization, electrical power generation and distribution, and fuel management) still hewed closely to their 1950s-era origins. They did not operate automatically. It was the cockpit crew's responsibility to manage these systems, to diagnose any problems and to execute emergency procedures.

System normal and emergency procedures had been developed over more than fifteen years of fleet experience. Each procedure was prescribed in the Naval Air Training and Operational Procedures Standardization Program's manual, *NATOPS Flight Manual: Navy Model P-3C Aircraft.* (The pilots' and flight engineers' version of the P-3 NATOPS manual, describing the aircraft and its systems, normal and emergency procedures, and performance was over eight hundred pages long.) The high workload in the cockpit—and its large size, putting many controls out of reach of the pilots—required a flight engineer to assist the two pilots. The division of labor was simple: pilots flew the aircraft and communicated with Air Traffic Control, while the flight engineer operated cockpit systems, subject to the plane commander's direction.

P-3 flight engineers were usually midcareer petty officers drawn from the ranks of the Navy's aviation electricians, mechanics and metalsmiths. As it happened, PO 2d Class Butch Miller, thirty-two, was an electrician and PO 2d Class Ed Flow, twenty-six, was a jet engine mechanic. Unlike Flow, Miller came to Patrol Squadron 9 from three years with Attack Squadron 195, from outside of the "community."

Advancement was sometimes difficult for flight engineers. Their work had little to do directly with their trade as electricians or mechanics, and "working outside of their rate" often had the effect of penalizing them on competitive advancement exams. Miller's advancement problems, however, had other causes. At the same point in life and time in service, many sailors would have been first class petty officers; Miller was still a petty officer second class. A break in active service and a disciplinary problem had slowed his progress up through the pay grades. It is likely that Miller's halting professional progress frustrated his father, a retired master chief jet engine mechanic.

Like Miller, Petty Officer Flow came from a Navy family too. All the male Flows of two generations—father, uncles, older brother—had spent time in the service, and even before his low draft lottery number (fifty-two) put the pressure on in 1971, Ed Flow was talking to the Navy recruiter in North Carolina, where he was living with his mother. Flow entered the Navy just about the time a Selective Service board in Georgia, where his father lived, moved to draft him.

Flow arrived at Patrol Squadron 9 via the flight engineer course at Patrol Squadron 31, after a tour with Patrol Squadron 22 in Hawaii as an aircrew second mechanic. (Flying P-3s clearly appealed to Flow. After twenty-six years in the Navy, Senior Chief PO Ed Flow would retire in 1997 and start flying Customs Bureau P-3As and -Bs from Corpus Christi, Texas, searching for drug smugglers.) Some pilots regarded Flow, overall, as the best flight engineer in the squadron, second only behind PO 1st Class Jim Crow in detailed aircraft systems knowledge, but infinitely more cooperative and congenial than was Crow. It is possible that things would have come out differently if Flow were in the seat four hours after takeoff instead of Miller.

Finding of Fact. Master Chief Shepard and Petty Officer Hemmer, assigned to Patrol Wings Pacific Detachment Adak, were assigned to the flight for flight pay purposes and for indoctrination purposes, respectively.

Master Chief Garland Shepard, thirty-four, and PO 1st Class Gary Joe Hemmer, also thirty-four, were not assigned to Patrol Squadron 9 or to the squadron's Adak detachment. Instead, they were both attached to the Tactical Support Center and under the command of its officer in charge, Cdr. Jim Hightower. Like his counterparts across the Pacific, Hightower was responsible to his headquarters at Moffett Field for the operation of the Tactical Support Center.

Garland Shepard was the small command's master chief, the senior enlisted man in the unit. He had been raised in tiny Trimble, Missouri, the seventh generation of his family in Clinton County. Shepard joined the Navy in 1962, and during his sixteen years had been an aircrewman on every postwar patrol aircraft model in the Navy's inventory. He even had some P-5 seaplane experience. In the TSC and around the hangar, Shepard was saltiness personified. He looked like a sea dog, too, crusty and bearded. As crusty as you could be in your mid-thirties.

Shepard, married and the father of two boys, was on Adak on an unaccompanied tour. Family housing was in short supply on the island, requiring a wait for accommodations as long as six months. The Shepards decided that she would move from their last duty station (Hawaii) to Missouri and wait for him there.

The decision meant that the focus of the master chief's life was the Tactical Support Center, freeing him for long hours in its confines. Such men, married but living alone during a tour of duty, were called "geographical bachelors." Often extraordinarily hard working, occasionally real problems.

Both men were observers from the TSC, volunteers along for the ride. Shepard was collecting flight pay, and Navy regulations at the time required that he spend a minimum number of hours in the air each month to remain eligible for this extra money. Urged on by his master chief, Gary Hemmer had volunteered for the flight as part of an informal campaign to improve professional cooperation between the Adak TSC and the sensor operators it supported. Hemmer was an ocean systems technician, the land-based counterpart of the two acoustic sensor operators on the crew, PO 3d Class James Brooner and Airman Randall Rodriguez.

Hemmer, born in Missouri but raised in Westminster, Colorado, was new on the island. He had only been there a few weeks, and his family was still camping out in their quarters with communal dishes and bedding, waiting for their own to arrive. Hemmer was not an aircrewman, and so he would be flying in borrowed flight gear and in a pair of his own low-topped, Corfram uniform shoes. He would not be the only one aboard AF 586 whose dress left him unprepared for what was coming. The Naval Safety Center would conclude in its closeout report on the accident that of the fifteen men on board "only one was properly/adequately dressed for the ensuing survival episode." That one was Garland Shepard.

As a master chief petty officer, Shepard was one of a handful of men at the very top of the Navy's enlisted manpower structure, one of roughly 3,700 master chiefs in an enlisted force of 462,000. That structure began at pay grade E-1, with apprentices in boot camp, and eventually proceeded through three petty officer grades (third, second, and first, E-4 through E-6, respectively) to chief petty officer, senior chief petty officer, and master chief petty officer. The Navy's chiefs, in all three pay grades, E-7 to E-9, were the heart of its noncommissioned officer corps. Their experience and expertise accounted in significant measure for the Navy's ability to perform in the face of constantly changing personnel assignments and with an average age in most operational units around 20.[9]

Garland Shepard would be one of the two oldest of the survivors to be rescued the next morning by the Russians (Hemmer was the other), and his age and salty appearance would confuse them into thinking that Shepard, and not the boyishly good-looking Lieutenant Caylor with fashionably long sideburns, was the senior American aboard their vessel. The reality was, however, that Shepard (like Hemmer) was a supernumerary on this flight, despite the fact that he had more experience as an air antisubmarine warfare technician than did the three young sensor operators together, and more time in the Navy than anyone aboard. He had another distinction. He had already survived one aircraft sinking, in a Patrol Squadron 40 Marlin off Cavite, in the Philippines, in 1967. During a night seaplane takeoff, the port bow hatch had sprung open. The aircraft quickly filled with water and sank. Everyone got out and was rescued from the warm waters of Manila Bay. Shepard would mention that biographic vignette to Grigsby, during the plane commander's last pass down the cabin before they ditched, sharing an experience that the crew's only other flying boat sailor would instinctively understand.

Shepard and Hemmer would both ride out the aircraft's impact into the water sitting at auxiliary ditching stations on the floorboards, wedged tightly in between ceiling-high equipment racks and facing the rear of the aircraft without intercomm. headphones and in the dark. Completely isolated with their thoughts. In the ninety minutes during which the emergency would unfold, both men would have ample time to regret the impulse that had urged them to go on this particular trip. Their survival, especially Hemmer's, who had none of the aircrew survival training the others had, would number among the greater marvels of the day. Gary Hemmer's oldest daughter later disclosed that memories of this flight formed the stuff of her father's nightmares for years after his rescue.

Finding of Fact. The officers scheduled for the tactical mission met in the BOQ at 0415, 26 October 1978, and proceeded to the Tactical Support Center for their mission briefing. Lieutenant (junior grade) Ball did not accompany them, having received permission from Lieutenant Commander Grigsby to arrive at the aircraft at a later time.

Adak provided few opportunities for distraction, much less entertainment. Some enterprising Marines assigned to the station's security detachment ran the Tundra Tavern, a popular speakeasy that featured their interpretation of Mexican food and appealed to those with adventurous palates on the island. But otherwise, practically nothing. So it was that Lt. (jg) John Ball, thirty-one, spent part of the night before the flight playing after-dinner bingo over "two or three beers" in the Chief Petty Officers Club with Lt. Cdr. Mike Harris and Lt. (jg) J. J. Skarzenski, a squadronmate. This was John Ball's second night on the island. He had arrived the day before with Petty Officers Miller and Brooner and Airmen Garcia and Reynolds in the aircraft they would fly today.

Ball was off to bed at nine. Sworn testimony from the other surviving members of the crew reveals them to all have been equally abstemious, at least that night. Harris later testified that "from close, intimate observation," he knew these men to be "an unusually sober, stable crew. . . . All men involved appeared to have very moderate personal habits." Nothing else in the accident investigation arose to contradict his impression, despite the fact that Harris knew some of the new men on the crew not at all.

Ball arrived at the aircraft at 7:00 the next morning and assisted with the ongoing preflight inspection. He would soon go before a squadron board that would examine his readiness to move from nav/comm into the tacco position, and this flight, under Gibbons' tutelage, would be a valuable extra training opportunity for him.

A P-3 preflight inspection for a tactical flight could take an experienced crew several hours, time used in fueling and loading the aircraft, aligning navigation systems, checking the operation of cockpit and antisubmarine avionics, inspecting the airframe and engines, and correcting whatever discrepancies might have been discovered.

In the early days of the P-3, the A and B models, the two functions, navigation and communication, were separate. The navigator was an officer, usually the junior pilot on the crew, and the communicator was an enlisted radio operator, who would tune and maintain radios and monitor frequencies. The actual content of the messages going out from the aircraft would come from the plane commander or another officer on the crew. This hierarchy and division of labor had its origins in World War II aircraft practice, passed down after the war through the P-2 and P-5 to the first P-3s.

The situation created a decade of bad navigator morale. Pilots saw themselves as airplane drivers, not navigators. The crew's third pilot wanted to be in the cockpit, not at the navigation table, but unless some other pilot relieved him, that is where he would stay. The patrol plane second pilot (PP2P), who had just left the nav table sometime in the last year, had no desire to go back to it, and the patrol plane commander had forgotten his nav skills or pretended that he had.

The automation of many navigation functions and the simplification of many communications functions (especially the introduction of crystal controlled tuning and the demise of manually keyed Morse code) made it possible to consolidate these dissimilar responsibilities in the hands of someone who would not resent them, the junior naval flight officer (NFO) on board. After a period as nav/comm, during which he was being trained to fleet up to tactical coordinator, this officer would slide directly across the aisle and become responsible for pulling sensor data together into a coherent picture of the submarine datum area.[10]

Lt. (jg) Bruce Forshay, twenty-four, was the junior NFO of the three aboard AF 586. Next to Wagner, Forshay had the least flight experience of the officers on the aircraft that morning, a total of only 264 hours in the air and just 159 in the P-3. Bruce Forshay had arrived at Patrol Squadron 9 at the end of September and a few weeks later was rushed off to join the detachment in Adak "to gain experience." He would be forever resentful of the perceived haste and eagerness with which he was thrown into the barrel in the Aleutians, even before the squadron's parachute riggers took the time to update the headset and microphone connections on his helmet. Like Wagner, Forshay would go from check-in at Moffett to afloat in a raft off Shemya in less than a month.

The senior NFO, Lt. (jg) Matt Gibbons, had eleven hundred hours in the P-3. Matt Gibbons, a New Yorker, would be the closest thing to a big-city boy aboard the aircraft today. The oldest of seven, he had moved with his family from Brooklyn, New York, upstate to Schenectady in 1962. Gibbons's father, a lawyer and World War II Navy vet with time as a rear-seat gunner in Curtiss Helldivers, worked for the state's attorney general in neighboring Albany, the capital. In 1975, Matt graduated from Marquette University, where he had held a Navy ROTC scholarship, and left Milwaukee for Pensacola, Florida, and active duty.

Matt Gibbons had a lot of time at Adak. He had gone to the island for the first time in early May with Crew 1, Bud Powers's crew. Although the plan was to rotate personnel through the detachment every six weeks, on 26 October he had been on Adak 107 days straight. Gibbons would later wryly joke about being a "centurion" on the island. (Centurions were naval aviators who had made one hundred carrier landings. The careful inventory of career carrier landings by attack and fighter pilots, like total flight hours, was the measure of manliness among carrier aviators.)

Gibbons was the victim of a common form of discrimination. As one of the few single officers in the squadron, his time in the barrel away from home tended to be elastic. Other squadrons did the same thing, and bachelors everywhere got a lot of night, weekend, and cross-country flight time while married men slept at home with their wives.

Finding of Fact. The mission brief took place at the TSC at 0500, 26 October 1978. The briefing officer was Lieutenant John Eger. The briefing lasted until approximately 0545 and there were no unusual questions and there was no unusual tasking. The flight was planned as a routine reconnaissance mission. The call sign assigned to the flight was AF 586.

The Tactical Support Center (the term is sometimes used interchangeably with ASW Operations Center) was one of the great innovations that came to patrol aviation at roughly the same time that the P-3C was introduced into the fleet in 1969. Its first function was as a brief/debrief site for flight crews. In the TSC the crew be would be informed of its mission, get intelligence on its target, and be provided information on the environmental conditions on station that could limit the effectiveness of the aircraft's sensors or otherwise affect tactics.

At the conclusion of the flight, the mission would be debriefed in detail and taped acoustic data collected could be replayed on the sophisticated spectrum analyzers the center contained for analysis by the TSC's staff of officers and enlisted ocean system technicians. The TSC's most important contribution, however, was not as a site but as a service. The Tactical Support Center made it possible to string a succession of flights together in real time, often evaluating one crew's flight results in time to send updated information to the next crew while it was still on station. In this way a submarine prosecution could be sustained from crew to crew, and day to day. Each crew's flight would become part of a campaign rather than an isolated event.

Lt. John Eger recalled the briefing of this flight as exceptionally smooth, probably because some on the crew had reviewed the briefing package the day before, while standing the Ready Alert duty, and were already familiar with its contents. (John Eger would also be the briefing officer for X-ray Foxtrot 675 and Delta Foxtrot 704, the two Ready Alert aircraft that were launched later in the day as part of the search and rescue effort for their squadronmate.)

In the late 1970s U.S. Navy intelligence on the location of Soviet combatant ships, submarines, and certain fleet auxiliaries (such as intelligence collection trawlers, AGIs) was so complete that it was very unlikely AF 586 would find one of these at sea in the mission area unexpectedly, even just off Petropavlosk, one of two major Soviet naval bases in the Pacific.

Although the auxiliaries would often spend long periods at sea, combatant ships of the Soviet Navy usually did not. Unlike the U.S. Navy, which routinely deployed its ships and squadrons out of their home ports for at least one-third of the time, the Soviets' usual posture was in port, *ready* to go to sea. Infrequent, large fleet exercises would flush out the ships, squadrons, and flotillas of the Soviet Navy into blue water, provoking an orgy of American tailgating and eavesdropping, but most often they were tied up at their piers, like runners crouching in the starting blocks before a long-delayed race.

Soviet ballistic missile submarines were an exception to the Red Fleet's modus operandi. These ships sailed regular patrols on stations within missile range of their target complexes in the United States. As longer-range missiles and more modern submarines entered the USSR's inventory, the close-in "Yankee-boxes," *Yankee*-class submarine patrol areas in the western Atlantic and eastern Pacific, were pulled back into midocean and beyond.

The Soviet's Baltic, Black, and Pacific Fleets were vulnerable to being choked off from open water. Only the large and powerful Northern Fleet, home-ported on the White Sea, had relatively easy access to the world ocean, and even it would have to penetrate past Iceland, through the Greenland–United Kingdom "gap" to take the offense.

Had the two countries gone to war before the mid-1980s, the U.S. Navy's offensive strategy and the Soviet Navy's defensive one would have ensured an apocalyptic sea battle in the waters off Norway's North Cape, or so the U.S. Navy thought. Despite the Navy's confidence, the outcome would have been entirely unpredictable. During the late 1960s and through the early 1980s, the U.S. Navy had a difficult time keeping its secrets to itself.

John Anthony Walker Jr. began passing some of the U.S. Navy's most sensitive communications secrets to his KGB case officers in December 1967, twelve years after he first enlisted in the Navy. One month after Walker walked into the

Soviet embassy and started his career as a spy, gunboats of the North Korean Navy stopped and seized the USS *Pueblo* during its very first mission, Pinkroot Operation One, while the ship was collecting signals and electronic intelligence off Wonsan Harbor. The KW-7 and more modern KW-37 crypto machinery that survived the crew's hasty destruction efforts and fell into Korean hands when *Pueblo* was captured almost certainly found its way to the Soviet Union, where it joined the stream of information just starting to come from Walker.[11] (*Pueblo*'s crew had time only to burn active KW-7 keylists and to destroy the KW-37's circuit cards.) Walker's keylists gave voice to the *Pueblo*'s KW-7 machine.

Walker, in uniform and out, would continue to spy for the Soviets for eighteen years, until he was finally arrested in Rockville, Maryland. During those years, Walker (eventually with three others he recruited into his ring, including his brother and son) provided the Soviets with enough technical manuals, encryption keys, and purloined paper-copy Navy classified messages to establish what amounted to a clandestine U.S. Navy message center in the Soviet Union. For nearly two decades, a small group of knowledgeable Russians read many sensitive U.S. Navy enciphered messages with essentially the same facility that their American addressees did.

Thanks to Walker's crypto key lists, the Kremlin knew much, perhaps all, that was being passed on the Navy's submarine and maritime patrol broadcasts, and certain other encrypted circuits. By the late 1970s, the Kremlin also knew more. It knew what the Americans' daily intelligence digest photography could be revealing.

In 1975, Christopher Boyce and Andrew Lee (the "Falcon" and the "Snowman" of the book and movie of the same name) started selling secrets about TRW's Rhyolite and Argus photo satellite intelligence systems to the KGB *rezident* in Mexico City. Boyce (the son of a retired FBI agent) stole them and Lee delivered them. It was two years before they were caught. The year after they were caught, 1978, a disaffected CIA watch officer named William Kampiles sold the operations manual of the KH-11 photo satellite system to the Russians, compromising the Talent-Keyhole (TK) intelligence compartment, which held information on the United States' most sophisticated space-based imagery system.

As a result of these breaches, in the late 1970s the Soviet Navy could have known more about its opposite number than anytime before or since. There is some evidence, however, that the KGB, in a fit of bureaucratic jealousy or compartmentation gone amok, never told the Navy what it was learning about the Americans from these sources.[12]

Finding of Fact. Since sufficient time was available during preflight, Lieutenant Commander Grigsby, Lieutenant (junior grade) Gibbons, Lieutenant Caylor, Ensign Wagner, Petty Officer Moore and Airman Garcia had breakfast at the Birchwood Enlisted Dining Facility. Lieutenant (junior grade) Ball also had breakfast

that morning with Lieutenant (junior grade) Mette from the on-coming Ready Alert crew.

Lt. (jg) Dennis Mette was the alert crew's navigator/communicator. Had things developed differently, worse even than they did, Denny Mette's voice on the HF (high-frequency) radio from X-ray Foxtrot 675 at 2:25 P.M. might have been one of the very last things Matt Gibbons or anyone else aboard Alfa Foxtrot 586 (AK 262's mission call sign) heard from the outside world.

Mette, whose prior enlisted service was as a nuclear power machinist's mate, was lucky to be where he was and not aboard AF 586 in John Ball's place. The two close friends—both got their commission as officers through the Navy's NESEP program for technically trained enlisted men—were near neighbors in Navy housing at Moffett Field. Ball had agreed to be the extra nav/comm on the flight today, the "PARPRO rider," backing up Bruce Forshay, because he knew Mette's tactical coordinator examination board was scheduled for Friday, the day after the flight. Putting Mette on the Ready Alert crew for Thursday, instead of in the air off Kamchatka, would give him another full day to study for the inquisition to come. A day ahead of herself in California, Mette's wife, Cindy, was planning to send the kids to bed early that night and wait by the phone to hear how Denny had done before the tacco board.

PO 3d Class Bill Miller was lucky, too. He was one of the acoustic sensor operators assigned to Crew 6, but he had left Adak on Tuesday with Crew 12 for Hawaii, so his place aboard the aircraft Thursday morning would be taken by a new man on the island, Airman Randy Rodriguez. PO Greg Bush, the crew's radar operator, was absent also. He was in California with his pregnant wife, due the following Monday, waiting for their baby to be born. Airman Rich Garcia would fill Bush's seat.

Historically, the U.S. Navy, like its Royal Navy model in so many things, kept the dining and living ("messing and berthing") spaces of officers and enlisted men apart, as far apart as was possible on the small, wooden ships of the eighteenth and nineteenth centuries, where so many of its modern traditions had their roots. Socialization, too, was explicitly forbidden, on the theory that familiarity would breed contempt, or if not exactly contempt then an unseemly camaraderie that inevitably would impair morale and erode discipline. The goal was that the two would meet only in the workplace, where the former would tell the latter what to do and when to do it. The latter was then expected to respond with a cheery "aye, aye" and move on.

By the late 1970s, however, these traditions of separation were beginning visibly to erode, at least ashore. As lifestyles changed, manpower declined, and the number of bachelors, even among junior enlisted men, plummeted, the cost of running separate "closed messes" (subsidized dining facilities) and "open messes" (clubs and bars) for both officers and enlisted men became prohibitive. Some facilities, especially in the continental United States, were simply closed. Others had their hours curtailed and services reduced, or were consolidated.

In one sense, Naval Station Adak was a special case. Valiantly fighting entropy out at the bitter end of a logistics pipeline that was as slender as Reeve Aleutian Airlines' flight schedule, and paying its civilian employees eye-popping, Anchorage-level wages, Adak was a difficult and hugely expensive proposition to support. In San Diego, the commander Naval Air Force, U.S. Pacific Fleet, must have gritted his teeth every time his staff paid the bills to support a handful of maritime patrol flight crews at this distant outpost of empire.

The "tailhookers" (carrier aviators) on the naval air force commander's staff at the air station on San Diego's North Island were not naturally inclined to be very supportive anyway. Someone whose life centered around the aircraft carrier and its embarked air wing of fighters and attack aircraft had, as a matter of faith, a low opinion of submarines; anything else suggested vulnerability to torpedoes. That low opinion became positive contempt when considering not submarines, but the hookless, land-based aircraft and their crews whose mission was antisubmarine warfare.

On Adak, things were not easy for station personnel—unless they were hermits, hunters, or fishermen—or for the deployed squadron detachments. The isolation was numbing. The weather was frequently hellish on the ground and in the air. The physical plant suffered from the weather, and from a combination of neglect, inadequate funding, and abuse found in public housing but nowhere else.

The only grace note was the bald eagles. The big, handsome birds were common over the island. Watching them soar majestically overhead, it was almost possible to imagine arrows and olive branches clutched in their talons, until they alit to roost, less majestically, on the garbage dumpsters that dotted open space. Peering, over hooked beaks as hard and glossy as antique ivory, with speculative interest at discarded, half-eaten box lunches.

Frustratingly, there was not any escape from the BOQ or the enlisted barracks, or from mess hall food. Living on the economy was impossible. You could not go "ashore," meaning outside the gate, for anything. There was no gate, no fence line, and nothing beyond the last, tired buildings but hard rock, dangerous bog, and, finally, the implacable Pacific. Closing dining or other personnel support facilities was out of the question. Consolidating them violated decades—no, centuries—of naval tradition, but it had to be done.

That is why four of Crew 6's officers—Gibbons and Grigsby, later joined by Wagner and Caylor—had breakfast in the Birchwood enlisted mess hall that morning. In October 1978, breakfast at Birchwood cost officers ninety-five cents. Enlisted crewmembers got by without the thirty-cent surcharge; they paid sixty-five cents. The Birchwood galley was known as a generous, if greasy, feeder. The smell of each morning's half-cooked bacon hung in the messhall's warm, humid air even during lunch and dinner. Most crewmembers remember eating a big breakfast, and were glad that they had. Walking out the door on the way to the flight line, John Wagner took an apple with him.

Finding of Fact. The flight crew, except for Lieutenant Caylor, Lieutenant (junior grade) Ball, Ensign Wagner and Petty Officer Miller had been assigned as the Ready Alert crew on 25 October. Lieutenant Caylor had been assigned as Duty Operations Officer; Lieutenant (junior grade) Ball had been scheduled to fly on a familiarization flight that was cancelled due to unsuitable weather conditions; Ensign Wagner flew on a tactical flight with another flight crew that returned to Adak at approximately 1700; and Petty Officer Miller had been scheduled for the same flight as Lieutenant (junior grade) Ball. In accordance with NATOPS guidelines, all flight crew personnel had sufficient crew rest time prior to the flight on 26 October 1978.

Under the most conservative interpretation of the flight manual's crew rest rules, John Wagner should have had a minimum of fifteen hours rest after landing on 25 October and before preflighting on the twenty-sixth; he actually had twelve. Whether or not Wagner had sufficient crew rest prior to the flight seems to have attracted more attention than the issue was worth, with both the squadron commanding officer and the wing commander commenting on the finding in the investigation. The latter then dismissed what he characterized as a "technical violation" by observing that Wagner's performance was not adversely affected in any way by fatigue.

Curiously, no one in the chain of command commented on another fact imbedded but apparent in the investigation's finding: the extent to which AF 586 was flying with a pieced-together crew, a collection of individuals, for the most part very young men, each individually qualified to fly in his position, but collectively without long experience on station together that would make them effective tactically or strengthen them in crisis.

In theory, in the 1970s each fleet patrol squadron was manned so that it could support and schedule twelve ASW aircrews, each crew at least eleven men strong. A contemporary rule of thumb suggested that this crew complement, coupled to the nine aircraft in each squadron's custody, its internal maintenance capability and outside support should permit one aircraft to be maintained on station one thousand to twelve hundred miles from base essentially indefinitely. (At that distance, one aircraft on station meant that three were in the air continuously, with another always outbound and a third always inbound. A fourth would be in preflight inspection, and a fifth in postflight maintenance.)

Depending on many factors, most beyond the individual squadron's control, recruiting and retention shortfalls and training perturbations kept the twelve-crew goal very difficult to achieve. Neighboring Silicon Valley's vigorous economy made the retention of young officers and enlisted men with any technical skills difficult. Outside the gate and out of uniform, the grass was greener. Life was easier and the pay higher; husbands were at home more; wives were happier. Flight engineers, too, were in chronically short supply. Patrol Squadron 9 did not have twelve crews on board. By one count, the total of formed and trained crews was really only nine or ten. Help was not on the way, either. The squadron's parent wing had assigned manning priority to those squadrons preparing for full-squadron deployments, not to Patrol Squadron 9.

Managing people to maximize the number of combat ready aircrews was one of the principal challenges of a squadron's operations officer, usually the senior lieutenant commander on board. The other factor affecting readiness was crew stability, meaning how long the same group of eleven men had flown and trained together. Stability was important because antisubmarine warfare in the P-3 was as much art as science, and only a crew that worked well together had a reasonable chance of putting together the clues that led from initial detection, through localization, to the target's position, course, and speed. To the so-called kill criteria that confirmed the submarine was within the lethal envelope of aircraft weapons.

When Crew 6 taxied out to the runway that morning, only half the members of the nominal crew were actually present. The other half, including all three sensor operators, came from other crews. This crew was like a pick-up ball team. Everyone had played his position before, but they had not practiced much together, and a few were real rookies.

Chapter 2

Papa Delta Two

The Lockheed Orion patrol aircraft program was as close to a license to print money as any Department of Defense contractor was likely to get. The P-3 Orion, named after the familiar, rectangular constellation of the hunter in the winter sky, was in continuous production for thirty years; 628 were built, including 327 of the P-3C model, like Buno. 159892.[1] (The acronym comes from Bureau Number, the aircraft serial number assigned by the Navy's Bureau of Aeronautics, itself called BuAer, until supplanted by the Naval Air Systems Command.)

Almost 250 P-3s were sold or otherwise transferred to sixteen countries. Only Africa was absent from the roll call of populated continents that were home to busy Orion squadrons. (Granted some foreign operators actually did not operate much. Such was the case with the half-dozen Imperial Iranian Air Force P-3Fs, beautifully painted in a unique, mottled blue camouflage scheme that made them especially conspicuous in their semipermanent parking spaces on the ramp at Bandar Abbas on the Persian Gulf. Inducted into the Ayatollah Khomeini's Islamic Iranian Air Force after the revolution and moved to Shiraz, they would fly even less.)

Its sales success numbered the P-3 among the few largest navy aircraft programs since World War II. Only the United Kingdom, France, Germany, and Italy had no interest whatever in the aircraft. Their national aerospace industries pushed them in different directions. The UK put its maritime patrol flight crews into the huge, four-jet Nimrod, a heavily modified de Havilland Comet 4 commercial transport in war paint. The transformation was not a natural one, but the

Nimrod's two cavernous bomb bays inevitably impressed allied flight crews.[2] The other three nations were partners in the French Briguet *Atlantique,* a big twin turboprop powered by Rolls Royce. Their hopes for rich NATO and world markets for the *Atlantique* were blown away by the UK's decision to go it alone and by Lockheed's highly successful international sales blitz for its P-3.

The popular Orion was derived from the unsuccessful Electra commercial transport (as was the EP-3 detained by the Chinese on Hainan Island twenty-three years later). The metamorphosis from commercial transport to Navy maritime patrol aircraft required only a relatively few major changes. The fuselage was shortened approximately seven feet. The nose was reshaped to accommodate a large, forward hemisphere search radar, and the tail was extended into a distinctive stinger shape that housed both the aft search radar and the sensor for the magnetic anomaly detection equipment, which needed to be isolated from the aircraft's own magnetic field as much as possible. As much as twenty thousand pounds of "kill stores" (torpedoes, mines, depth bombs, and missiles) could be carried in an eight station bomb bay cut into the belly and on ten racks mounted at hard points on the wing. In the P-3C "search stores," the expendable sonobuoys that formed the acoustic link between the aircraft and the target submarine, were carried in forty-eight external launch tubes. Reloads, required because a submarine search could easily consume more than just four dozen buoys, were stacked horizontally in a storage rack behind the starboard overwing escape hatch and could be fired or dropped from four other launch tubes that penetrated the pressurized fuselage. The flight crew, normally eleven to twelve men, included an ordnanceman to provide the muscle for this process.

Eager to succeed its own antiquated P-2V Neptune and to freeze everyone else out of this lucrative market, Lockheed proposed the P-3 (then P-3V, the *V* identifying Lockheed as the manufacturer) to the Navy in 1957, even before the first Electra flew, in response to the Navy's Type Specification No. 146. Lockheed's initiative was highly successful. In mid-1958, the Navy awarded the company an initial research and development contract. The P-3 aerodynamic prototype (a modified Electra, FAA civil registration number N1883) flew for the first time after just three months. The last P-3 would come off the production line thirty-three years later.

Like the airframe, the Orion's propulsion plant design also had its roots in the old Lockheed Electras. Each of the P-3's four turbine engines turned a planetary reduction geartrain, the output of which spun its prop shaft. The huge prop—thirteen feet six inches in diameter, more than two feet broader than the fuselage itself—rotated at constant speed in flight, varying blade angle rather than rpm to adjust to changes in engine power. The turboprop combination—a jet engine driving a prop—was ideal for the P-3's mission. It gave the aircraft reasonable cruise speed (328 knots, just over 370 miles per hour) and ceiling (up to twenty-eight thousand feet), so it could reach out one thousand miles from its base and operate for four hours on station. It also gave the P-3 good fuel consumption at the low altitudes typical of end-game antisubmarine warfare. In the dense atmosphere below eighteen thousand feet, a propeller is the most efficient way to convert jet engine heat to forward thrust.

There is no prop rpm control or condition lever in the cockpit of the P-3, both familiar to reciprocating engine or other turboprop pilots, only four oddly colored, azure blue–topped power levers. Pushing forward on the power levers—the cluster fits easily across your palm—sprays more fuel into the engine combustion cans, and the result is instantly visible on the big shaft horsepower and turbine inlet temperature gauges above the center pedestal: higher temperature and more power. The props, however, remain at 1,020 rpm, 100 percent. Taking a larger "bite" out of the air absorbs power increases; conversely, reductions in power are translated into a smaller bite. Prop revolutions remain the same.

Propeller rpm control in the P-3 is effected by automatic changes in the angles of the blades, controlled in turn by hydraulic pressure on one side of a pitch change piston housed in the prop dome, located behind the conical spinner. A mere five hundred pounds per square inch (psi) of hydraulic pressure against the piston is enough to change blade angle in the face of the enormous aerodynamic forces playing against the spinning prop. These fine blade angle changes maintain the propeller at constant rpm in flight, regardless of engine power. By 1978, the P-3's propeller was a very well known system, with a long service history documented by rooms full of data. At the manufacturer, Hamilton Standard, in Windsor Locks, Connecticut, it was possible to conceive of a full career spent entirely inside of the long-lived, high-volume program.

Because almost every propeller malfunction could have a serious effect on control of the aircraft, the P-3's propulsion system featured a variety of prop safety devices. These governed rpm, locked blade pitch to prevent a loss of control, and prevented a prop from creating drag by being driven like a windmill by its passage through the air.

Finding of Fact. PD-2, Aircraft Bureau Number 159892, a P-3C (U) assigned to Patrol Squadron Nine, was scheduled to fly on the tactical flight 26 October 1978.

The mission aircraft was a P-3 from Patrol Squadron 9's rotating detachment in Alaska of four crews and three aircraft. The remaining crews and six other aircraft remained at Moffett Field, and formed the reservoir from which the small Adak detachment was supported through regular exchanges of people and aircraft.

PD, Papa Delta in the phonetic alphabet of the armed services, painted on the vertical stabilizer identified the aircraft belonging to Patrol Squadron 9. The two-letter aircraft identification system had its roots in early naval aviation history.

During the 1970s, Pacific Fleet patrol aircraft carried identifiers beginning with *P*, *Q*, *R*, or *S*. Less confusingly, all Atlantic Fleet patrol aircraft designators began with an *L*.

PD-2, Grigsby's assigned plane, was only twenty-five months old the day of the flight. The new car smell was certainly gone from the vinyl-covered bench at its galley and four-place dinette table seats, but everything in the $16.5 million aircraft was still new enough to look good and work well. With luck and attentive corrosion control, Buno. 159892 would still be flying well past the turn of the century.

Mike Harris, a second-tour naval flight officer and the detachment's officer-in-charge, later explained that PD-2 had been put on the schedule for Event AK 262 because it was the best systems aircraft of the three he had available in Adak. It had come from the parent squadron at Moffett Field on 24 October and flown a 7.5-hour-long operational flight the day after arrival. A slow-to-retract nose gear had been corrected, and this morning PD-2 would pass the preflight inspection by POs Edwin Flow and Harold Miller without discrepancy.

The second of Harris's three aircraft would be spending 26 October in Hawaii, finishing a torpedo loading and delivery exercise, and the third would be assigned to the Ready Alert crew.

Finding of Fact. Aircraft Buno. 159892 was transferred to Patrol Squadron 9 on 27 September 1976. Number One Engine, Model T56-A-14 Turboprop, Serial Number AE-109860, had a total of 1,407.8 hours operating time as of 12 October 1978 and was original equipment. The propeller assembly, Model Number 54H60-77, Serial Number N223919, was placed on Number One Engine on 18 September 1978. It had undergone rebuilding at the Naval Air Rework Facility Norfolk, Virginia, on 12 June 1978 and build-up at the Aircraft Intermediate Maintenance Department at Moffett Field, California, on 15 September 1978.

Buno. 159892 rolled out of Lockheed's Burbank, California, construction hall and flew its Navy acceptance check flight on 15 September 1976. It was the 143d P-3C built and delivered. By the end of the month, 159892 was parked on the Patrol Squadron 9 flight line, with the 1.2 hour flight from Burbank to Mountain View in its otherwise blank logbook.

Two years later the airframe had logged only 2,038 flight hours and all four of 159892's engines were still first run, that is, none had been overhauled yet. No. 1 was the low-time engine, 1,441 hours; no. 3, with 2,050 hours, was high time. The no. 1 propeller assembly had more time (3,555.6 hours, nearly 900 since its overhaul in Norfolk, Virginia) than its engine, but the difference was not uncommon and had no significance. Props and engines are not matched units and almost always are removed and replaced individually, as required. The overhauled prop had been hung on its engine by squadron mechanics at Moffett

Field on 18 September, and a successful check flight was flown two days later, confirming that the installation had been done correctly.

A turboprop engine is unavoidably complicated because the pairing of a turbine engine with a propeller doubles, in a sense, the range of potential problems. Unlike a turbojet or turbofan engine, the turboprop exposes you to all the problems endemic to jet engines and also to those of propellers and prop controls. More complicated yet, because the engine spins at relatively high speed and the prop at relatively low speed, the two must be connected by a hefty reduction gearbox, which is subject to problems all of its own.

Despite this triple threat, modern turboprop engines are remarkably trouble free. Compared apples to apples, there are no appreciable reliability or safety differences between turboprops and turbojets. But when something does go wrong, the situation can deteriorate very quickly and the problem can become serious fast. Such is the case with the P-3's T56-A-14: a big engine, turning a big gearbox, spinning a thirteen foot six inch, four-bladed propeller. Pilot error and not material failure, however, was the cause of most serious P-3 problems, and that unhappy constant—true of most aircraft types—was confirmed by experience in the months before PD-2 went down.

Finding of Fact. Aircraft Buno. 159892 had undergone an 1,800-hour, A-phase inspection 10–12 October 1978, at which time both number one and two propeller control assemblies were serviced with MIL-H-83282 hydraulic fluid vice MIL-H-5606 hydraulic fluid. There were no outstanding discrepancies that could have affected the performance of the aircraft.

During the 1970s, the Navy worked toward the goal of a single hydraulic fluid to service all aircraft systems. At the time there were two approved fluids, the familiar MIL-H-5606, oily and bright red, and the new MIL-H-83282, described as "fire resistant." The Navy's goal was to be able to use -83282 everywhere on the aircraft, in the basic hydraulic system but also in landing gear struts, viscous dampers, and prop controls.

Two test campaigns were conducted before -83282 was approved for use in prop controls. The Navy conducted an in-house flight test program at the Naval Air Test Center Patuxent River, Maryland, to compare the fluids under real world, in-flight conditions. For its part, Hamilton Standard evaluated the effect of the fluid on the prop control's many seals, and ran functional evaluations. In June 1977 the Naval Air Test Center was ready to report that the new fluid was suitable for fleet use in all models of the P-3. That same September, Hamilton Standard concurred. In November 1977, operators in the Pacific Fleet were informed that -83282 was approved for use in prop controls and that the new fluid could be mixed with the old without restriction.

Two weeks before PD-2 went to Adak, its no. 1 and 2 props were serviced with

MIL-H-83282 hydraulic fluid as part of a routine maintenance inspection. These two were the only propellers of the thirty-six in the Patrol Squadron 9 fleet that did not contain the familiar MIL-H-5606 fluid.

Finding of Fact. A No. 1 Engine propeller leak had been discovered and reported during post-flight of Aircraft Buno. 159892 on 25 October 1978. A thorough inspection by maintenance personnel revealed no discrepancy.

PO 2d Class Donald Tullar, an aviation metalsmith, was one of the two flight engineers with Crew 11 in PD-2 on its flight on 25 October, the day after it came from California and the day before it was lost with Crew 6 aboard. Tullar and PO 1st Class Leonard Northrop, the other engineer, had shut down and restarted the no. 1 engine twice during that scheduled eight-hour flight, both times without problems. "Everything operated smoothly," Tullar recalled later.

After landing around 5:00 P.M., Tullar discovered what he thought might be a small prop leak on the no. 1 engine during his postflight inspection. He reported it to the maintenance night shift supervisor, a parachute rigger by training, who then sent a jet engine mechanic, PO 2d Class Jerry Aquistapace, to investigate. Aquistapace did not find a leak after running up no. 1, so PD-2 went on the schedule for Event AK 262 the next day with Crew 6.

Tullar, who left the squadron ops area after his postflight and would not get back to the hangar until midmorning the next day, unknowingly dodged a bullet in the afternoon. He was originally supposed to fly PD-2 again on 26 October, but Operations removed him from the schedule because the required 5:00 A.M. preflight inspection did not permit adequate crew rest. Sometime late on the twenty-fifth Tullar's named was literally scratched off the already-signed flight schedule and PO Butch Miller's inked in. That casual act shaped the future and altered lives.

Butch Miller did not discover the swap—and that he was now flying early the next morning—until 8:00 or 9:00 that night. The news did not put him to bed early; however, he was up until 1:30 in the morning talking to Northrop. "Crew rest" provided the opportunity for adequate sleep before a long day but could not guarantee it. The late notification must have really annoyed Miller, because he was still bitching about it to Lieutenants (junior grade) Gibbons and Ball when the three met at the aircraft for preflight several hours later.

Butch Miller's frame of mind during his last day alive was to get a lot of posthumous attention as people looked back on the accident in the months to come, including consideration of reports that he had argued with his wife, Karen, a few days before the fatal flight. No one ever suggested that Miller's mood had anything to do with what happened. In his personal review of the investigation four months later, the commander of the Pacific Fleet's patrol wings specifically dismissed psychological and emotional factors as playing any role.

The Adak detachment's ops officer was not as fastidious about crew rest requirements in the case of Ens. John Wagner as he was with Tullar. John Wagner was on the 25 October flight with Tullar, but he was scheduled for the tactical flight the next day too. So it was that Wagner showed up at the aircraft at 5:00 A.M. on the twenty-sixth, ready to go again. A junior officer's first few weeks in a fleet squadron were no time to be heard complaining about being on the flight schedule too much, and no one had much interest anytime in the complaints of ensigns.

The crew would be conducting PD-2's preflight inspection against the backdrop of a mystery and tragedy. Three older model P-3Bs belonging to the Atlantic Fleet's Patrol Wing 5, located at Naval Air Station Brunswick, Maine, had been lost in the preceding ten months, taking everyone—twenty-eight air crewmen—aboard down with them.

In December 1977, Patrol Squadron 11's LE-8 (Buno. 153428) operating from Naval Station Rota, Spain, was lost in the Canary Islands, with thirteen aboard. It had hit a mountain in the clouds over tiny Hierro Island. LE-8 was pulverized by the impact. So little was left that, according to one report, the P-3 was first tentatively identified as an American aircraft only through a scrap of paper in the wreckage with the word "Florida" on it. The following April, LJ-4 (Buno. 152724) of Patrol Squadron 23 went down silently and unobserved into the water off the Azores, with its crew of seven. Then in September 1978, a Patrol Squadron 8 P-3, LC-7 (Buno. 152757), lost its wing and disintegrated in the air over Paris, Maine, on the way to an air show in Canada, killing eight more.

According to Emmett Eggleston of the *Palo Alto Times,* by the fall of 1978, people were getting spooked in the fleet. Writing about PD-2 on its front page, dated 27 October 1978, the newspaper quoted Rear Adm. Ralph Hedges, the senior Navy commander in Maine, as having said, "There's a feeling that the Wing has been hexed, jinxed or under some supernatural spell, and it's almost impossible to fight because we don't know why our planes have crashed." Congress was interested, too, and asking questions about the losses. It was unlikely anyone on the Hill would sign on to an answer that drew on supernatural spells as an explanation for the deaths and destruction.

There is no indication whatever that anyone preparing to fly on Event AK 262 spent any time pondering this unnerving recent history. To the contrary, observers reported after the fact that, with the obvious exception of Butch Miller, crewmembers appeared enthusiastic about the flight, and eager to get into the air.

Finding of Fact. Preflight inspection of aircraft Buno. 159892 went very smoothly. Lieutenant Caylor and Ensign Wagner shared pilot preflight duties while Petty Officer Miller and Petty Officer Flow shared the Flight Engineer preflight responsibilities. Both flight engineers had visually inspected the engines and noticed no discrepancies. The aircraft had received a proper daily inspection the previous evening, fuel samples had been taken, preflight had been completed, and the aircraft had been released for flight. Petty Officer Miller had completed all required forms and a weight and balance form (DD 365F) had been approved. There were no known discrepancies that could have affected the performance of the aircraft.

A P-3 preflight typically unearthed two kinds of problems, those characteristic of *any* aircraft and those unique to the antisubmarine warfare avionics suite of *this* particular model aircraft. Navy aircraft reliability calculations took into consideration all discrepancies, but it was common that an aircraft would be merely flyable (referring only to airframe, engines, and nav/comm systems) somewhat more often than it would be operational mission-ready. Today's flight required a mission-ready aircraft, and PD-2's comprehensive preflight inspection confirmed that it was.

According to the weight and balance form filled out by Butch Miller prior to the flight, PD-2 would weigh 136,521 pounds at takeoff. The "basic airplane" comprised almost 69,000 pounds of this total. Oil (275 pounds), the crew (2,700 pounds), sonobuoys (2,326 pounds), and fuel (62,561 pounds) made up the rest. Curiously, the total shown on Miller's DD 365F form was 1,521 pounds over the 135,000-pound maximum written in the form's Limitations block.[3]

The plan was that PD-2 would return to the flight line with at least 23,000 pounds of fuel aboard—roughly five hours worth to dry tanks. Because of the island's famously unpredictable weather, this amount had been established as the on-top requirement back at Adak, to ensure sufficient fuel to get to a distant alternate if required. Miller's center of gravity calculation showed that the aircraft CG at takeoff would be well within the permissible range. Grigsby reviewed Miller's calculation as part of his own preflight inspection and signed it.

Hours later, long after Senior Chief Gerald Lenhart had supervised AF 586's departure from the flight line, he heard that PD-2 was going to ditch. Rightly anticipating the investigation to come, Lenhart then collected all of Buno. 159892's maintenance records and delivered them for safekeeping to Mike Harris's office.

Chapter 3

On Station

Weather is a player in everything that happens near the Aleutians. It claims new victims, occasionally aircraft, usually fishing boats and their crews, every year.

Sometime between 10:30 P.M. 1 April 2001 and 3:35 the next morning, the Alaskan fishing vessel *Arctic Rose* vanished from the Zemchung Flats fishing grounds in the Bering Sea, north of the Aleutian Islands. The steel-hulled, ninety-three-foot vessel silently disappeared over the midwatch, between a routine evening call to its sister ship and the transmission of an alarm from its Emergency Position Indicating Radio Beacon.

Arctic Rose's accident, as mysterious as the simultaneous capsizing of *Americus* and the sinking of its sister ship *Altair* in February 1983 near Dutch Harbor, was described as "the deadliest single accident in the U.S. fishing fleet in half a century."[1] Fourteen had died aboard *Americus* and *Altair*.[2] All fifteen of *Arctic Rose*'s crew were lost, coincidentally the same number of men as would climb up AF 586's boarding ladder to go flying this morning.

Finding of Fact. While the aircraft preflight was taking place, Lieutenant Commander Grigsby received a thorough weather brief and filed a DD 175 Military Flight Plan that would take him to his assigned operating area west of Shemya Island via reserved airspace and return him to Adak when the mission was terminated.

Caylor and Wagner conducted the cockpit preflight and pilot's walk-around inspection, freeing Grigsby to get the weather briefing and file their flight plan.

The preflight inspection identified a few minor discrepancies, but the maintenance launch crew quickly fixed these.

For reasons of operations security, AF 586's canned flight plan told the air traffic control system as little as possible, just enough to get the aircraft out of Adak at 9:00 A.M. and back nine hours later. For eight hours and twenty minutes of the nine hours in the air, AF 586 would be operating in Roughcut Delta, a reserved block of oceanic airspace. The FAA's local facility would control the aircraft only for the first and last twenty minutes of the flight, within one hundred miles or so of Adak. Elsewhere, the flight plan's notes said, the cockpit crew would be responsible for safe separation from other aircraft. This assumption of responsibility was largely an air traffic control formality; no one expected other aircraft to be flying under visual flight rules in AF 586's remote operating area. If a Soviet aircraft were to materialize, it would be up to the two crews to stay far enough apart from each other to avoid a midair collision.

Among other things, the flight plan remarks also told ATC that the aircraft had fifteen crewmembers on board and was equipped with standard Navy survival equipment, meaning anti-exposure suits and life vests, the usual two seven- and one twelve-man rafts, and a sonobuoy set to a frequency reserved for emergency homing beacon use. As a pilot with a special instrument rating, Grigsby could approve his own flight plans and on this one he followed the usual practice and signed as the approving authority, not as pilot in command.

The weather briefing was routine, too. At takeoff and on his return, Adak's weather would be seasonal. Occasional snow and rain showers aside, afternoon weather in the Central Aleutians would not be appreciably worse than early evening weather on the mainland, at Elmendorf and Anchorage, the two choices for an alternate should the crew not be able to get into Adak for some reason.

Finding of Fact. The forecast weather for the area in which the flight would be operating to the west of the island of Shemya was as follows:

Ceiling: 2,000–4,000 feet with multiple layers extending to 31,000 feet

Wind: variable southwest at 30 knots to northwest at 40 knots

Turbulence: light to moderate at all altitudes in vicinity of low pressure system

Icing: trace to light mixed icing between 1,000 and 10,000 feet vicinity of low pressure system

Precipitation: rain and snow showers en route

There was a rather strong occluded frontal system spawned by an intense low-pressure system forecast to be approximately 80 miles east of Shemya by 0001Z 27 October 1978.

The seas off the Aleutians are one of the globe's great weather battlegrounds. Here dry, cold polar air pours east out of Siberia to flow over the relatively warmer waters of the North Pacific and the Bering Sea. Heated by this contact at the surface, the now-humidified air rises, triggering powerful squalls, small snow or rain showers that sweep furiously across the waves one after another, or dense fogs that move with the speed of the wind across the islands, occasionally bringing visibility down to inside the span of your arms.

Near-permanent low atmospheric pressure over the archipelago makes the central Aleutians into a sort of "storm sump," drawing the big systems that form regularly off Japan (or, in late season, even mid-Pacific typhoons) into a great semicircular track that has its terminus in the Gulf of Alaska. As these systems, the Pacific equivalent of the infamous Atlantic nor'easters, race past Kamchatka, they spin up howling winds and mountainous seas. Immediately behind the weather front everything is confused, with high seas often running against strong winds.

On 26 October, the major swell system in AF 586's operating area was from the north-northwest, 330°, with waves running from twelve to twenty feet trough to crest, perhaps even higher. Some accounts have suggested that the waves were as high as thirty feet, which would have made them enormous and very rare in most of the waters of the world but not exceptional here. A minor, overlying wind-driven swell system was coming from the southwest, 220°, pushed along by a wind just above the surface as high as forty-two knots, nearly fifty miles per hour and just under gale force. A heading into the wind would put an aircraft parallel to the major system.

Grigsby's weather briefing packet for the mission, prepared by Adak's Naval Weather Service Office early that morning, included all the usual charts. The surface chart showed a deep low (29.29 inches atmospheric pressure, compared to the standard 29.92 inches) off Petropavlosk, circled by forty-knot winds, with layered clouds all the way from the Central Aleutians west to over the Sea of Okhotsk. In days to come, the low would get deeper still. Forty miles north of Kiska Island and sailing through what amounted to a hurricane, Coast Guard Cutter *Jarvis* would record a barometric pressure of 29.05 inches the next day, with the notation "falling rapidly."

The packet also included the usual page of recommended ditch headings for each 5-degree square of latitude and longitude. (Absent any better information, a pilot could align his aircraft on the recommended magnetic heading and have some chance that he would hit the water parallel to the major swell system in the area. As it happened, the recommended heading, 150°, was 70° off.)

Although on station weather was not expected to be good, Grigsby's special instrument card attested to his skill flying on instruments, and based on the briefing, he would not have expected to find anything west of Shemya that the cockpit crew and the aircraft's superb foul weather systems could not handle easily. Destination weather at the time of return was not forecast to be bad: for the two hours around Crew 6's estimated time of arrival, Adak anticipated seven miles visibility under a four thousand foot overcast, with scattered and broken cloud layers below that, and winds from the south-southwest at fifteen knots gusting to thirty-three. The weather at Anchorage, the alternate selected, two and a half hours later would be better, if only because the winds would be lighter.

Finding of Fact. Engines were turned at 0825 and the aircraft was in position, ready for takeoff, by 0840. Takeoff commenced at 0845 with Lieutenant Commander Grigsby in the pilot's seat, Lieutenant Caylor in the copilot's seat and Petty Officer Flow in the Flight Engineer's seat.

Everything the flight crew and other Detachment personnel had done that morning was with one goal in mind: to get AF 586 into the air on time, as prescribed by commander, Task Group 32.2's PARPRO event schedule. A late takeoff would have provoked instant criticism that would have flashed along the operational chain of command to the squadron and crew, and confirmed the bitter observation that "shit always flows downhill." Takeoff was scheduled for 9:00 A.M. but could be as early as 8:45 and still fit into the flight's window.

The cockpit crew would have completed the short takeoff checklist prior to taking the runway. The first item on that checklist is "Set Condition V." The P-3 Flight Manual defines five crew readiness conditions, to be set by the mission commander, as appropriate, during flight. Condition V is set for takeoff and landing, and also for ditching. It requires everyone aboard to be in his assigned ditching station with headrests in place, seat belts and shoulder harnesses fastened, and with gloves on for fire protection. The patrol plane commander may also prescribe helmets. Ordinarily, helmets were not worn for takeoff or landing. A P-3 crewmember could go twelve months, check ride to check ride, between one wearing of his hard hat and another.

Once on Runway 23, nose wheel aligned on the centerline and parking brakes set, everyone on board would have waited, impatiently watching the minute hand. At a busy air station, an aircraft could not be permitted to block the instrument runway while the clock ticked, but Adak obviously had no other operations at the field. No one was inbound, and the next departure was by a Coast Guard C-130 in half an hour, heading back home to Kodiak.

When Grigsby released the brakes, pushed the four power levers forward, and commanded Ed Flow to set "max power," and after Ed Caylor announced they had passed through "refusal" airspeed, PD-2 with Crew 6 aboard was going flying. Event AK 262 had begun.

Some airplanes want to fly. Sailplanes want to so much, they do it without an engine. Others, like helicopters, have to be tricked into the air. A quick, surreptitious tug on the collective, and they are in the air before there is time for protest. Most other aircraft lie somewhere in between gliders and helicopters in their natural enthusiasm for flight. These others get light on their landing gear as they accelerate down the runway, and then seem to rise spontaneously into the air at the end of the takeoff roll.

Not so the P-3, it must be told when to fly, but after that, it responds eagerly. The P-3's stance is level at rest, but as the takeoff roll progresses, it squats purposefully, becoming increasingly nose down and tail high. When the copilot announces "rotate," the pilot responds by pulling back on the yoke decisively with both hands. Only then does his airplane lift itself into the air, all signs of reluctance gone. Happy to be in the air. So it must have been for AF 586; "rotate" at just above 130 knots (150 mph), and off Adak fifteen minutes early. Even before the landing gear hooked into their up-locks, Matt Gibbons would log the time of takeoff in the appropriate blank of his draft of the mission report, and Bruce Forshay would report "out" to Elmendorf over the radio.

After the landing gear came up and the flaps were retracted, and after power was reduced for the climb, Condition IV would have been set, a one-man inspection of the aircraft during climb-out by Butch Miller, the off-duty flight engineer, searching for leaks, smoke, fumes, loose equipment, or other obvious discrepancies. (All more common in the days of unpressurized aircraft and reciprocating engines.) Then Condition III, this would have released the rest of the crew to check the status of their equipment. And once on station, Condition II, with all positions manned as necessary for routine patrol.

Finding of Fact. The flight to the tactical on station point, in the vicinity of Shemya, was uneventful and the weather proved to be somewhat better than forecast. Once in the tactical operating area, two ships were identified visually. They were a Liberian tanker and a Soviet fishing vessel, the Mys Sinyavin.

AF 586 climbed through cloud layers to twenty thousand feet, the flight plan altitude for the transit to the on-station coordinates, along the track prescribed by the standard instrument departure from the field. Inside the cabin Condition IV gave way to Condition III.

Although the P-3's minimum crew is four (the cockpit crew plus an observer in the tube), that minimum is for pilot training, maintenance tests, and repositioning flights over land only. Doing anything else with the aircraft requires more crewmembers.

Unlike PO 3d Class James Brooner, twenty-three, and Airman Randall Rodriguez, nineteen, the two acoustic sensor operators, Airman Richard Garcia, twenty, at Sensor Station 3, actually had something to do on the flight. Sensor Station 3 is the crew's non-acoustic sensors operator, responsible for operation of the aircraft's radars, the magnetic anomaly detection (MAD) equipment, electronic intercept

(ESM) equipment, and, when installed, the forward-looking infrared search sensor. What sounds like an impossible job is made possible because these systems are usually used one at a time, during different phases of flight.

On this flight, Rich Garcia would record all the Soviet electronic emissions intercepted by his ESM gear and use his radar to help Lieutenant (jg) Gibbons establish a plot of all shipping on the surface in the operating area. The goal was a position, course, and speed for every vessel in the area. When time and the weather permitted, the aircraft would descend to a few hundred feet to "rig" and photograph the contact, adding a name and home port and comments about the ship's appearance and deck cargo or other details to the end-of-mission report.

By contrast, Brooner and Rodriguez were aboard PD-2 on 26 October because the aircraft flight manual prescribed a minimum crew of eleven for all operational flights, not because they had any particular role to play during the next hours in the air. Brooner and Rodriguez were the Sensor Station 1 and 2 operators on the made-up crew that flew AF 586. Had this been an antisubmarine warfare training flight, they would have operated the aircraft's paired acoustic sensor equipment, responsible for displaying, evaluating, and recording the ocean sounds picked up by the sonobuoys—expendable sonars—dropped by the aircraft.

One of the aircraft's two long range frequency analysis and recording displays was located at each acoustic sensor station, a piece of equipment poetically called "Jezebel."[3] Jezebel was used to detect and identify submarines by the distinctive acoustic "signature"—a characteristic pattern of discrete frequencies and broadband noise—that each class put into the water. Under absolutely ideal conditions, and conditions in the North Pacific were rarely ideal, Jezebel could detect some submarines one hundred or more miles away from a buoy.

During a flight on top of a submarine, Rodriguez, Brooner, and the tactical coordinator, Gibbons, would have formed the core of the tactical crew. The aircraft's success on such a flight would depend almost entirely on the ability of these three crewmembers to sift submarine-generated noise from the cacophony of the ocean.

On a PARPRO mission such as Event AK 262, however, there was no submarine to search for and there would be no buoys in the water. Brooner and Rodriguez must have had little to do. On this flight they would have been as much passengers as were Master Chief Garland Shepard and PO Gary Hemmer, the flight observers from the Adak Tactical Support Center.

Airman Dave Reynolds, twenty-four, the crew's ordnanceman from Charlotte, North Carolina, also would have been underemployed. AF 586 would not be searching for submarines today. Unless they unexpectedly stumbled over one, no sonobuoys would be expended. With no buoys in the water, the banks of sonobuoy radio receivers and the pair of acoustic analysis recorders would remain in standby after preflight. The usual, pungent smell of burning thermographic paper from the twin recorders would not be wafting through the tube once the aircraft got to its station.

The crew found only two ships. Because of the lax standards of the Liberian merchant marine registry, vessels flying Liberia's one-star flag, with "Monrovia" painted on the stern, were ubiquitous in the world's sea lanes. It would not necessarily have surprised the crew to find a Liberian-registered tanker here on the opposite side of the world from West Africa.[4] The other ship was *Mys Sinyavin* ("Cape Sinyavin"), one of several stern trawlers at sea under the control of the Far Eastern Fish Association (the Dalnevostochnaya Ryba), the Soviet North Pacific fisheries authority. Two more Soviet trawlers, *Mys Belkina* and *Mys Gorodok,* were out of PD-2's radar range up track. A fourth, *Tajikistan,* was farther north still, in the Bering Sea. Crew 6 never knew these ships were there. *Mys Sinyavin* was proceeding southwest, with all of its trawl gear out of the water and stowed away.

Finding of Fact. At approximately 0930, Ensign Wagner relieved Lieutenant Commander Grigsby in the pilot's seat.

Grigsby had been in the left seat since takeoff, forty-five minutes earlier. Once relieved, he would remain out of the seat for almost two hours, likely spending most of his time in the cockpit, but now free to walk aft, to the galley for a cup of coffee or to the head (the aircraft's toilet), just forward of the dinette. The break would also have given him time to visit with the members of the tactical crew, busy—or not—at their stations along both sides of the aircraft's center aisle.

Finding of Fact. At 1050, No. 1 engine was loitered for fuel conservation. Prior to shutdown, a successful Negative Torque System (N.T.S.) check was obtained at 165–170 knots at 8,000 feet. There were no abnormal indications present either during the N.T.S. check or during the loitering of No. 1 engine.

The maximum advertised endurance of the P-3 is twelve hours and twenty minutes, assuming takeoff with all six tanks full (a total of 62,500 pounds of fuel) and an aircraft weight of 135,000 pounds. It is possible, however, to extend that endurance significantly, by as much as five hours, by shutting down first the no. 1 engine and then the no. 4, as fuel is burned and the aircraft loses weight. Operating with one or two engines shut down is called "loitering." The technique is not unique to the P-3; Coast Guard C-130s do it, too, on maximum endurance missions, but other aircraft do not. Ships at sea that spot a passing P-3 with one or two props feathered often wrongly assuming that the aircraft is in distress when it is simply conserving fuel. Their confusion is natural. Flying around with good engines shut down is a quixotic thing to do.

Lieutenant Commander Grigsby's decision to loiter the no. 1 engine was entirely routine, as was the negative torque sensing check performed by the flight engineer. The flight manual requires an NTS check when "mission flight plans call for feathering shutdown and subsequent air start of an engine or engines" before the shutdown.

The successful check at 10:50 A.M. confirmed that the NTS system was likely to operate on restart, if required by a prop malfunction that resulted in negative torque, a condition where the prop would be attempting to drive the reduction gearbox. If such a situation were not corrected, propeller drag could become great enough to threaten control of the aircraft.

Crew 11 had flown PD-2 on a tactical mission the day before, twice shutting down the no. 1 engine and restarting it uneventfully and after their successful NTS check on 26 October, Crew 6 had no reason to expect that their experience would be anything different.

Finding of Fact. At approximately 1100, Petty Officer Miller relieved Petty Officer Flow as Flight Engineer.

In the days of the P-3A and B, the flight engineer enjoyed a special status as the de facto leader of the enlisted crewmembers, irrespective of seniority. In part this status adhered to the engineer because of his proximity, hour after hour, to the patrol plane commander in the left seat in the chummy confines of the cockpit.

The P-3C, with its complex and often (at least in the early years) cranky central processor, changed that. The computer and its associated systems required a full-time in-flight technician on the crew, and an experienced IFT eventually became a natural rival to the flight engineer for leadership. The engineer's forte gave him little leverage to understand the mysteries of the P-3C's complicated, computerized system, and little time to learn them. On this flight, however, the two flight engineers would rightly expect no challenge to their leadership from any enlisted man on the crew.

Miller was six years older than Flow and had five more years of Navy service than the younger man. Plane commanders liked the cheerful Miller, who obviously loved to fly. Nevertheless, in the aircraft Ed Flow was the more experienced of the two. Miller had 680 hours in the P-3; Flow had nearly 1,100 hours. Despite that imbalance, the differences in age and seniority might have lent Miller more authority than they should have. Back at Moffett Field, Miller had benefited from being the backup flight engineer on Crew 1, the commanding officer's crew. He had learned the practical factors of his trade from Bud Power's handpicked flight engineer, but he had flown his first evaluation as a flight engineer only the preceding March and so could count just six months of real world experience in the cockpit's center seat.

Finding of Fact. At approximately 1120, Lieutenant Commander Grigsby relieved Lieutenant Caylor in the copilot's seat.

Once on station, the cockpit fell into a routine, with the autopilot doing most of the work by keeping AF 586 straight and level. Unlike an antisubmarine warfare training flight, in the hours to come PD-2 would require little maneuvering and relatively little flight at very low altitude. With just two ships in the area, only the three naval flight officers in the tube, carefully navigating down the prescribed track and reporting AF 586's progress by radio in laboriously hand-encrypted messages, would stay busy. Before takeoff, Gibbons and Forshay had agreed on a general division of responsibilities: Gibbons would communicate and Forshay would navigate. In general, that is exactly how the two NFOs spent their remaining hours in the air.

Grigsby evidently planned on rotating his cockpit crew every two hours or so. That schedule would give him a well-rested and alert cockpit for the entire nine-hour flight, especially for the descent, approach, and night landing at Adak just before six that evening, where the greatest challenge for the pilots was likely to lie.

After he settled into the flight engineer's seat, Miller took advantage of the tranquility to quiz the new no-P, Wagner, on aircraft systems. Although both Miller and Flow had completed the RAG's instructor flight engineer syllabus, this kind of interrogation was not unique to instructors. It was commonplace on any flight deck when nothing much was going on. Their conversation soon got around to the prop.

Finding of Fact. Between 1050 and 1220, altitudes varied between 300 and 8,000 feet, as the aircraft was maneuvered for surface ship reconnaissance and surface search. During this period, neither icing nor precipitation was encountered. Outside air temperatures were purposefully checked and never fell below 0°C.

Until just after noon, AF 586's on-station weather was actually slightly better than forecast. The freezing level had been forecast to be at five thousand feet, which would have put PD-2 in and out of icing during the early hours of the flight. In fact, however, icing was not evident at aircraft altitude until almost 1:00 P.M.

PD-2 would have been maneuvering during this hour and a half to remain clear of clouds and icing, dipping down low to identify and photograph the only two ships on its track. Of the two, *Mys Sinyavin,* the big Russian refrigerated processing stern trawler heading southwest, would have been by far the more interesting. The distinctive Soviet stack insignia, a yellow hammer and sickle on a red field, always sent a quick frisson through the observers at the windows on any flight. It would have done that today, too, even though these Russians were harmless fishermen. Matt Gibbons logged the ships' position, course, and speed. He would need the information for his postflight "purple" report (one of the Navy's color-coded operational reports) to the task group commander.

PD-2 was equipped with two, identical AN/APS-115B surface search radars, one forward and one aft, each searching one hemisphere around the aircraft. The raw radar picture was available only to Airman Garcia, the Sensor Station 3 operator, and to Gibbons on his multifunction CRT display at the tacco station. Radar contacts could be passed to the cockpit only as "fly to" points on the patrol plane commander's small tactical display or orally as heading instructions over the intercom.

The arrangement worked adequately for tactical applications, like surface search or mining, but was awkward when the radar was used for weather avoidance or navigation. Denying the pilots' their own radar display, however, was a deliberate design decision. Cockpit workload was thought to be heavy enough, especially at low altitude, without adding one more potential distraction.

The best that could be said about the -115 radar was that it was a compromise, optimized for nothing. The radar was unusable against either a submarine periscope or snorkel mast except in the glossiest sea states. Against nuclear submarines, the threat after the 1960s, radar was simply superfluous: the nukes never had to expose themselves, and with a single, small ESM mast above the surface, they could detect the distinctive APS-115 radar emission long before that radar could threaten them with counterdetection. The -115 was somewhat more useful in navigation, weather avoidance, and surface search applications.

In today's sea state, however, even surface search would be seriously degraded looking in the direction of the swells and Garcia's radarscope would have a bright bloom of sea return clutter at its center. He would have to adjust the antenna tilt all day long, to get the best picture possible. Finding *Sinyavin* on radar a second time—even under these conditions it would not be difficult—would become Garcia's unknowing, essential contribution to saving the lives of his crewmates.

Finding of Fact. At 1250, as the weather was deteriorating, the flight crew elected to restart No. 1 engine. While the aircraft commenced a slow descent from 7,500 feet to remain below the weather, the restart checklist was commenced.

The P-3's twenty-eight-thousand-foot ceiling prevents it from climbing above most weather, as turbojet- or turbofan-powered aircraft can do everywhere but in the tropics, where clouds occasionally rise to stratospheric heights. Moreover, the maritime patrol mission frequently requires flight at lower altitudes, in clouds and icing. By an accident of geography, the maritime choke points that could hold major units of the Soviet Navy, its nuclear submarines and large combatant surface ships, locked in their home waters are all in northern latitudes, too.

Happily, the Orion is an excellent foul weather aircraft. Anti-ice systems (to prevent the formation of ice) and de-ice systems (to remove it once formed) are very effective. The aircraft has operated successfully and safely for decades from Iceland, Newfoundland, and Alaska in U.S. Navy livery and in Norwegian and

Canadian colors through the extremes of winter weather found in those countries.

Its powerful engines provide copious amounts of high-temperature engine-bleed air to de-ice the wing leading edges and engine inlets, at the cost of a small reduction in power available. The props, tail planes, and forward windshields are kept clear by electrical heating. The P-3's electrical power generation capability (three engine-driven generators with a fourth available, driven by the auxiliary power unit located beneath the copilot) has enormous margins. Not until the aircraft is down to a single generator and the propeller or empennage de-icing system is actuated does the aircraft begin automatically turning off some non-essential electrical loads to conserve power for flight-essential systems.

The P-3 flight manual highlights operating procedures, practices, or conditions which may damage equipment with a "Caution" legend, and such a caution placard precedes the discussion on all weather operations with engines shut down.

> CAUTION. Anti-icing protection is not available for engines secured for loiter operations. Two- or three-engine loiter in icing conditions may cause ice build-ups in the feathered engine, leading to damage or possible engine failure upon restart. Two- or three-engine loiter should not be utilized in conditions where visible moisture is present at ambient temperatures below +10°C because of possible ice build-up in the shut down engine.

Now that the weather was getting worse, Grigsby prudently instructed Petty Officer Miller to restart no. 1. With the engine running, hot air could be bled from its compressor, and used to de-ice the lips of the engine airscoop and the compressor inlet. (Electrical de- and anti-icing systems had been entirely unaffected by AF 586's three-engine operation because, by design, the P-3 has no generator on the no. 1 engine.)

When the no. 1 engine was shut down at 10:40 as prescribed by the loiter shutdown checklist, the cockpit crew would have immediately gone on to do the first ten items of the restart checklist. With those items accomplished in advance, restarting the engine in an emergency could be done very rapidly.

At 12:50 Grigsby, in the right seat, would have been the one to read the restart checklist beginning with item 11, with Miller performing the required actions and reporting their completion. Wagner was flying the aircraft from the left seat, autopilot momentarily off for the engine restart, with Caylor sitting directly behind him on a large, boxy housing that contained a radar component, the usual perch for off-duty pilots. From that position he could easily see the no. 1 engine while he overheard Grigsby reciting the checklist.

Four hours into its nine-hour flight, PD-2 weighed approximately 115,000 pounds when no. 1 was restarted. Start, taxi, takeoff, and climb-out, two hours on four engines and two on three had burned up nearly twenty thousand pounds of fuel.

Because it is located ahead of the plane of the propellers, under usual conditions the cockpit of the P-3 in flight is fairly quiet, quiet enough so that the pilots and flight engineer normally talk to one another directly at a conversational volume rather than using the intercom system. The restart checklist took seconds, literally, to accomplish. It is possible that Miller had done this procedure in an aircraft or flight simulator 150 times before. It is probable that Grigsby, veteran of a tour of duty as a maintenance check pilot at a P-3 overhaul facility, would have had even more experience in restarting a T-56 engine in flight.

Finding of Fact. Petty Officer Moore was stationed as observer for the start, while Petty Officer Flow watched the start from a position immediately next to Moore. Lieutenant (junior grade) Gibbons and Lieutenant (junior grade) Ball observed the start from the tacco's window. Lieutenant Caylor observed the start from a position directly behind Ensign Wagner.

PO 3d Class Howard Moore, twenty-two, the crew's in-flight technician, was in training for two years before he arrived at Patrol Squadron 9 in August 1978. Years later he would say candidly that the long course of Navy training—boot camp in Illinois, electronics in Tennessee, aircrew in Florida, and survival in California— was the first thing he ever completed in his youth. Howard Moore, from Hoover, Alabama, had drifted through Berry High School in Birmingham, and one year of college at Jacksonville State, in Jacksonville, Alabama. As his father hoped, he settled down quickly in the Navy. Nancy and Wayne Moore proudly watched their son graduate at the head of his advanced avionics course.

When he was not out of his seat, peaking and tweaking the complex system in flight or helping the ordnanceman wrestle buoys, Moore was assigned as an observer to Station 10, just aft of the main cabin door on the port side of the aircraft. Today he would sit there backing up the nav/comm on the radio receivers, by copying incoming encrypted radio messages. Atmospheric conditions could infect HF communications with maddening static, making transmissions very difficult to understand. Having two people listening and writing down the phonetic alphabet stream that crackled through the ether improved the chances of getting a message right. Moore was also to watch no. 1 relight.

An observer in the tube is always posted to watch an in-flight engine start, usually at one of the aft lookout windows, where he will have a clear view of what the flight station cannot see, the top of the nacelle and up the engine tailpipe. Once the prop begins to spin, he is looking for anything: leaks, flames, or smoke, anything out of the ordinary that cannot be seen from the cockpit.

Six would watch this engine start, but only because with just two surface contacts in the area, there was not much else going on at the time. Otherwise, things were quiet enough that Dave Reynolds was sleeping in one of the two bunk beds on the starboard side aft, across from the galley. The characteristic, twitchy motion of the aircraft as the propeller spun up, just before Miller turned on the no. 1 fuel and ignition switch to relight the engine, woke Reynolds up.

Matt Gibbons and John Ball were both at the tacco's station, with Ball in the seat and Gibbons looking over his shoulder. Gibbons remembers telling Ball, who seemed uninterested at first, to watch the start with a comment to the effect that "look out[side] . . . you can never tell what you're going to see."

No one had any reason to believe that this start would be any different from the others they had witnessed.

Finding of Fact. At approximately 1253, No. 1 propeller was unfeathered and No. 1 engine restarted. It started normally, although several of the crew thought it may have been somewhat slow to achieve stabilized rpm. There were no indications of propeller fluid leakage, no prop pump warning lights or other indications of an impending problem. The engine was operated at minimum power for several minutes until oil temperature rose to 0°C, then at 1,000 shaft horsepower until oil temperature climbed to 40°C.

Once Grigsby decided he wanted no. 1 back, engine restart from loiter shutdown was basically Miller's show. Even on a normal restart, things happen very quickly between restoring fuel and ignition and achieving 100 percent rpm. If something malfunctions on the way to 100 percent, things happen even more quickly. Either way, everyone in the cockpit knew the procedures, and knew who was to do what.

Both pilots would have glanced up briefly when Miller announced, "Unfeathering No. 1," reached for the far left-hand feather button above Wagner's head, pushed the guard away, and then pulled the button down, starting the feather pump. (Their confirming glance was a reflex, a habit embedded to ensure that the flight engineer had his hand on the correct feather button to restart the loitered engine, because the next four steps of the restart checklist would happen in a rush, without the usual challenge and reply.)

Ensign Wagner would then look out at the wing and announce what he was seeing. On the port wing, visible just beyond his left shoulder, no. 1's blades would have twisted off the high-pitch stops toward lower pitch (Wagner: "Blade angle"), been caught by the wind, and started to spin slowly clockwise (Wagner: "Rotation"). The NTS System, tested at 10:50 A.M. before no. 1 was feathered, would catch the prop as it spun up through 20–30 percent and hold it there. (Miller, with his eyes on the no. 1 tach: "Stabilized r.p.m. . . . ignition"; as he turned on the fuel and ignition switch: "Lightoff.")

Miller's hand would then drop quickly to the no. 1 emergency shutdown handle, ready to pull it if something—oil pressure, turbine inlet temperature, rpm—went wrong. Everyone's eyes would finally settle on the no. 1 rpm gauge, watching it to confirm that the hydro-mechanical governing system would catch the prop and hold normal rpm.

As usual, it did. The flutter of activity was almost over.

Grigsby resumed reading the checklist, with Miller responding suitably to each challenge. Then Miller would have scanned the engine instruments one final time and announced, "Normal start, no. 1" to both pilots. A seasoned engineer, knowing he had a no-P in the left seat, would now move his right hand discreetly to the copilot's no. 1 power level to block its forward motion. The momentary gesture would prevent a premature application of power to a cold engine by an overzealous young pilot on the other side of the cockpit.

Ed Caylor was one who thought no. 1 came out of feather slowly. John Ball, at the tacco's window in the line of no. 1 and 2 props and attentive only because Gibbons had prodded him to be, was another. Next to him, Gibbons thought it was "sluggish" too. All their judgments were subjective. The difference between "slow" and "normal" might have been a heartbeat or two. Ed Flow, who knew more about it than the others and who watched the restart from behind the tailpipe, hunched over Moore's shoulder at Station 10, did not see anything out of the ordinary. Neither did Bruce Forshay, who knew less and whose station across the aisle from the port wing gave him only a reflected view of the start, mirrored in the tacco's large scope.

During the two hours no. 1 had been shut down, engine oil would have cooled to well below the normal operating temperature range of 60–90 degrees C. Wagner's cautious restoration of power was intended to ensure warm engine oil and good lubrication before the engine was taxed.

Finding of Fact. At approximately 1300, Ensign Wagner adjusted the power level on No. 1 engine to marry all four power levers at a cruise setting. Aircraft altitude was approximately 6,500 feet. As he did so, No. 1 engine r.p.m. went offspeed, climbing in a fluctuating manner, and accompanied by an audible offspeed. There were no other indications of a prop malfunction, either visible fluid or warning lights.

At 40 degrees C oil temperature in the no. 1 engine, Miller would have announced "pilot's power number one." Wagner then pushed the power lever forward, looking for approximately 1,500 shaft horsepower on each engine, to hold 205 knots indicated airspeed.

The most powerful aerodynamic force acting on a rotating propeller is called centrifugal twisting moment, which acts to twist the blades to flat pitch (flat as compared to the direction of flight) and toward higher rpm. Mechanical governing, the coarse control of rpm between 99 and 101 percent, is accomplished by using high-pressure hydraulic fluid to counteract centrifugal twisting moment. At this instant, that delicate balance—hydraulic pressure offsetting CTM to hold the prop near 100 percent rpm—was upset inside the dome of PD-2's no. 1 prop.

While fluid leaked internally from the face of the pitch change piston, rpm ratcheted up. Passing 103.5 percent, another safety feature of the prop engaged, locking blade pitch at around 25 degrees and setting an upper limit to rpm. No. 1 was now a fixed pitch propeller, a large, aluminum four-bladed version of the small wooden props of yore. Once all hydraulic pressure was lost, the only way to control prop rpm below that pitch-locked limit would be by putting an aerodynamic load on it through the selection of airspeed and altitude.

No instrument in the cockpit reports propeller blade angle. Hamilton Standard investigators later inferred the 25-degree position from what they were told by Ed Caylor and Ed Flow, and what they knew of their design. Had pitch lock not caught and held the blades near 25 degrees, they reasoned, centrifugal twisting moment would have twisted the blades even flatter, toward 0 degrees. On the way, the snap toward a flat blade angle would have finally been arrested by a mechanical low pitch stop, set at 13.5 degrees, but in that case rpm would have shot to near 200 percent and stayed there. At that speed, the twelve-hundred-pound prop would be rotating at more than two thousand revolutions per minute, probably fast enough to shed its blades.

Such a catastrophe would sling the four heavy blades through the air like scimitars, almost certainly fatally damaging the aircraft. (When a Patrol Squadron 47 P-3 lost its no. 4 propeller near Masirah, Oman, in March 1995, one blade sliced through the lower fuselage, severing thirty-five of forty-four engine- and flight-control cables, instantly shutting down all four engines and forcing a dead stick ditch, six miles offshore, in the warm, calm waters of the Gulf of Oman. Rescue came in ten minutes and, incredibly, all survived.)[5]

PD-2's no. 1 prop would soon exceed 129 percent, the limit of its tachometer gauge, but eventually stabilize below that limit. AF 586 had suffered a serious malfunction, but the aircraft was still in the air and flyable, and the overspeed could be controlled.

Chapter 4

Emergency

For the next hour and a half, every thought, every spoken word and motion in PD-2's cockpit would be accompanied by the furious, high-pitched screaming of the overspeeding no. 1 prop and the shuddering of the airframe, buffeted by turbulent airflow over the outboard half of the port wing and by drag from the prop. Much of the time the aircraft would be imbedded in clouds and picking up ice, shaken by moderate turbulence. "Hand tooling" PD-2 (flying autopilot off), often on instruments and in icing, heightened the pressures on the pilots as they groped to manage the cascading emergency while they tried to nurse their aircraft hundreds of miles to land.

The smallest change in the wind or aircraft attitude instantly produced a change in prop rpm. It took a lot of muscle on the rudder and ailerons to keep PD-2 straight and level under these conditions; each pilot could manage only ten or fifteen minutes of this wrestling before he became exhausted and the other had to take over the controls.

No one aboard had heard the howling sound of supersonic prop tips before. This incessant, shrill keening in the cockpit, which forced the cockpit crew into unfamiliar flight helmets and onto the intercom system, must have been unnerving and exhausting, even more than was fighting the flight controls to maintain straight and level flight against the drag of the runaway prop.

Finding of Fact. Petty Officer Miller conducted a warning lights check and turned the No. 1 synchronizer switch to Off. It had no effect on r.p.m. As r.p.m. climbed through 103.5–105%, Lieutenant Commander Grigsby and Petty Officer Miller

decided to feather the No. 1 engine utilizing the Emergency-handle (E-handle). As Petty Officer Miller pulled the E-handle, fuel flow and horsepower dropped to zero and turbine inlet temperature started to fall rapidly. However, r.p.m. continued to climb to approximately 131%. It was accompanied by a very loud audible offspeed.

Miller's quick check of the center panel annunciator lights was an informal but common addition to the established emergency procedure. He was checking to ensure that a statistically improbable dual light bulb failure in one of the caution lights was not masking an inoperative propeller pump. The pumps provided the hydraulic pressure to move the pitch change piston; a failure could mean a total loss of control when the E-handle was pulled.

All the lights tested good. Miller thought that he could now refeather the prop with confidence. Switching off the synchronizer switch freed the no. 1 prop from following the lead of the master propeller. Turning the switch on had been the last step in the restart checklist, finished just a few minutes ago. Normally the three other props were carefully synchronized to either no. 2 or 3 as a master reference, to avoid annoying beat frequencies—rhythmic "wah, wah, wah" sounds reminiscent of a muted jazz cornet—caused by minor rpm or phase differences drumming through the fuselage. A malfunction in the system, however, could pull a prop off speed. Miller was isolating the no. 1 prop from the synchrophaser system, in case the system was sending spurious, increase rpm signals to its governor.

No help. No. 1 rpm continued to climb.

The first two steps on the P-3's engine emergency shutdown checklist are done by the flight engineer from memory. The copilot will not start reading from the checklist until the third step. First, the flight engineer reaches forward and pulls the yellow-and-black-barred emergency shutdown handle. Then he discharges fire extinguisher agent into the nacelle, if it is on fire.

The functions of the E-handle, and which of them are performed electrically and which mechanically, perennially appear as questions on pilot and flight engineer written and oral exams. It is certain that everyone in the cockpit, even Wagner, knew exactly what was supposed to happen when Miller pulled the handle out to the stop.

Fuel would be shut off at the engine fuel control both electrically and mechanically, and the fuel tank emergency shut-off valve would close mechanically. Suddenly starved of fuel, the fires in the engine's combustion section would immediately flame out, and PD-2's no. 1 engine would cool and coast to a stop, as confirmed by a rapid drop in turbine inlet temperature. (Under normal flight conditions, it is so quiet in the P-3's cockpit that one can hear the rotary numerals in the turbine inlet temperature gauge rattle down toward four zeros when fuel is cut off. Today, their faint, mechanical clatter would be overwhelmed by the prop's noise.)

Propeller feather would be initiated electrically and mechanically, and the blades would slap to high pitch (past 90 degrees) and stop rotating. No. 1 engine's bleed air shutoff valve would close electrically, isolating the engine from the manifold that carried hot, high-pressure air from one wingtip to the other for de-icing, bomb-bay heating, and engine start. The oil tank shutoff valve would also close electrically, denying this potential source of flammable fluid to any nacelle fire.

Normally, once an engine is shutdown ("caged") the immediate problem goes away while the crew turns the aircraft for home or the nearest suitable airfield. Loss of an engine is a mission abort criterion. Today was not normal: the no. 1 engine shut down on command, but its prop failed to feather.

Finding of Fact. Lieutenant Commander Grigsby, who had taken control of the aircraft, reduced power and climbed in an attempt to slow r.p.m. in accordance with NATOPS procedures. He called "fails-to-feather" and ordered everyone in the cockpit to don his helmet. The noise created by the overspeeding propeller was quite loud and it was very difficult to hear. Petty Officer Miller checked the feather button in and Lieutenant Caylor noted that the light in the feather button was on. Lieutenant Commander Grigsby and Petty Officer Miller discussed something that no one could overhear because of the noise. The procedures for operating with a propeller that fails to feather were not completed, i.e., the E-handle was not reset, the oil tank shut-off circuit breaker was not pulled, and the E-handle was not pulled out again.

Grigsby would have immediately announced, "I've got it," grabbing the yoke and putting his feet on the rudder pedals, and so taking physical control of the aircraft from the junior no-P in the left seat. The zoom climb and power reduction were intended to slow the aircraft and put an aerodynamic load on the no. 1 prop, slowing it as much as possible.

Some initial confusion in the cockpit could be expected under the circumstances. A moment before Ed Caylor had heard Miller yell, "It's pitchlocked," and someone else, almost certainly Grigsby, yell back, "No, it's not." It is not clear, either, who announced "Fails to feather" seconds later. John Wagner said he did not hear anyone ask for the checklist. Ed Flow, now back in the cockpit from having watched the restart over Moore's shoulder, recalled hearing "Fails to feather" about the time the pointer pegged at the top of the no. 1 rpm gauge, but he did not know who said it; Caylor thought it was Jerry Grigsby. It probably was him.

With the abrupt change of aircraft control, Wagner had become Grigsby's copilot. He, not Grigsby, was now responsible for reading the checklist. Just audible above the rising noise of the prop (Flow estimated it was now spinning at over 130 percent), Grigsby's critical phrase would now morph into an observation rather than a command, and the fails-to-feather procedure, designed specifically to provide gearbox lubrication by freezing the oil tank shutoff valve in the open position, would not be completed.

Flow watched Miller start through the emergency procedure, but then stop midway to consult with the patrol plane commander. Miller and Grigsby would have had their heads together on the copilot's side of the cockpit, shouting in one another's ear to be heard over the roaring prop. Caylor had just gone aft to get Wagner's helmet. (Two separate searches for Wagner's misplaced hardhat bag would keep Caylor out of the cockpit during the critical few minutes when the key decision was being made.) Flow and Wagner, isolated to their own thoughts by the noise, did not hear the exchange. No one would know for certain what Grigsby and Miller said to each other.

But based on a hurried statement Miller then made to Flow, it is not difficult to make a reasonable guess about that conversation. Miller turned to tell Flow that he was not really certain what pushing in the E-handle would do to rpm. What he must have meant was—unsure about what exactly had gone wrong, or why rpm had increased when he had pulled the shutdown handle—he and Grigsby had concluded that they might lose what little rpm control they seemed still to have by mechanically resetting prop controls momentarily back to unfeather. Rather than "tease the animals" (another of the animal metaphors that color cockpit vocabulary and hint at pilots' appreciation of the forces they hold in check), the two evidently decided to leave the E-handle out and halt the checklist where it was.

Flow—after he relieved Miller and was back in the flight engineer's seat, he would rethink all that had happened—told Miller he was not certain what pushing in the E-handle would do now either, and then Flow went aft to get Miller's hardhat.

Finding of Fact. At 1305, aircraft was stabilized at 140–150 knots at approximately 10,500 feet. r.p.m. on the No. 1 propeller was stabilized at 115%. The aircraft had been turned towards Shemya and Lieutenant Commander Grigsby requested a heading directly to the island.

Bruce Forshay's nav/comm station, like Matt Gibbons's station across the center aisle, put him just behind the cockpit, separated from the flight station only by a step up and a bulkhead that was open at the aisle for access. (Unlike airline practice, there was no door to the cockpit that could be closed and locked to isolate the flight station from the tube, only a gray cloth curtain that could be drawn closed at night to control light from the cabin.)

Even so, Forshay's first hint of a problem came a short time after the restart, but only because the flight station unexpectedly called him on the intercom and asked for a heading direct to Shemya. At the time, Alfa Foxtrot 586 was at 51°50'N, 161°50'E, approximately 460 miles from Shemya and about twice that far from Adak. Gibbons's first encrypted mission abort message left the aircraft a few minutes later. It did not describe the malfunction or report that the aircraft was in distress.

All of his nav systems were working well, and so Forshay, one of the newest of the "FNGs" on the aircraft, was able to respond nearly immediately with a heading to steer and an estimated time of arrival for the tiny island: 100 degrees true and 4:00 P.M.[1] It would be another twenty minutes before prop noise and airframe vibrations rose to the point where Forshay grew concerned, and wearing an unaccustomed helmet at the time, he would miss hearing the first fire warning horn in the meanwhile. (Forshay was not alone in this. John Ball, too, discounted the noise and vibration and missed the first fire warning horn. Ball would only start to feel "real alarm" when he joined a small group destroying crypto near the galley after the second fire.) From engine restart to splashdown one hour and thirty-seven minutes later, Forshay stopped working and left his seat only once, and that was to don his anti-exposure suit.

Alfa Foxtrot 586 now was off its PARPRO track, heading for Shemya. A quartering tailwind would slowly blow them off course to the north, forcing Forshay to adjust with a series of small heading changes to the right. They would end up heading 108 degrees true, tracking directly for the island but crabbing slightly into the wind.

Only a chamber of commerce booster would call Shemya by one recorded nickname—"the Black Pearl of the Aleutians," presumably an admiring reference to the color of the hard rock underfoot—with a straight face. Others, more accurately although less rhapsodically, call the small, seven-square-mile island near the far tip of the Aleutian chain "the Rock." The prisoners at Alcatraz, the isolated federal maximum-security prison in San Francisco Bay, had the same nickname years ago for their home. No point on Shemya is as much as one mile away from salt water.

The Rock is located approximately fifteen hundred miles west-southwest of Anchorage (equivalent to New York City to Austin, Texas), but less than nine hundred miles from Magadan, the Russian port city on the Sea of Okhotsk. At 52°43' north latitude, 174°07' east longitude, Shemya shares its day with the rest of the United States only because of an enfolding bend to the west in the International Date Line. Were it not for this convenient distortion, the island's few residents would forever be in tomorrow.

Like Adak's, Shemya's weather is dominated by the persistent Aleutian Low. Also like Adak, Shemya's surrounding waters, the Bering Sea to the north and the Pacific to the south, moderate air temperatures as compared to those at the same latitude on the vast Siberian landmass to the west. The mean temperature in late October is 40 degrees F, and only during January, February, and March is the mean temperature below freezing. However, it is not the cold, but the wind and fog, the isolation and earthquakes, that give Shemya its special character of life on the edge, the edge of the Pacific tectonic plate. On Shemya the wind can blow without respite at forty knots for a week at a time, strong enough, it is said, to knock the Simichi foxes that forage the island clean off their feet.[2] On Shemya, especially at water's edge, it is easy to believe that at any moment the island could slip down a few feet and disappear under the waves, unnoticed and unmourned.

In October 1978, Shemya Air Force Base was home to the still-new Cobra Dane phased-array tracking radar that peered far into the Soviet Union, monitoring space activities and missile shots, and to a detachment of RC-135S Cobra Ball intelligence-collection aircraft from the parent squadron at Eielson Air Force Base, at Fairbanks, Alaska. Shemya's proximity to Siberia drew the big Boeings, special mission military versions of the 707, to this isolated outpost, from which they would openly spy on the Soviets.

In 1978, life on the Rock was not too bad, not as bad as it had been but not as good as it would get. Damage to Shemya's runways and hangars from the major earthquake in February 1975 had been repaired, but the facilities upgrade program that was to take down and replace the bedraggled World War II structures that dotted the low-lying island was still a few years away.

Grigsby rolled AF 586's nose around to 100 degrees true heading, toward Shemya on the first heading Forshay had passed to him. The island lay more than four hundred miles to the east, just behind the cold front draped in a sweeping arc from the low pressure center now located near 55° N, 179° E. They were indicating only 140–150 knots airspeed. Adjusting to this slow transit speed, one more appropriate to the landing pattern than to cruise, Grigsby lowered wing flaps to the Approach position, effectively increasing wing area and reducing his stall speed. He dared not fly any faster lest the increased airspeed let the prop spin even faster.

En route, they would be pushed along by a helpful tailwind, but even with that boost AF 586's ground speed would be less than two hundred knots. About thirty minutes after they had settled on the new course, when Matt Gibbons radioed Elmendorf that AF 586 had a propeller malfunction and was proceeding direct to Shemya, the island was still about 350 miles away.

At AF 586's estimated time of arrival at Shemya, the surface wind would be out of the south-southeast at thirty knots, with gusts even higher. Shemya had only one runway, a 9,990-foot-long, cement-paved monster oriented almost east-west. When they were heavy, the RC-135s needed every foot of it to get off the ground.

On this heading, Grigsby would be approaching Shemya from behind Attu, with its central ridge of 3,100-foot hills. Once across Agattu Strait and past Alaid and Nizki (each islet about the size of Shemya), Grigsby would have to land east on Runway 10 into a powerful right crosswind, perhaps near the edge of the aircraft's thirty-five-knot maximum crosswind component. He had been on the island only once before. In July Crew 6 had evacuated a badly battered Air Force meteorologist from Shemya after a hiking accident to the hospital at Elmendorf.

A three-engine landing at dusk at an unfamiliar airfield, with no. 1 pitch-locked, decoupled from the engine, and windmilling freely, would test Grigsby's airmanship. Before that test were to happen, however, Crew 6 would face another trial, an endurance contest. They would need to keep the no. 1 prop intact and AF 586 in the air and on course for two hours or so.

Earlier in the flight, on occasion AF 586 had been close enough to land so that the cockpit crew could just make out the bleak profile of the Kamchatka Peninsula, low and gray under the bottom deck of clouds, with occasional sharp peaks punching up through the layers. Every crewmember came up to the cockpit to look out at it. They had pointed it out to each other, investing the faint smudges and bumps on the horizon sixty miles away with an ominous, threatening character that weaker eyes would have missed. Shepard, who had seen the same coast several times before, thought the many distant volcanoes were beautiful. So did Grigsby. He had brought his Nikon camera along on the flight to take telephoto shots of the distant shore.

Nineteen seventy-eight was midway through the Carter presidency, years before the USSR was memorably characterized by President Reagan as "the Evil Empire" and twelve years before its implosion, but everyone on board AF 586, staring out the windows at the imagined eastern palisades of the Empire's defenses, would have accepted Reagan's description.

AF 586's emergency came out of sight of the Soviet Union, but not far off the Kamchatka coast, little more than an hour's flight time into a quartering head wind to the airfield at Yelizovo, fifteen miles northwest of Petropavlovsk. Established procedures for a prop overspeed required Crew 6 to land at the nearest suitable airfield, but no one aboard ever considered landing at Yelizovo, and risking turning over the aircraft to the Soviets.[3]

Finding of Fact. At approximately 1310, a thin film or sheen of what appeared to be propeller hydraulic fluid was seen on the No. 1 propeller afterbody.

PD-2 was bleeding to death from a very small cut. Matt Gibbons saw it through the window at his station, no more than a glossy shine on the normally dull-black, composite ring that formed the propeller's conic afterbody. None of the other survivors aboard would later comment on the evidence of a leak in their testimony, but only John Ball would have been able to see the no. 1 prop from Gibbons's perspective. It is possible that no one else saw the leak.

The fact that the prop was now visibly leaking could not have been a surprise. The overspeed had dramatically signaled an internal failure in the pitch change mechanism ten minutes before. The film of fluid being spun out from the prop control now simply confirmed what the flight station crew had known since the prop failed to feather—something had gone terribly wrong.

During the next hour and twenty minutes, PD-2 would exhibit other symptoms of its failures. The prop spinner would start an eccentric wobble, evidence that the reduction gearbox was disintegrating. The fire warning horn would sound repeatedly, as friction heated and reheated the dry gears to above 400 degrees F, the threshold temperature for the warning. A chips light would come on, and several other amber caution lights would flicker. Among these signs of growing distress, the prop's hydraulic leak could look like a minor problem, but that leak was the trigger for everything that followed.

Finding of Fact. At approximately 1310, Lieutenant Caylor relieved Lieutenant Commander Grigsby in the right seat. Lieutenant Commander Grigsby immediately relieved Ensign Wagner in the left seat. Condition Five was ordered set in order to keep traffic within the cabin to a minimum. Aircraft was in instrument and icing conditions.

Jerry Grigsby now had the first team of pilots in the seat, but it would be another half-hour before his most experienced flight engineer, Ed Flow, joined them there. Condition V, putting everyone into his assigned ditching station, was first ordered at Flow's suggestion, to reduce foot traffic up and down the tube and into the cockpit, although there is no indication that anyone was wandering about the tube aimlessly. This would be the flight condition in which the crew would ride AF 586 into the water approximately one hour and twenty minutes later.

After he was relieved, John Wagner would remain in the cockpit for the next forty minutes or so, sitting directly behind Jerry Grigsby, watching what was going on from atop the radar box that had been Ed Caylor's off-duty perch. Wagner would be back in the left seat once again, for a few minutes only, while Grigsby belatedly put on his QD-1 anti-exposure suit and then walked the length of the tube for a last word with each crewmember. He paused at Shepard's station, and stooped to listen while the other man told him about the Marlin going down off Cavite; two P-5M sailors signaling each other they were going to make it. Gibbons overheard them agree that Shepard would take special care of Hemmer when the aircraft stopped.

After Grigsby got into his seat, Wagner went back into the cabin and to ditching station 15, on the floor between Shepard's and Brooner's stations.

Finding of Fact. Lieutenant (junior grade) Gibbons prepared an encrypted message to Elmendorf Airways indicating that they were aborting the mission. He was assisted by Lieutenant (junior grade) Ball. He also ordered the crew to begin donning QD-1 survival suits.

Tactical communications were normally encrypted off-line by the nav/comm into three letter groups using a manual encryption/decryption pad checked out from the Tactical Support Center. The process was slow and laborious, and prone to error, which explains why Patrol Squadron 9 scheduled two communicators for flights such as this one.

Gibbon's priority precedence message of twelve groups ("India Hotel Tango, Lima Juliet Sierra, Victor Golf Bravo") carried the first report of what had gone wrong on station. He and Ball encrypted it, one verifying the other's work, to ensure that no error had been made in composing the message from the glossary of single words and blunt, descriptive phrases in the system then in use.

Gibbons ordered the tactical crew into anti-exposure suits, anticipating the instructions from the cockpit to do the same by some minutes. By the time the order from the flight station came over the intercom to don QD-1s, everyone in the cabin already had his on.

Getting into a QD-1 in the confines of a P-3's few unobstructed spaces was a lot like bargain basement shopping. There would have been the same air of controlled desperation; the same pile of identical, ill-fitting garments; the same flurry of arms and legs penetrating arm and leg holes; the same grim satisfaction when the task had been completed successfully. Only the sense of competition would be missing. PD-2 carried 23 QD-1s. Everyone would get his own.

Finding of Fact. Crew had set Condition Five. Several of the flight crew helped distribute QD-1 suits and secure loose objects within the aircraft.

The Navy's QD-1 "quick-donning" anti-exposure suit (and the Air Force's essentially identical CWU-16/P) of the 1970s was a one piece, one-size-fits-all waterproof coverall rolled into a tubular, protective container the size of a sofa pillow.

The big difference between the QD-1 and the CWU-16/P anti-exposure suit models was color. The Navy wanted its crewmen, presumably downed over waters where it held sway, easily seen for rescue. For this reason, Navy suits were high-visibility orange. The Air Force had no such confidence about which side would come upon its downed aircrew first and specified that its suits be colored dark green for evasion, thinking that the grounded flyer had many ways to make himself conspicuous, if he wanted to be. Patrol Squadron 9 had gotten some ex–Air Force suits from surplus racks at a West Coast air base about a year before the Adak detachment started and added them to its own inventory of Navy survival equipment.

Once out of its container, the rubberized suit was entered through a shoulder-to-hip waterproof zipper, after which the head and arms were extruded past tight rubber cuffs and the torso zipper sealed. Inside, for any but the largest-framed air crewman, the effect was rather like wearing an oversized, awkward full-body baggie. Flow, 6'4" and 200 pounds, and Ball, 6' and 190 pounds, would have fit into their QD-1s reasonably well. Garcia, 5'8" and 140 pounds, and Rodriguez, 5'8" and 150, enveloped, like the Michelin Man, in rubberized folds, would have had ample room for company.

"Quick-donning" did not describe the suit; it described the circumstances.

QD-1s were too uncomfortable to be worn continuously, which meant they had to be put on in a hurry. Although the Naval Air Systems Command asserted then that less than three minutes was required to enter the suit, the seven step entry process described—even omitting the second step, delicately described as "void"—could only be done this quickly under ideal test lab test conditions, or during a drill.[4]

After the return of the survivors in November, early reports seemed to confirm that the poor condition of the suits had led to the three deaths from exposure. These first reports of tattered and torn survival suits, and the image of young sailors using (and dying in) Air Force hand-me-downs, created a furor that was to take months and a sidebar investigation to put down.

Finding of Fact. At approximately 1320, people noticed that the prop spinner or prop itself appeared to be wobbling somewhat.

Bruce Forshay saw the wobble reflected in Matt Gibbons's scope. Glancing out of a window toward the prop just before the first fire warning, Ed Flow decided, rightly, that the dry reduction gearbox was tearing itself apart, driven by the prop blades extracting energy from their passage through the air. He must have said something about the new development, because Caylor, now in the right seat where he would have been unable to see the no. 1 nacelle, knew about the wobble, too.

The wobble meant that the planetary gear train, which normally supports the prop, inside the gearbox had come apart. Half an hour later, after the second fire warning, Gibbons thought the wobble had become so bad that the prop itself could come apart any minute. If it did, the blades might narrowly miss the neighboring no. 2 nacelle, but past experience had shown that when a turning prop disintegrated on the port side of the aircraft, one or two blades would almost certainly knife into the fuselage somewhere between the tacco's station and the cockpit.

Finding of Fact. At 1326, the aircraft passed its first message to Elmendorf Airways, who held flight guard, over HF radio. It was an encrypted message and Elmendorf was asked to relay it to the T.S.C.

The P-3's long-haul communications system was designed around two identical high-frequency transceivers, HF1 and HF2. Two long line antennas, stretched taut like clotheslines from the forward fuselage to the top of the vertical stabilizer, were a key part of the system. Depending on atmospheric conditions and the frequency in use, HF radio ranges of hundreds of miles were routine and ranges of several thousand miles and more were uncommon but not extraordinary.

Elmendorf Aeronautical Station, at the Air Force base outside of Anchorage, held AF 586's communications flight guard, meaning that while AF 586 was on its mission, all of the aircraft's air-to-ground communications went to Elmendorf. From this ground station, aircraft messages would be relayed as necessary to air traffic control agencies (such as Anchorage) or to command centers (such as the Adak TSC). Responses from both would flow back to the aircraft the same way, relayed through Elmendorf.

Gibbons's message text (this was the second encrypted message after the abort, not the first), thirty-six apparently random letters from the phonetic alphabet, would have been meaningless to the radio operators at Elmendorf or to any eavesdropper. Elmendorf would have relayed it to the TSC, where after manual decryption, the reverse of the laborious process on the aircraft, its meaning would first become clear to Lt. Floyd Warren, who less than an hour earlier had relieved John Eger as the TSC watch officer. Now, twenty-one minutes after the first abort message left the aircraft, the TSC would know what had gone wrong, but not how serious it was.

Warren would have relayed both messages to Group, Force, and Fleet command centers, so that everyone concerned would know that AF 586 was coming home early, and why. That news would trigger the complex process by which PARPRO flight support would stand down in the Pacific.

Seven minutes later, Gibbons sent Elmendorf essentially the same information, unencrypted:[5] "Elmendorf, Alfa Foxtrot 586. We're a Papa Three aircraft, ah, we have a propeller malfunction at this time. Present position five two two two north, one six four three zero east. Our altitude is one one thousand feet; true airspeed one five four; ground speed one niner four. We are departing direct Shemya at this time, over."

The P-3's hand-held cabin microphones are keyed by a press-to-talk thumb switch on their side, but the boom mikes attached to each hardhat can only be keyed by a foot switch at each station. Helmet now on, Gibbons was broadcasting into the mike pressed against his lips, keying the HF transmitter with the switch under his foot. After he finished this transmission, his QD-1 bootie, nearly as big as a swim fin, must have inadvertently remained atop the foot switch. That mike stayed hot, transmitting background noise from the aircraft ("Fuck it; we're going plain voice") out to the world and inadvertently jamming the frequency. Elmendorf would now call AF 586 15 times unsuccessfully. Then, discovery and Forshay's urgent shout, "Get off the mike. Get off the mike. I can't talk on the radio." And finally, two-way communications were reestablished:

ALFA FOXTROT 586: Elmendorf, Elmendorf, Alfa Foxtrot 586, over.
ELMENDORF: Alfa Foxtrot 586. Have you readable. Readable. How me, over?

ALFA FOXTROT 586: Elmendorf, Alfa Foxtrot 586. I have you five by five.[6]
Present position five two two five north, one six four four eight east.
We are proceeding direct Shemya at this time. We are 337 miles west
of Shemya. Proceeding direct with a propeller malfunction, over.

Finding of Fact. At approximately 1335, r.p.m. indications began falling to 0%,
although the prop was still turning in excess of 100%. This was accompanied by a
slight audible decrease in r.p.m. No annunciator lights were illuminated and the
lights were verified as operable.

As he watched the no. 1 tach unexpectedly begin to unwind counterclockwise off
the stop, Ed Caylor let himself hope that the prop was finally going to feather,
but the pointer was lying to him. The sight and sound of the prop, confirming
that it was still out of control, belied the instrument's seemingly good news.

Grigsby's cockpit crew would get a number of confusing indications from
PD-2's engine instruments as the emergency played itself out, and this was one of
them. No. 1's rpm was not decaying, as the indications on its tachometer seemed
encouragingly to suggest, rather the tach's rpm pick-up sensor in the nacelle had
finally failed.

As prop and gearbox instrument sensors were progressively destroyed by the
overspeed, the information they provided on what was going on in the nacelle
was lost, or became misleading. So it was with the engine chips light, which
under ordinary conditions would signal metal fragments afloat in its lubricating
oil, an early sign of impending failure potentially so serious that illumination of
the chips light was grounds to shut down its engine, unless the crew was coping
with another emergency that required engine power.

There was no oil in AF 586's dry gearbox to transport chips to the sensor
plug, so the warning light did not illuminate until molten metal from some liq-
uefied bit flowed into the sump and closed the plug's normally open electrical
contacts, passing power to the light.

Both parts of the aircraft, the cockpit and the cabin, now became preoccu-
pied with what they were doing: flying the aircraft and trying to deal with an
emergency not fully understood forward; terminating the mission, talking to
Elmendorf, and preparing the aircraft for ditching aft. Intercom communications between the two halves of the aircraft died off to the bare minimum, each
implicitly trusting the other to do what was necessary.

Finding of Fact. At 1336, T.S.C. Adak received the message, passed from Elmendorf, that AF 586 was aborting its mission due to a major propeller malfunction.
The Ready Alert crew was called immediately to prepare for a possible launch, as
directed by the Officer-in-Charge, Patrol Squadron 9 Det. Adak.

AF 586's plain language (unencrypted) abort message was transmitted from the aircraft at 1:33, and received at the Tactical Support Center at Adak three minutes later. The entry in the TSC's log summarizes what Elmendorf passed on: "From Elmendorf Airways: Propeller major breakdown divert Shemya Island 051 50N 161 50E 2308Z." By happenstance, the detachment's officer in charge, Mike Harris, was in the TSC when AF 586's message came in. He immediately ran over to the detachment's offices and called in Pat Conway's Crew 11 to go fly the intercept mission. Conway had last seen some of Crew 6 early that morning while the two crews were preflighting their aircraft side by side on the ramp. He had helped the others solve a software problem, and then gave no further thought to Crew 6 until Mike Harris intercepted him on the way to the TSC with news of what was happening.

In the minutes between the call to Crew 11 and takeoff, their mission would change character. What began as an intercept and escort would quickly become a search and rescue (SAR). Crew 11's mission briefing was over at 2:15 and they were off Adak and in the air at 2:32, fifty-nine minutes after Crew 6's first unencrypted distress message.

Finding of Fact. At 1338, AF 586 declared an emergency through Elmendorf Airways. They said that they were not in extremis however. Elmendorf relayed this information to Anchorage Center (A.T.C.).

> ELMENDORF: 586, Elmendorf, roger. Copy all, copy all. Are you declaring an emergency at this time?
> ALFA FOXTROT 586: . . . That is affirmative. We, ah, we . . . we are not in extremis at this present time. We are proceeding direct Shemya, over.

Grigsby immediately cut in on the intercom to Gibbons and corrected him. AF 586 *was* in extremis, he told his tacco.

> ELMENDORF: Requesting your souls on board forward and aft, forward and aft. How copy?

Elmendorf and Anchorage wanted to know how many crewmembers ("souls") were aboard AF 586. The location of each in the aircraft, cockpit or cabin, would be important information to a crash crew on the ground trying to pull survivors from wreckage. In this case, however, it was not relevant—not yet, anyway—and Gibbons had been asked the question out of sheer habit. ATC had the information anyway, filed hours ago in the flight plan:

> ALFA FOXTROT 586: Ah, One five. I say again, one five souls on board. We're a Papa Three aircraft, over.

ELMENDORF: . . . Requesting number of souls fore and aft, fore and aft, over.

ALFA FOXTROT 586: . . . Ah, roger. There are three souls fore and one two souls aft, over. . . . Ah, thank you much for your assistance, out.

Finding of Fact. At approximately 1340 the aircraft had its first fire warning. It was accompanied by a small amount of smoke emanating from the top of No. 1 engine. Petty Officer Miller discharged the fire extinguisher and the fire went out immediately. Lieutenant Commander Grigsby started to descend the aircraft, slowing in order to control r.p.m.

The shrill shriek of the fire warning horn does more than announce a probable fire in an engine nacelle. It interrupts everything else, and dumps adrenaline into the bloodstream of anyone within earshot. An engine fire warning in the P-3 compels urgent attention. In flight, a horn goes off directly above the pilot's head and four red lights illuminate on the engine fire warning panel just about at eye level for the flight engineer. The lights surround the hot engine's E-handle, cueing the flight crew to action.

The horn may be muted, once it has sounded, but the lights remain lit until the detecting element in the nacelle no longer senses an abnormally high temperature. Even in AF 586's noisy cockpit, the warning horn would have been heard instantly.

Finding of Fact. At 1342 AF 586 requested launch of S.A.R. aircraft to intercept. Altitude was 8,000 feet.

The fire changed everything, sharply increasing the possibility that AF 586 would not make it to land and impelling the crew to ask for help:

ELMENDORF: Alfa Foxtrot 586, Elmendorf.

ALFA FOXTROT 586: Elmendorf, Alfa Foxtrot 586, go ahead, over.

ELMENDORF: Roger, sir. I have an A.T.C. clearance. You ready to copy?

ALFA FOXTROT 586: . . . Go ahead.

ELMENDORF: Roger, sir. A.T.C. clears AF 586 direct Shemya via present position direct Shemya. Maintain one zero thousand feet. Requesting souls on board, amount of fuel and time. How copy?

ALFA FOXTROT 586: Elmendorf, Alfa Foxtrot 586, ah, roger. We have one five souls on board. Approximately six plus zero zero hours fuel, and we are presently at eight thousand. Trying to maintain eight thousand feet. Request you launch S.A.R. aircraft to intercept us. We are presently heading one zero zero true. Present position five two two eight north, one six five one six east. We are three hundred

and twenty miles west of Shemya and, ah, we're requesting you
launch S.A.R. aircraft at this time, over.

ELMENDORF: . . . Roger, copy. Understand requesting an intercept at this
time.

ALFA FOXTROT 586: . . . That's a Charlie, Charlie. Thank you, out.

"J. S." and "R. N.," the Elmendorf radio operators who were AF 586's contact with
the rest of the world throughout the emergency, had just become busy men. At
the same time they were keeping up their end of a near-continuous conversation
with the aircraft, they were also talking to three Anchorage Center controllers by
telephone, getting clearances and answering questions from the Sector 11 air traffic controller ("S. G."), and keeping the adjoining Sector 9 ("L. P.") and ten controllers informed. When the command center at Moffett Field joined the net, as
it soon would, Elmendorf would be asked to repeat transmissions unintelligible
in California.

Finding of Fact. At approximately 1345, Petty Officer Flow relieved Petty Officer
Miller as flight engineer so that the latter could put on a QD-1. Petty Officer Miller
left the cockpit and did not return.

Butch Miller's last act as a flight engineer turned out to be putting out the first no.
1 engine fire. As soon as the pilots finished their own seat switch, Flow swapped
with Miller, who left the cockpit to go aft, put on an anti-exposure suit, and settle
into a ditching station. By the time he left the cockpit, Miller was ashen-faced
and extremely agitated. (Watching him step into the cabin, Caylor thought that
Miller might be having a heart attack.)

Walking aft down the aisle, through the quiet preparations for ditching
being managed by Gibbons, Miller almost certainly knew what some of his
younger crewmates still did not: PD-2 could not reach Shemya. The systems that
were disintegrating inexorably in the no. 1 nacelle were his expertise, his spe-
cialty, and his last glimpse around the cockpit would have told him that their
wounds were mortal.

Miller is almost off-stage. He will reappear briefly, first in an odd observation
by Dave Reynolds that describes him (Miller) as "very excited and nearly hyper-
ventilated" when he gets to the rear of the aircraft. John Ball will see the same
thing minutes later.

Reynolds's and Ball's characterizations of the off-duty flight engineer as
intensely anxious are two of only three comments that even hint at normal
human emotions in the abnormal world that AF 586 has become. (The third
comes from Denny Mette, who hears Bruce Forshay's voice crack while transmitting the first Mayday message to Elmendorf and then recognizes that Matt Gib-

bons has taken over the radios. Forshay soon collects himself, and the two will share transmissions to Elmendorf. Gibbons, however, will do most of the talking.)

Miller then seemingly recovers, and just as Moore, still seated at Station 10 watching the no. 1 nacelle, reports a second fire, Miller will help a small team finish stowing loose gear and begin systematically destroying communications and cryptographic equipment. Sitting at the galley, tearing crypto into shreds by hand, Miller will look "very scared" to Ball. Ball (by his own admission and with this example in front of him) will now become very frightened, too.

Miller will choose to ditch in Station 21, perhaps without thinking, because that is where he sat while he shredded crypto. The choice will prove to be a bad one. Station 21 is one of two aft-facing bench seats at the P-3's small galley. In this seat he would have had to turn his head to see John Ball, in Station 23, a long arm's reach across the aisle in the forward, outboard seat of the four-person dinette. No one else would have been visible to either man; both were as far back in the aircraft as it was possible to be, with nothing facing them but the gentle concave curve of the aft pressure bulkhead. Their ditching stations would have been a snug fit for both men, enrobed in the loose-fitting QD-1s and trussed up in the LPA life vests' harnesses with their collapsed, inflatable lobes.

Finding of Fact. At 1346 the Adak Air Traffic Control Facility received word that AF 586 had declared an emergency. They, in turn, notified the T.S.C., the squadron and Search and Rescue at 1348.

In the cockpit, Grigsby reached to the center pedestal and turned on the search power switch, enabling the sonobuoy jettison system. When he's instructed to, Reynolds would now be able to ripple fire all forty-eight sonobuoys into the water, item 4 on the ditching checklist. Each buoy will be blown out of its tube in the belly of the aircraft and into the water by a small, explosive charge. The memory of these staccato reports—forty-eight, one after the other until the buoys are all gone, like a bundle of firecrackers sharing a single fuse—will stick in his and Moore's minds as an exciting highlight in a day that had many of them.

Finding of Fact. At approximately 1348, Petty Officer Flow received permission to restore oil to the No. 1 engine reduction gearbox by completing the fails-to-feather procedures. When oil was restored, he noticed no indication of oil pressure on the gauge, although 6.5–7 gallons remained in the tank. Simultaneously, white smoke was observed to billow from the no. 1 engine and a caramel colored fluid flowed along the lower portion of the nacelle, aft of the propeller. Lieutenant Commander Grigsby ordered the oil tank shut-off circuit breaker reset, and as it was, the smoke stopped. Very shortly thereafter, flickering prop pump no. 1 and chips lights illuminated along with either a prop pump no. 2 or oil pressure light.

They were too late. The oil that would have been an effective lubricant and coolant immediately after the prop ran away was now just fuel for a fire in the hot, dry gearbox. Heavy, white smoke immediately streamed from the nacelle and tailpipe. No surprise. Grigsby had half-expected a flash fire. He had discussed with Flow the risk of putting oil back into a hot gearbox just before he told the flight engineer to do it, reasoning that the emergency was serious enough now that anything might help.

The decision to push the E-handle in and to resume the fails-to-feather checklist had been a difficult one for another reason: the fear that the prop, somehow unleashed from any restraint, might now simply spin off into the fuselage. Grigsby even considered first moving Gibbons and Forshay out of the plane of the props before pushing the handle back, but he did not do it. To everyone's relief, the handle went in and the prop stayed on.

Although the smoke stopped right after the valve was closed again, within a few minutes the second fire warning would go off, and the crew would be forced to discharge its last fire extinguisher on the port side of the aircraft to put out the fire.

Normally, oil is circulated in the reduction gearbox at the rate of sixteen gallons a minute. When the no. 1 engine E-handle was pulled out at 1:01 P.M., all oil to the gearbox was shut off at the valve at the bottom of the oil tank, and the flow was not restored until Flow's unsuccessful experiment at 1:48 P.M. In the meanwhile, the gears ran dry for forty-seven minutes, generating tremendous heat and building to an eventual catastrophic failure of the assembly.

Those forty-seven minutes were on Lieutenant Caylor's mind. Only after Petty Officer Flow raised the issue with the PPC did Caylor realize the fails-to-feather checklist had never been completed at the onset of the emergency, while he was hunting for Wagner's helmet. Caylor now concluded that the gearbox had been without oil for too long and realized that they would eventually have to ditch.

Ken Harris, a representative of Allison, the engine manufacturer, later speculated in unsworn testimony that by 1:48 P.M., when lubricating oil was briefly restored, the catastrophic gearbox failure had already happened. The massive gearbox housing had likely cracked also, letting the oil leak out of the housing freely into the nacelle.

Finding of Fact. Between 1350 and 1430, there was some confusion on the part of both Elmendorf Airways and Anchorage Center, as to whether the aircraft had actually already ditched or not. This word was relayed to the T.S.C. and Adak A.T.C., and caused some internal confusion.

On three separate occasions, Alfa Foxtrot 586 told Elmendorf that the aircraft was ditching, first at 1:53, again at 2:01, and finally at 2:24 (six minutes before water entry, prefacing its last announcement with the arresting phrase, "this is no drill"). After each of the first two times, as the emergency peaked and receded, the situation momentarily stabilized and hope returned in the cabin (if not necessarily in the cockpit), Gibbons corrected himself, and Elmendorf acknowledged the change.

Even so, given the number of parties eventually aware of the desperate drama playing out west of Shemya (including Elmendorf Airways, Anchorage Center, the Coast Guard at Juneau, the detachment and its parent squadron and wing in California, U.S. joint service headquarters at Yokota, Japan, and the Adak TSC as well as Navy and joint service command centers from Oahu to Washington), confusion was probably inevitable.

None of this would make much difference to the crew's chances or the conduct of the rescue, and only Yokota came in later for any open criticism. Looking back on events just four days after the ditching, Mike Harris said he believed that Yokota's continual requests for information over the primary SAR radio frequency impeded the rescue effort.

Finding of Fact. At approximately 1352 the aircraft had its second fire warning, accompanied by sparks and flames from within the nacelle and what appeared to the crew to be glowing metal. It was extinguished by utilizing the second fire bottle.

Petty Officer Flow had anticipated the second fire. When he got back into the FE's seat at 1:45, one of the first things Flow did was to break the safety wire that guarded the red-capped fire extinguisher transfer switch in the usual "direct to engines" position. When the inevitable second fire came, he would be immediately ready to put it out. (He had also depressurized the aircraft, item 3 on the ditching checklist, in anticipation of what was coming. If the aircraft did go into the water, it would be impossible to open the escape hatches if its cabin were still pressurized.)

Then the horn went off again. Matt Gibbons watched the sparks fly out of the nacelle from behind the prop. He saw "bright yellow or amber" flames color the edges of the nacelle's access panels.

The P-3's engine fire extinguisher systems are simple and effective. One system protects the port side of the aircraft (engines 1 and 2) and the other the starboard (engines 3 and 4). They are identical but not interconnected. Each system includes two, 10.5 pound charges of bromotrifluoromethane extinguisher agent held in two spherical, pressurized bottles located forward of the firewall in no. 2 and 3 nacelles.

With the transfer switch in the "direct to engines" position, each engine is protected by its own fire extinguisher. In the "transfer to adjacent engines" position, a second shot of agent is available to fight another fire in the same nacelle.

All that is required to discharge a bottle is slight pressure on a button hidden behind each E-handle. With the handle pulled out, the discharge button lies exposed and conveniently to hand. If the second shot is not enough, there is no third and fourth chance.

Ed Flow later believed that the second fire, which used up the last fire-extinguishing agent, got Grigsby thinking seriously about ditching. Another fire, one that did not blow out by itself but instead breached the nacelle firewall and started eating the wing, would quickly send the aircraft spinning uncontrollably into the ocean and kill them all instantly. They had to ditch before they lost control, but no one was in a hurry to decide that now was the time.

The macabre joke among P-3 flight crews flying the North Pacific in winter was that the correct speed for ditching in those waters was 405 knots (465 mph), the aircraft's redline (limit) airspeed. By hitting the water at this speed, called V_{NE} (velocity not to exceed), the aircraft would surely break up on impact and sink, killing the crew immediately and sparing them the pain of a less abrupt ending.

In the cockpit Grigsby, Caylor, and Flow started to talk in earnest about ditching, but decided to try to continue to Shemya. The aircraft was now at one thousand feet, five hundred feet below the base of the clouds. Grigsby resumed their descent, down to five hundred feet. The new, lower altitude was a compromise. He elected to give up some radar range (a function of altitude) to be able to put the aircraft in the water very quickly, in case the situation deteriorated suddenly.

Finding of Fact. At 1353 the aircraft transmitted a MAYDAY to Elmendorf. The message stated that they were ditching 290 miles west of Shemya.

AF 586's encrypted abort message had been transmitted to Elmendorf at 1:27 for relay to the Tactical Support Center, where it was to be decrypted and passed on. Twenty-four minutes later, at 1:51, Elmendorf asked the aircraft to verify the last, three-letter group. Was the last group "Victor Tango Oscar"? It was, but the TSC's question would never be answered.

At 1:52 P.M., Alfa Foxtrot 586 reported that it was ditching. The exchange took three minutes:

> ALFA FOXTROT 586: Elmendorf, Elmendorf Alfa Foxtrot 586, Mayday, Mayday, Mayday. Position five two two seven north, one six five five niner east. Heading one two three degrees true. Ground speed one four three. We are ditching, ditching, ditching. Position five two two seven north, one six six zero east. Mayday, Mayday, Mayday.[7] Alfa Foxtrot 586. We are ditching, ditching, ditching. One five souls on board. Three orange life rafts. Three orange life rafts. Over.
>
> ELMENDORF: Five Eight Six, Elmendorf, roger, copy. Roger, copy.

ALFA FOXTROT 586: Elmendorf, Elmendorf, Alfa Foxtrot 586. We are
ditching, ditching, ditching. U.H.F.D.F., U.H.F.D.F. three four five
decimal five. Three four five decimal five. We have three, I say again,
three orange life rafts. . . . We are two niner zero miles west of Shemya. . . . Position five two two five north, one six six zero eight east.
I say again, Position five two two five north, one six six zero eight
east. Over.

Naturally the aircraft had been moving the entire time. At a ground speed of 140
knots, AF 586 would cover a mile in just under thirty seconds. The new reported
position is two minutes of latitude and one minute of longitude away from the
one in the initial Mayday report. It is easy to picture the tacco glancing up at his
scope, reading the coordinates as they change before his eyes knowing that each
mile of position error, an impossible distance to swim under these conditions,
could mean the difference between rescue and loss:

ELMENDORF: . . . roger, copy. Roger, copy.
ALFA FOXTROT 586: . . . Position five two two five north, one six six one
zero east. Over.
ELMENDORF: . . . roger, copy. Roger, copy.
ALFA FOXTROT 586: . . . Request you relay nature of our emergency. We
had a propeller number one . . . propeller . . . propeller number one
overspeed. Would not decouple. Runaway prop. Engine fire. We are
presently level one thousand feet. Position five two two six north.
One six six one zero east. Position five two two six north, one six six
one one east—
ELMENDORF: Five Eight Six, Elmendorf, request you say again reason for
number one propeller, reason for number one propeller. Over.
ALFA FOXTROT 586: Roger, Elmendorf. Number one propeller. Runaway
propeller on restart on engine. Propeller would not decouple,
resulting fire in number one engine. Over.
ELMENDORF: Five Eight Six, Elmendorf, roger, copy. Roger, copy.

Gibbons had misdiagnosed the emergency, and his report to Elmendorf was in
error. But it did not matter. The essentials of what he was saying were correct:
AF 586 was telling the world, through Elmendorf Aeronautical Station, that it
was going down, and taking fifteen men with it.

In fact, the propeller probably *had* decoupled from the engine. Robert Mad-
sen and George Nesky, both from Hamilton Standard, the propeller manufacturer, later said they believed the reduction gearbox had decoupled from the
engine, based on survivors' reports. The prop was spinning wildly on its shaft,
churning the dry planetary gear train and the spur gears behind it, separated

from the cold, inert engine by a parted safety coupling. The coupling is designed to fail, mechanically separating the engine from the gear train and prop, whenever drag from the propeller enters the –500 to –1,700 shaft horsepower range.

Finding of Fact. At approximately 1353, Lieutenant (junior grade) Gibbons, Lieutenant (junior grade) Ball, Petty Officer Miller, and Airman Reynolds destroyed and jettisoned all cryptographic materials as well as tactical publications. This was accomplished in the galley area. Petty Officer Miller remained in ditching station No. 21 during this time. The aircraft descended to 1,000 feet.

Destroying your own cryptographic equipment has special significance to military and naval units. On the ground, at sea, or in the air, it means not only that you have lost control of events, but also that they have taken a very ominous turn, and you are preparing to be overwhelmed by great force. It can be seen as an act of sacrifice: you're giving up your own ability to communicate securely with your headquarters so that others who are more fortunate may continue to do so.

The act has the same significance in embassies and consulates, and evidence that an embassy is doing it—Japan in Washington in 1941, the United States in Tehran in 1979—is a pretty convincing signal that some kind of denouement is coming.[8] In civilian terms, destroying crypto is less akin to updating your will than it is to rolling your casket out of storage.

Crew 6 had carried cryptographic materials from the TSC aboard PD-2, the daily settings and codes that would allow secure communications with its operational control center, in this case as relayed through Elmendorf. By the standards of squadrons whose full-time business was intelligence collection—the Navy electronic warfare squadrons of EP-3s at Guam and Rota, Spain, for example—AF 586's crypto and other classified holdings were very modest, roughly two briefcases full.[9]

Once they were in QD-1s and loose gear had been stowed, Crew 6 had ample time to destroy its fairly small holding of crypto and classified material (by dropping the torn scraps out a chute and into the ocean), and not much else to do but compose themselves. By the time the crew turned to destroying crypto, AF 586 was only thirty-seven minutes from water impact. No one aboard knew how much time remained to him, but as the scraps of paper fell into the sea most must have suspected that they, too, would soon follow.

Finding of Fact. At 1357, AF 586 notified Elmendorf that they intended to continue to Shemya at 1,000 feet.

If AF 586 had ditched at 1:54 P.M., heading south-southeast (generally with the primary swell system and crosswind) with 143 knots ground speed, it is likely that no one aboard would have survived the impact.

ALFA FOXTROT 586: Elmendorf, Elmendorf, Alfa Foxtrot 586, revise our intentions. We are level, level one thousand feet. We are still proceeding direct Shemya. Will revise as our status changes, over.

ELMENDORF: . . . Roger, copy. Roger, copy.

ALFA FOXTROT 586: . . . New position. North five two two seven. East one six six two three, over.

ELMENDORF: . . . Roger, copy. Roger, copy.

Finding of Fact. At 1359, AF 586 reported to Elmendorf that No. 1 engine gearbox had a total failure. The aircraft was then at 500 feet.

ALFA FOXTROT 586: . . . It appears the Number One engine gearbox has total failure. I say again, Number One engine gearbox has total failure, over.

ELMENDORF: Five Eight Six, Elmendorf, roger, copy. Five Eight Six, Elmendorf, have A.T.C. request. You ready to copy?

ALFA FOXTROT 586: Roger, roger, Elmendorf. Five Eight Six ready.

ELMENDORF: A.T.C. requests Alfa Foxtrot 586 verify inbound Shemya and level, over.

Matt Gibbons had turned over the radio to Bruce Forshay and then left his seat to review ditching station responsibilities individually with every man in the tube. Forshay answered: "Roger, roger. Alfa Foxtrot Five Eight Six is estimating Shemya at time zero two zero zero [Zulu, Greenwich Mean Time] and now at two hundred feet. I say again, now at five hundred feet, five hundred feet and position five two two eight north one six six three five we . . . east, over." While Forshay spoke to Elmendorf, Gibbons slowly moved aft from station to station, reminding each grim-faced sailor what he had to do when their aircraft splashed to a stop. Reminding them, too, that Grigsby was a seaplane pilot; he had put planes down in the water safely many times.

Forshay's estimate came from PD-2's navigation system, and his quick response to Elmendorf's query was automatic. It would also prove to be meaningless. AF 586 was at five hundred feet, and still more than two hundred miles from Shemya, with no chance of reaching the island. Elmendorf Airways blandly took the reply at face value: "Five Eight Six, Elmendorf, roger, copy. Roger, copy."

Seconds later:

ALFA FOXTROT 586: Elmendorf, Elmendorf [pause], Elmendorf, Elmendorf, Alfa Foxtrot 586. One minute to ditch. Position five two two eight north, one six six three five west . . . east, over.

ELMENDORF: . . . Roger, copy. Roger, copy.

ALFA FOXTROT 586: . . . Condition has stabilized again. We're now five hundred feet, five zero zero, position five two two niner north, one six six four five east. Uh, we're going to try to drag it on in to Shemya at this time. I'll keep you posted on ten minute advisories or if our situation changes. This time, uh, request verification that you have alerted S.A.R., over.

ELMENDORF: . . . Charlie, Charlie, Charlie, Charlie.[10]

Finding of Fact. At 1405, AF 586 reported that all persons aboard were wearing bright orange or green anti-exposure suits.

The survival of the crew depended on their rescuers knowing exactly where to look and what they were looking for. Gibbons would tell them that again and again. Alfa Foxtrot 586: ". . . Roger, roger. Again for S.A.R., we have sonobuoys U.H.F.D.F. homing on frequency three four five decimal five. . . . Three orange life rafts, fifteen souls on board, all wearing bright orange or dark green anti-exposure suits." Gibbons described the CWU-16/P as "forest green" or "dark green," a color that standing alone would have been practically invisible in the dark water that surrounded the rafts.

Finding of Fact. At 1414, AF 586 reported that all crypto gear had been jettisoned or destroyed. Aircraft was still at 500 feet.

Forshay's voice came back on the net, clear and controlled: "Alfa Foxtrot 586, still with you. Position five two three three north, one six seven two five east. I report all electronics, all cipher gear . . . I say again, all crypto gear has been jettisoned or destroyed, over."

Finding of Fact. At 1415, Coast Guard 1500, a C-130 en route from Attu to Kodiak, was diverted to the P-3 position, 52°40'N 167°30'E. CG 1500 diverted to Adak for fuel and briefing.

At 2:11, the Coast Guard command center at Juneau, Alaska, reported on the SAR radio net that there were no American flagships near AF 586 in its computer, but it "believed" there were Soviet vessels in the area. Three minutes later, the center directed the diversion of an aircraft, Coast Guard 1500, to the site.

In the grainy, black-and-white photograph, the seven men are arrayed in a ragged line in front of the bulbous nose of their aircraft. Behind them on the nose is the distinctive double chevron of the U.S. Coast Guard alongside the number "1500," which is painted above the legend "Kodiak." All but the copilot, Lt. (jg) Rick Holzschu, on the far right, are wearing the same leather jackets Crew 6 has on.

"Kodiak" explains the loose gravel on the tarmac and the sheen of standing water on the ground. It probably also explains the long hair and slightly bedraggled appearance of the crew, or perhaps that is just the effect of the baggy, wrinkled flight suits. Pierce Brosnan himself could not look well groomed in a flight suit. "Kodiak" does not explain the self-satisfied look on the crew's faces. That comes from the rescue mission they have just flown.

Years later, Senior Chief PO Barry Philippy, second from the left in the cocky stance of a bantam rooster, then a petty officer first class and Coast Guard 1500's navigator, would describe the flight on top of AF 586's rafts as the most rewarding mission he had flown in twenty-two years of Coast Guard service. Lt. (jg) Bill Porter, the aircraft commander, and the rest of the crew felt the same way. The crew's shared memory of their participation in a successful, life-saving mission would connect them together for decades, long after each one left the service for civilian life.

On 26 October 1978, Lt. (jg) Bill Porter, thirty-two, was bringing his crew back to Coast Guard Air Station Kodiak from Adak (not Attu) after three days away from home on foreign fisheries patrol. They had left Adak around 9:17, half an hour after AF 586 took off on its mission, on the last low-level leg of their trip. Porter's crew had spent much of the last three days in their C-130H at five hundred feet, over the Japanese, Russian, and Korean fishing fleets, with two young "scanners" and a National Marine Fisheries Services agent aboard, counting boats and recording what was going on inside the two-hundred-mile fishing limit. (On top of the rafts, hours later, Porter would be startled to see the scanners, Butch Miconi and Dan Mallot, stretched out on the cockpit floorboards near his feet, peering through deck-level windows and trying to keep the survivors in sight.)

Porter's C-130 "Hercules" was another of Lockheed's great success stories, even a bigger commercial triumph than the P-3 Orion. The first C-130A was delivered to the Air Force in 1956, in response to a design specification for an intratheater cargo aircraft, capable of operating from dirt or gravel airfields. The boxy, high-winged, four-engine transport was not pretty, but it did have a certain get-the-job-done, utilitarian look to it, and crews loved the airplane.

The 219 A-models were followed, in rough alphabetical order, by B through J models. Each successor represented some improvement or special capability not available in earlier versions. For a while, the world appeared to have an insatiable appetite for the rugged, flexible transport with the thirty-six-hundred-cubic-foot cargo bay and forty-five-thousand-pound payload capability. When that hunger seemed to be approaching satisfaction, the powerful Georgia congressional delegation—the C-130 was assembled in Marietta, northwest of Atlanta—always found a way to force-feed a few more new aircraft into the federal budget.

Four hours after takeoff and an hour out of home plate, CG 1500 got a radio call from the Kodiak Rescue Coordination Center. PO 3d Class Ray Demkowski, the radio operator, recorded the transmission by hand in his radio log: "0013Z. 1500 de [from] Kodiak Air/P-3 ditched at 00[illegible]Z 5228N 16630E. Request you proceed and assist/1500 R[oger]."

The position they were being diverted to, actually AF 586's coordinates thirty-one minutes before ditch, was thirteen hundred miles west and into the wind, more than four hours away at the C-130's sedate 330-knot maximum cruise speed. Porter had only thirty-five thousand pounds of fuel on board, seven hours to dry tanks, and not enough to get to AF 586 and stay long enough to do any good. They would have to fly back to Adak, refuel, and then head for AF 586's last known position.

Finding of Fact. At 1415, the VP-9, P-3 Ready Alert crew had completed its brief and was ready to start engines.

X-ray Foxtrot 675 would have a more than three-hour head start on Coast Guard 1500 getting off Adak and heading for the SAR area.

Finding of Fact. At approximately 1420, the radar operator aboard AF 586 reported a ship at 290° true and 16 nautical miles. Lieutenant Commander Grigsby turned the aircraft in that direction.

The no. 1 nacelle caught fire for a third time about fifteen minutes after the second fire was extinguished. Although the fire blew itself out seconds later, it triggered two minutes of airframe convulsions, what Ed Caylor would later describe as "sickening" vibrations.

Gibbons had expected that their track toward Shemya would take them toward or even near both of the surface contacts they had plotted when AF 586 first arrived on station, but when he destroyed his crypto, he had also destroyed the draft postmission report. That report, long since shredded, tossed out the free-fall chute and into the water with the rest of Gibbons's tacco bag, was the only record the crew had of the position, course, and speed of both contacts. They had to find the *Mys Sinyavin* again. Garcia reassured Gibbons that he could do it. Just as the third fire warning blared, Airman Garcia reported radar contact on the *Mys Sinyavin,* behind them slightly to port and some five or six minutes away.

On the flight line at Adak, Denny Mette is now in the ready alert aircraft, going through his final equipment checks at the nav/comm station. He tunes an HF transmitter to Elmendorf's frequency, 11,176 kilohertz, and calls up for a radio check:

> X-RAY FOXTROT 675: Elmendorf, Elmendorf, X-ray Foxtrot Six Seven
> Five, over.

ELMENDORF: X-ray Foxtrot Six Seven Five, if you have traffic, 8,989 or 13,201 [kilohertz]. Mayday traffic this frequency, over.

X-RAY FOXTROT 675: Six Seven Five, wilco, out.

Elmendorf has told Mette to clear the frequency. Chastened, Mette will stop transmitting but he will keep one HF receiver tuned to 11,176 KHz and eavesdrop on the action while he waits impatiently for his inertial navigation systems to align. (These essential systems are the basis of the P-3's over-water navigation system and one source of attitude and heading information for the pilots. Unaligned, they would be unusable.)

In the cockpit, Jerry Grigsby has taken back control of the aircraft from Ed Caylor. Keeping AF 586 under control is exhausting work, and the two have been exchanging duties. At Grigsby's direction, Caylor will spend the next few minutes futilely trying to raise the ship on the VHF emergency frequency, 121.5 MHz. Nothing; the P-3's communications suite does not include a VHF-FM radio, and the *Sinyavin* is not guarding 121.5. Commercial airliners normally do monitor this frequency as they fly, but evidently there is not one in range on the transPacific great circle route, and Caylor gets no answer.

Finding of Fact. At 1424 AF 586 reported they would ditch in two minutes at position 52°34' North, 167°47' East. They reported a Soviet trawler within 20 nautical miles.

ALFA FOXTROT 586: Elmendorf, Elmendorf, this is Alfa Foxtrot Five Eight Six. We are ditching. At this time we are passing through 500 feet. Position five two three five north, one six seven four five east. How copy? Over.

ELMENDORF: Five eight six, Elmendorf, roger, copy. Roger, copy. Roger, copy.

ALFA FOXTROT 586: Elmendorf, there is a ship in the immediate vicinity within 20 miles of us. We believe it to be a Soviet trawler. [Fade out.]

Gibbons's one item of volunteered, offhand information was the piece of data the system needed—confirmation of the Coast Guard's belief that Soviet ships were in the area—to save him and nine members of the crew. During the next several hours, Washington would work furiously, and ultimately successfully, to get Soviet agreement to direct the ship to the ditching coordinates to search for Grigsby's crew.

ALFA FOXTROT 586: Elmendorf, Elmendorf, Alfa Foxtrot 586. Request status of S.A.R. aircraft, over.

ELMENDORF: Five eight six, Elmendorf, stand by. Stand by.

Gibbons's ability to "stand by" was very limited; AF 586 would be in the water in only three minutes, but XF 675 was still on the frequency.

Finding of Fact. At 1425, X-ray Foxtrot 675, the S.A.R. P-3 from Adak, contacted AF 586 on the Elmendorf frequency. AF 586 reported that No. 1 prop had dried up and was vibrating wildly. XF 675 passed that they were rolling on take-off.

Mette spoke up again:

> X-RAY FOXTROT 675: Alfa Foxtrot Five Eight Six, Alfa Foxtrot Five Eight Six, this is X-ray Fox Six Seven Five, over.
> ALFA FOXTROT 586: Hi guys, this is Alfa Foxtrot Five Eight Six. Lieutenant jaygee Gibbons. Position five two three seven north, one six seven three eight east. We have one five souls on board. Three orange rafts. U.H.F.D.F. three four five point five. Our number one prop has dried up. It's vibrating wildly and we'll be going down in the near future, over.
> X-RAY FOXTROT 675: Uh, roger, Matt. This is Denny. We're rolling on takeoff. How copy? Over.

Denny Mette's encouraging report to Matt Gibbons was stretching the truth. In fact, XF 675 was just then completing its hurried preflight inspection and would not be off the ground for another six minutes. Lt. Ron Price, XF 675's PPC, could not begin to taxi for the runway until the finicky inertial gyroscopes had finished their alignment to true north and local vertical.

> ALFA FOXTROT 586: Roger, roger, Denny. We're two hundred and thirty five miles west of Shemya, by our best guess. There's a Russian fisher factory in the immediate vicinity, over.

During the last forty-six minutes, AF 586 had managed to close the gap between it and Shemya by only one hundred miles. Elmendorf came back up on the frequency:

> ELMENDORF: Alfa Foxtrot Five Eight Six, Elmendorf.
> ALFA FOXTROT 586: Elmendorf, Alfa Foxtrot Five Eight Six, go ahead, over.
> ELMENDORF: Roger, sir. The intercept, A.T.C. advises it is one zero minutes off Adak. One zero minutes off Adak. How copy?

Finding of Fact. Between 1425 and 1430, AF 586 talked almost continuously to Elmendorf Airways, providing updated positional information. The final position report was 52°39' North, 167°24' East while passing through 150 feet.

Air Traffic Control at Anchorage knew better. Aboard AF 586, Gibbons knew better, too; he had just talked to Mette. Like Mette's premature report of XF 675's takeoff, this report from Anchorage two minutes later that XF 675 had been in the air for ten minutes must have been a piece of well-intentioned fiction, evidently meant to encourage the crew of AF 586 as their ordeal moved to its crisis. AF 586 would be down in the water two minutes when XF 675 got off Adak.

> ALFA FOXTROT 586: Elmendorf, this is Five Eight Six. Roger, Elmendorf. We just talked to them. Thank you much. Our present position five two three niner north, one six seven three four east, and we are ditching momentarily. I'll be talking to you as we hit the water, over.
>
> ELMENDORF: Five Eight Six, Elmendorf. Roger, copy. Roger, copy.

During this final exchange over the radio, AF 586 will suffer its fourth and last fire warning, accompanied by even more powerful airframe vibrations. Again, the fire horn and lights will come on. Unlike the third fire, this fourth one will not blow out. Seconds later:

> ALFA FOXTROT 586: And Elmendorf, this is Alfa Foxtrot Five Eight Six. We are passing through three hundred feet. Position five two four zero north, one six seven two niner east. We're, ah, we've got a ground speed of one three zero knots. Time zero zero two niner. We are, ah, preparing to ditch at this time, this position. We're about ten miles from a ship, over.
>
> ELMENDORF: Five Eight Six, Elmendorf. Roger, copy. Understand ten miles from the ship, over.

At about two hundred feet, descending, and perhaps thirty seconds from water impact at nearly 115 miles per hour, Gibbons thinks again of his responsibility as the crew's tactical coordinator: "Roger, Elmendorf, also request that you pass to, ah, Adak, that all, ah, classified material and cryptographic material has been destroyed on board, over."

Forshay radioed this information to Elmendorf fifteen minutes ago, but Gibbons does not know that, and the thought surfaces in his mind during the last few seconds of flight: "Elmendorf, Five Eight Six. Twenty seconds to ditch. Position five two four zero north, one six seven two five east; position five two four zero north, one six seven two five east; position five two four zero north, one six seven two five east. Passing through 200 feet. We have one five souls on board. Three orange rafts, and all personnel in either orange or forest green anti-exposure suits. We are passing through 150 feet. Position five two three niner north, one six seven two four east. This is Five Eight Six, out."

Gibbons goes off the air. He has narrated events for ninety minutes as coolly as if he were doing the play-by-play for some other team's championship game. His voice sounds no different at 100 feet above the water than it did at 11,000.[11]

Finding of Fact. At 1430, a Patrol Squadron 9 P3-C(U), Buno 159892, ditched near position 52°39' North, 167°24' East with fifteen people on board.

Back in California days after the rescue, Dave Reynolds described his crewmates as having been "in good, high spirits and excited about the flight" as they headed out to preflight their aircraft on the ramp in front of the detachment hangar at Adak. Now, each one was strapped to his seat, alone with his thoughts, mouth dry and heart racing, while Grigsby wrestled the yoke to keep control of AF 586's heading, airspeed, and rate of descent during the last and most important seconds of the flight.

Five hours and forty-five minutes after a routine takeoff, it all came down to Jerry Grigsby. During the next few seconds, until the aircraft hit and stopped, no one else had anything to do but pray or worry.

In the cabin, only Gibbons, Forshay, Moore, and Reynolds could really see what was happening while AF 586 descended toward the water and the ocean rose up to meet them. They were the only four sitting alongside true observation windows. The two officers, Gibbons and Forshay, sat face forward, so they could also scan their displays and see the aircraft's position and its altitude, read the wind's direction and velocity, and check their ground speed. Moore's and Reynolds's seats faced aft for ditching, at blank, gray bulkheads.

At two hundred feet and below, the swells visible out the windows would have looked enormous. Back at the galley, Miller and Ball could peek out at a corner of the sky through what amounted to small, high portholes, too small to do much more than admit light and combat claustrophobia. None of the others— Garcia, Brooner, Rodriguez, Shepard, Wagner, or Hemmer—had a window, and three of them (Wagner and the two passengers) sat on the floor, crouching in a tight space between electronic equipment racks and held in place by seat belts bolted to the deck.

Gibbons had patched the HF into the crew's intercom system. The enlisted aircrewmen in the cabin sat listening to the clipped conversation between their aircraft and the ground, wondering if they would live through what was being discussed with such clinical detachment.

The ditching checklist in 1978 did not call for shutting off electrical power to aircraft systems not essential to flight prior to water entry, and so AF 586 hit the water with three engine-driven generators on the line and all eleven electrical busses fully energized. It did not make any difference. The generators tore away on impact, shutting down electrical systems as the water quickly rose up in the fuselage to drown them. Unexpectedly, the same impact shut off all four battery-operated emergency lights, suddenly throwing the interior of PD-2 into near-total darkness.

Chapter 5

Ditching

A "water landing." A mandatory part of the senior flight attendant's safety briefing to airline passengers on every over-water flight is a cheerful explanation of the braced, head-down posture they should assume in the event of what is glibly described as a "water landing." The phrase is a marketing euphemism for a controlled crash into the water. Only seaplanes make water landings. Land planes ditch.[1]

Jerry Grigsby would set up AF 586's ditching as a flat, straight-in descent into the water. His goal was to put his aircraft down, wings level and slightly nose high, flying as slowly as possible without risking a stall and with a minimum rate of descent. As difficult as this would be under the circumstances, it was the easy part—just basic airmanship under extreme conditions. The hard part was a key decision, the wind versus the waves. On which heading should he fly PD-2 into the water? A misjudgment could quickly kill them all. The even more difficult decision was when, when to give up trying to reach land and to put AF 586 down?

During those last forty minutes, while AF 586 ran out of alternatives to ditching, Grigsby would have been trying to pick the primary swell system, the biggest and most powerful rollers running across the sea beneath them, out of the confused chop on the surface. The P-3's navigation system could give him the wind's direction and speed down to the degree and knot, but Grigsby would have to analyze the surface the old-fashioned way, by seaman's eye. The lower the aircraft got, the harder it became to pick out the underlying, high-energy wave system from local disturbances and surface chop.

Ditching procedures are described in Section V, Part 1 ("Emergency Procedures—General") of the P-3 flight manual. The manual makes the consequences of a bad decision by the patrol plane commander very clear. "Except in extremely high wind conditions," the text says, "the aircraft should be ditched parallel to the primary swell system. Model tests and actual ditchings of various aircraft indicate that ditching into the wall of seawater created by a major swell is roughly analogous to flying into a mountain. Accordingly, a careful evaluation of sea condition is essential to successful ditching."

Jerry Grigsby's experience as a Marlin seaplane pilot, worth little to anyone since before he left Patrol Squadron 50, suddenly seemed priceless.

Finding of Fact. At time of actual ditch, personnel aboard the aircraft were in the following ditching stations:

Station 1—Lieutenant Commander Grigsby (pilot)

Station 2—Lieutenant Caylor (copilot)

Station 3—Petty Officer Flow (flight engineer)

Station 4—Lieutenant (junior grade) Gibbons (Tacco)

Station 5—Lieutenant (junior grade) Forshay (NAV/COMM)

Station 6—Airman Garcia (Radar)

Station 7—Petty Officer Brooner (SS1)

Station 8—Airman Rodriguez (SS2)

Station 9—Airman Reynolds (Ord)

Station 10—Petty Officer Moore (IFT)

Station 13—Master Chief Shepard

Station 15—Ensign Wagner

Station 17—Petty Officer Hemmer

Station 21—Petty Officer Miller

Station 23—Lieutenant (junior grade) Ball

No other ditching stations were utilized. Ditching stations were not assigned according to NATOPS recommended priority.

The flight manual's explicit "Priority of Ditching Station Assignment" is in a table by that name in Section V of the book. With fifteen aboard, it directs that the first twelve stations be filled first, then puts the remaining three into stations 21, 22, and 23. Stations 21 (where Miller ditched, and almost certainly died without ever leaving his seat) and 22 are side by side at the galley bench, facing the rear of the aircraft. Fortunately, Station 22 was left vacant. It is likely that any occupant of that seat, Ensign Wagner was the logical choice, would have died alongside Miller.

As he set up for the final descent, Grigsby invited Flow to leave Station 3, permitting the flight engineer, whose duties were completed once he toggled the cabin outflow valve controller to the closed position, to ditch somewhere in the presumed heightened safety of the tube, closer to the rafts and other emergency equipment.[2] Flow declined, and remained where he was.

The Navy's P-3 training and standardization program requires pilots to undergo an annual evaluation, examining the pilot's knowledge of aircraft systems and procedures, and his airmanship. (All other crewmembers undergo an analogous annual evaluation.) The evaluation includes four parts: open and closed book exams, an oral examination, and a flight check in the aircraft.

Ditching is one of the flight check's "critical" subareas, meaning that the pilot under examination must receive a grade of "qualified" in his demonstration of ditching technique to pass the check ride. To be qualified in ditching, the pilot must call for and complete his items on the eleven-step checklist, and be able to control airspeed within five knots and heading within ten degrees, and sustain a rate of descent less than three hundred feet per minute. Simulated water entry must be made flying straight ahead with wings level.

Grigsby did all that. He did it on 11 July, when he flew his annual check, and he did it to perfection on 26 October, when he put PD-2 down.

Finding of Fact. The configuration of the aircraft at time of ditch was as follows:

Landing Gear—Up

Wing Flaps—Approach

No. 1 Engine—Windmilling

Airspeed—120 Knots Indicated Airspeed

Rate of Descent—50 Feet per Minute

Heading—220° True (approximate—directly into the wind)

Shortly before the third fire warning, PD-2, flying at five hundred feet altitude, with visibility not more than several miles, must have unknowingly crossed *Mys Sinyavin*'s bow. The ship would have been off to port, too far away to be seen behind the low clouds and rain showers that filled the sky around the aircraft. In a few minutes, Rich Garcia would pick the trawler up behind them on his radar, by which time they had further opened the distance between them, but why he did not pick up the contact while PD-2 was approaching it is not clear. The answer probably lies in some combination of sea return clutter at low altitude,

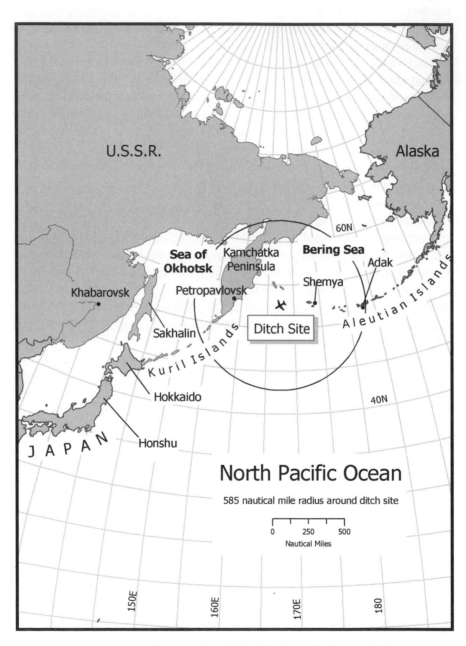

Alfa Foxtrot 586's ditching site

suboptimum performance by the forward radar set, and (perhaps) operator distraction.

Until the third fire warning, Grigsby had been heading generally east, toward Shemya. The third fire warning went out by itself after a few seconds, just before Garcia reported a surface contact almost directly behind them and now sixteen miles away. Garcia's news coupled to the blare of the horn must have solidified Grigsby's resolve. With the prop surging noisily in reaction to every attitude and airspeed change, Grigsby would have rolled gently away from the dead engine, through a right-hand, 180-degree turn, and headed directly at the ship six to eight minutes flying time away. Halfway there—Ed Flow says closer, actually within sight of the ship—the fourth fire warning forced Grigsby to turn away, into the wind and parallel to the tall, rolling waves of the major swell system. They could fly no farther; now was the time.

Later, Grigsby's seaplane experience in Patrol Squadron 50 would become the accepted explanation for his skillful touch in the final minutes of flight. In truth, there was nothing in that distant experience—his last flight piloting a seaplane was perhaps ten years in the past—that truly prepared him for this. With perfect recall, Grigsby might have remembered the P-5M flight manual's short discussion of "Rough Sea Landing." The two techniques for landing on a long, fast swell, illustrated by line drawings captioned with advice about when to hold the yoke back, when to "push the nose down with full force." You could not do either one in a P-3 and survive. It is possible that he recollected its advice to "survey" the sea and swells, to "drag" the surface repeatedly on different headings, searching for the ideal place to land; the former was essential, the latter impossible. He might have also remembered the manual's descriptions of the types of surface conditions; the encouraging information that the best landing areas may be found in the tranquil (and perhaps imaginary) place where swell systems are out of phase, and the troughs of one are filled by the swells of the other. "Wind chop waves always travel with the wind and the wave line is perpendicular to the wind line," the Marlin flight manual explained. It continued:

> The interval between [wind chop] waves is very short and their height and velocity is directly proportionate to the force of the wind and the time it has been blowing. . . .
>
> In open sea there is seldom only one swell system. The direction of open sea swell is usually away from heavy storm areas or low atmospheric pressure areas. The interval between swells is very long and depends on the source of the swell and the distance the swell has traveled. Height and speed of the swell are independent of the wind . . .

As he stared out the window in front of him at the tempest churning the surface, he might have remembered, too, the manual's recommendation that landing the Marlin, a *seaplane,* in seas more than four feet high—just *four* feet high—be limited to emergency conditions. The watery peaks in front of him were five, six, or perhaps seven times that big.

But all this counsel had to do with a plane designed to land in the water, to touch down between 75 and 88 knots (86–101 mph). The P-3 was an airliner; it had a cylindrical fuselage, designed for the repeated pressurization and depressurization cycles of scheduled commercial transport service. It lacked the stout ventral keel, the slab sides, the high wings, and the wingtip floats, everything that might have made a "water landing" survivable. Nothing in the Marlin's flight manual spoke about putting a *landplane* down into the water in a state 7–8 sea.[3]

In the cockpit with two men next to him, and twelve others close behind, for the next minute or so Grigsby would be completely alone.

The squadron's Aircraft Accident Report recorded conditions at the time of ditch as "1,500 foot ceiling. One and one-half to three miles visibility in rain showers, wave height 12–20 feet, winds 223 degrees at 43 knots." At 120 knots indicated airspeed into a 43-knot head wind, Grigsby's aircraft would hit the water at a ground speed of 77 knots, about 89 mph. A fifty-foot-per-minute rate of descent would have produced a barely perceptible "squeaker" on a normal landing. Perfect.

In fact, PD-2's airspeed on final approach might have been much slower. Even before the first fire warning, Grigsby and Caylor had talked about ditching speed. They wanted to go in at the slowest speed possible, and agreed that, wings level, a few knots below stall would be about right. It was a tradeoff: Grigsby would give up his safety margin on final approach in exchange for lower impact forces on splashdown.[4] At current weight, it would take 800–1,000 shaft horsepower on each good engine to keep PD-2's nose high and its rate of descent low, as Grigsby took the aircraft downhill for the last time.

Sinyavin, plodding resolutely down track on the same heading since it had left the Bering, never saw anything.

Finding of Fact. The aircraft impacted three distinct times, coming to rest on the final impact. It immediately started to fill with water. The three crewmembers in the cockpit exited the aircraft through the flight station overhead hatch. The three crewmembers who ditched aft, Lieutenant (junior grade) Ball, Petty Officer Moore and Airman Reynolds, exited through the port overwing hatch. The remaining crewmembers, except for Petty Officer Miller, exited through the starboard overwing hatch. Petty Officer Miller was not observed to exit the aircraft.

Everyone aboard remembered the instant that AF 586 stopped flying. Years later, salty Garland Shepard casually likened it to a "bad P-5 landing," but it must have been much worse.

The consensus was that there were two bounces, although Ed Caylor, Bruce Forshay, and Ed Flow were among members of the crew who recall three. The first, relatively gentle, must have been a carom off the crest of a swell still at flying speed, the way a flat stone hitting the water at just the right angle will skip off the surface of a pond and continue in flight.

Alone in one of two side-by-side ditching stations, boxed in between electronics compartments fore and aft, and across the aisle from the blank face of the main electrical load center, Wagner had little idea of what was happening after he left the cockpit for the last time. Sitting in the plane of the props, he could not hear Gibbons or Forshay on the radios and had to crane his neck to see Rich Garcia at the radarscope. No one else was visible. The first bounce told him everything. The moment of that glancing contact is when John Wagner realized that their flight was over.

The next, or perhaps third, impact was much harder as the aircraft hit tail first and then decelerated to a sudden stop, dragged to a halt by further contact with the water. John Ball said it felt like being hit by an uncontrollable force or power. Dave Reynolds's recollection was more apocalyptic: a severe impact, a bright orange fireball on the starboard side (probably as the wing tore away, carrying both hot engines past Reynolds's window), and a momentary, furnace blast of heat. At first Reynolds thought he was dead. Matt Gibbons remembered it in less hellish and more earthly terms, as similar to riding an amusement park flume ride.

The flume ride metaphor for a P-3 ditching, a jarring deceleration amid a huge cloud of spray and splashing water, must be especially apt because it was used again seventeen years later. Lt. Jeff Harrison, the Patrol Squadron 47 plane commander who ditched Buno. 158217 just offshore the Royal Air Force base at Masirah, Oman, in March 1995 described his experience as "similar to a log ride at an amusement park, but with more of a kick in the pants."

AF 586 was now down. Launching the three rafts and getting out of the aircraft quickly had just become the most important thing in every crewmember's life. Everyone aboard would now have to move amidships, where the life rafts were stowed, and execute survival procedures they had practiced before, but never performed. The three from the cockpit would get there by running down the wet, arched top of the fuselage. The twelve inside the tube would make their way forward or aft along the aisle, toward the escape hatches over the wings.

In one hour Crew 6 had gone from limping to Shemya to going down in a storm at sea. For the men in the cabin, even in extremis PD-2 had been a familiar place, dry, lit, heated, and, thanks largely to Gibbon's remarkable sangfroid, orderly. Each one would soon take a step, literally a single step, and find himself in a watery, near-frozen bedlam with his life at risk. All the survivors would be surprised by how fast PD-2 took on water and sank.

After he declined Jerry Grigsby's invitation to occupy another ditching station, as the aircraft descended through one hundred feet Ed Flow dropped his seat down and full aft prior to impact, positioning it away from the center pedestal and nearly under the overhead escape hatch, and locked his shoulder harness while he started to recite the Lord's Prayer to himself. Trussed up in this protected position, for the first time during the flight he could no longer see the water. Flow does not remember getting out of the seat, opening the hatch (as prescribed by the flight manual), and pulling himself to the top of the fuselage, but he does remember the cold rush of wind that blew past him on its way out the hatch as soon as it dropped open. He still wonders if the aircraft would have floated longer had he left the overhead hatch closed, trapping the air inside the fuselage and forcing the three of them out the midships hatches.

Ed Caylor was dazed by the impact, perhaps even knocked unconscious for seconds. When he came to in the cockpit and reached down to release his lap belt and shoulder harness buckle, he was shocked to find his hands underwater, and more water pouring in around the floorboards under his boots. He went out the hatch right behind Flow, a step or two ahead of Grigsby. Caylor estimated that the three of them were out of the cockpit in less than one minute.

The aircraft must have been sinking nose down, because at about the same time, when Matt Gibbons yelled, "Let's go," at the injured Bruce Forshay and pulled him out of his seat, there was a foot or two of water in the aisle.[5] John Wagner, buckled in at Station 15 a few feet behind Gibbons, between smoking and sparking electronics cabinets, said two feet of water rushed into the aircraft immediately after impact. When John Ball came to and got out of his seat at Station 23 (the farthest aft in the aircraft), he was in water that was already past his knees and rising.

Just forward of Ball but on the opposite side of the aircraft, Howard Moore unbuckled his harness, rose, and turned (Station 10 faces aft for ditching). He could see nothing ahead of him but the glitter of small electrical fires in the smoky, dark cabin of the aircraft. All the battery-operated emergency lights had unaccountably gone out on impact. Unable to see, Moore ran headlong into the aircraft boarding ladder, still erect in its storage position directly across from the main cabin door, and then disentangled himself. He arrived just behind Rodriguez at the port escape hatch, with others forming a line across the aisle at the starboard hatch.

Rodriguez, who had ditched in his seat at the Sensor Station Two operator's position, was responsible for jettisoning the port side emergency hatch and launching the no. 1 raft. Moore remembers that Rodriguez opened the port hatch and immediately went out after it.[6] After fumbling ineffectually himself with the clips to release the no. 1 raft while the water rose, Moore recalls that he then gave up and followed Rodriguez's lead out the hatch, onto the wing and into the water, ahead of Reynolds and Ball.

The actual sequence of events at the port overwing escape hatch in the minute after forward motion stopped was somewhat different, as substantiated by Dave Reynolds's statement on 8 November and Matt Gibbons's recollections since. Reynolds remembered Moore jettisoning the hatch while Rodriguez attempted unsuccessfully to launch the no. 1 raft, even as the water rose rapidly above it while the fuselage filled. With the cabin half-flooded and the raft still stowed firmly in place, Rodriguez would have been compelled to duck down, fully submerging his helmeted head in the dark water to continue fumbling with the reluctant release catch. Before Rodriguez gave up trying, Gibbons grabbed him by the back of his life vest, pulled him across the aisle and shoved him out the starboard side hatch ahead of Bruce Forshay. This switch explains Rodriguez's presence in the Mark-7 with the other two sensor operators.

Reynolds's Station 9 faced aft, too, directly at the forward bulkhead (wall) of the P-3's head and across the aisle from Howard Moore's seat. When he came to after impact, the bulkhead of the head compartment was lying on top of him, pinned in place by the heavy backpack parachute stowed at its top and by the loose galley equipment that had been secured in the head. He wrestled himself free, following Moore up the aisle through the water flooding into the aircraft, and then dropped past his knees into the open well of the hydraulic service center. Its hatch had failed on impact, opening a mantrap into the small below-deck compartment that housed the hydraulic systems' pumps and reservoirs. Hauling himself out of the hole, Reynolds, minus the emergency water bottle and first aid kit that were Station 9's responsibility, waded another few steps forward and then escaped the aircraft out the port side behind Moore, urging Moore out the hatch ahead of him.

By the time Ball freed himself, first from the galley table that had collapsed around him and then from a large crack in the floorboards that had opened up aft of the main cabin door and momentarily trapped one of his feet, the tops of the escape hatches were already underwater. Ball, who had yelled to Miller before he started moving and got no answer, was now breasting chest-high water that was rising fast, head and shoulders in the big bubble of air momentarily trapped in the top half of the cabin but flowing swiftly out of the open overhead hatch in the cockpit. He thought that he was the last one still inside the aircraft, and he probably was the last one alive. A lucky roll exposed the top of the port hatch, and he swam to it and out, following Moore and Reynolds into the cold water. When Ball popped up alongside the sinking aircraft, its cabin was probably completely full of water.

AF 586 was now down to a maximum of two rafts, capacity nineteen men according to Navy specifications. If both were launched, they would be adequate for the fifteen men on the aircraft. Things had gone better on the starboard side, where everyone else from the tube had congregated, although the problem was the same. The raft tie-downs proved very difficult to release.

Finding of Fact. The Mark-7 and Mark-12 life rafts, located on the starboard side of the aircraft, were launched by Airman Garcia and Lieutenant (junior grade) Gibbons. The Mark-7 life raft located on the port side of the aircraft was not launched because of difficulty encountered releasing its retaining straps and rapidly rising water.

Gibbons and Forshay were seated across one of the two fault lines in the aircraft after impact. (The other was at the galley.) The impact at water entry cocked the nose of the aircraft over to port, popping out both officers' observation windows and opening up a large hole in the fuselage at the navigator's station, through which pieces of the shattered nav table and all the gear stowed inside it now washed out into the ocean. Bruce Forshay's flight jacket went with it, flushed off the back of his chair by a wave. Surrounded by small bits of floating debris, he submarined under his lap belt, back and right side wrenched or possibly battered by a collision with something unknown.

Across the aisle, Matt Gibbons was uninjured, despite the fact that his tactical display had imploded noisily, sucking glass shards from the shattered screen into what had been the vacuum in the interior of the big tube. Gibbons stepped across the aisle, yelling, "Let's go." He slapped Forshay's lap belt open and pulled the other man up from his seat to join the distressed procession midships—Brooner, Garcia, Shepard, and Wagner, not in that order—heading through the smoke and the dark, past the "shambles" (Gibbons's description) at the aircraft's main electrical load center, to the overwing escape hatches. They would all cluster at the starboard side, even Gibbons, whose station assignment put him in the no. 1 raft with the plane commander.

Hemmer fell into line ahead of order. On impact he had been thrown out of Station 17, which he later described as "completely destroyed," and directly across the aisle into the sonobuoy storage area next to the starboard side hatch. He got up, remarkably uninjured, and went through the hatch, now completely covered with water, in the middle of the line.

The faint light of an overcast, gray afternoon filtering through a few small windows (or through where windows had been) and caught in dense smoke was all the illumination the crew had. As PD-2 settled into the water, the cabin became progressively darker.

Finding of Fact. The emergency lighting in the aircraft, which had been turned on prior to ditch, failed and the aircraft was completely dark.

Ed Caylor glanced quickly down the length of the cabin as he stepped out of the water and onto a circuit breaker panel pedestal, heading out the overhead hatch. The tube was dark and full of smoke, and the groans of metal flexing and breaking carried forward to him from out of the shadows beyond the cockpit. He would flash back to these sounds and images of drowning machinery years later, when he saw the artfully staged scenes of RMS *Titanic*'s last hours on the movie screen.

Battery-operated exit lights beside the emergency exits had been turned on as part of the crew's preparations for ditching, a precaution in case the g-switches that should automatically illuminate the lights on impact did not work. The reverse happened. All of the lights went out, perhaps knocked free from their retaining clips next to the hatches by the impact.

This failure provoked Recommendation No. 6 in the JAG investigation, that "Naval Air Systems Command evaluate the emergency exit lights aboard the P-3 aircraft for reliability and examine the retention capability of the emergency exit light holder." The wing commander passed this recommendation up the chain of command with the unassailable and somewhat vacuous observation that there was a "critical need for emergency equipment to function as designed when needed." His superior, rather more forthrightly, called for "a more reliable internal aircraft emergency lighting system."

So it must have been a surprise to many when the commander of the Naval Air Systems Command the following July informed everyone that a contractor investigation (presumably by the lights' manufacturer) "has shown that the emergency exit light holders are adequate to withstand ditching loads. The lights are designed to come on during ditching loads, and have an expected life of 30–40 minutes." He did not comment on the fact that none of this had worked that way on 26 October, the year before.

Finding of Fact. The aircraft sustained the following exterior damage as a result of the ditch:

The starboard wing was torn from the aircraft at the fuselage.

The aircraft had a large crack in the fuselage aft of the main cabin door.

The magnetic anomaly detector boom had broken off at impact and was floating near the aircraft.

Despite Grigsby's extraordinary airmanship, the laws of physics still governed what was happening west of Shemya. Force still equaled mass times acceleration, and PD-2 hit the water at around sixty to seventy knots or more and weighing approximately fifty-two to fifty-three tons. The resulting impact was enormous and battered the aircraft powerfully, immediately wreaking major structural damage and speeding its sinking.

Adrenaline seems to have distorted everyone aboard's sense of the passage of time, creating in each man's mind the illusion that he was moving with unnatural, almost superhuman, speed through a very slowly unfolding disaster. Crew estimates of the length of time PD-2 remained afloat, however, do not show this same attenuating effect. By all accounts, PD-2 went down very quickly. Ed Caylor thought it might have been only one minute after impact before the tube completely filled with water and just ninety seconds altogether before the tip of the vertical stabilizer disappeared under the surface. Bruce Forshay agreed, ninety seconds until PD-2 was gone. The consensus in the Mark-7, however, reached after a quick muster to find out who was aboard, was two minutes. The longest estimate was three to four minutes. PD-2 hit the water and sank, and very quickly there was nothing on the surface to mark where it had gone down other than the rafts. Almost nothing.

Hours later, while orbiting overhead the rafts, crewmembers in XF 675 thought that they observed AF 586's crash position locator floating in the water. (The device is a small, floating airfoil containing a radio beacon set to 243.0 megahertz, the UHF distress frequency. It is designed to fall away from the aircraft automatically on high-impact shock and to immediately transmit an emergency signal.) Possibly they did see it. At 4:15, still half an hour away and miles from the ditching site, they had heard an emergency beeper on 243.0, but the source could have been one of the PRT-5 beacons, too.

Days later, delayed by the weather, the Coast Guard cutter *Jarvis* finally got to the scene, too late to do anyone any good. It did, however, steam past what some believed was the pen-shaped magnetic anomaly detector boom housing floating in the water. That is what it looked like in the grainy photos the crew took. The weather was too bad to attempt a pick-up of the flotsam, however, so whatever it was, it was allowed to float away. Gibbons's empty Mark-12 raft was still afloat, too. Nothing else was visible. PD-2 had vanished into the sea.

Finding of Fact. The aircraft sustained the following significant interior damage as a result of the ditch:

Copilot's flight instrument panel came loose and hit copilot's legs.

Floor panels beneath copilot's chair started to come loose.

Tacco station window imploded.

Nav/Comm station navigation worktable disintegrated and struck Lieutenant (junior grade) Forshay on the right side.

A section of the aircraft, including the Nav/Comm window, approximately two foot by four foot, exploded on impact, leaving a large hole in the starboard side of the fuselage.

Ditching Station 17 broke loose from its mounts.

The forward bulkhead of the lavatory broke loose at impact and hit Airman Reynolds.

The Hydraulic Service Center door broke loose or popped open, allowing water to enter the aircraft at a rapid rate.

The aircraft cracked aft of the main cabin door and forward of Ditching Stations 9 and 10. The crack resulted in a 4–5 inch gap in the deck of the aircraft.

The bench seat opposite (aft) of Ditching Station 23 broke loose and canted forward toward Ditching Station 23.

Remarkably, all eight cockpit windows remained in place. Had they, the three front windows especially, failed, it is likely that Grigsby, Caylor, and Flow would have quickly drowned in their seats under a tidal wave of cold water.

In view of the destruction that occurred in the cabin, it is surprising that only Miller was killed and Forshay injured. Hemmer, Reynolds, and Ball could have quickly been victims of structural failure, killed on impact or trapped inside as the aircraft went down.

Finding of Fact. The channel 15 emergency sonobuoy was not removed from the aircraft because of difficulty releasing its retaining straps and rapidly rising water.

Crouching amid the cluster of bodies at the starboard escape hatch, the injured Bruce Forshay could not release the restraining straps that held the emergency sonobuoy securely in place next to the no. 3 raft, on the forward end of the storage rack that held buoy reloads. Even during crew emergency drills under ideal conditions, the clips and nylon webbing could stick and tangle, defeating attempts to release survival equipment. Forshay was defeated by them now, as Rodriguez, Moore, and Wagner had been. By the time Bruce gave up the struggle, water was already covering the hatch. He stepped through it and popped up to the surface, lifted there by the air trapped in his anti-exposure suit.

The AN/SSQ-83 emergency buoy that Forshay had just reluctantly abandoned was little more than a microphone attached to a battery-operated VHF radio transmitter sealed into a watertight canister. When the sonobuoy sank with PD-2, the survivors' only ability to talk to an aircraft overhead went down with it.[7]

The choice of this particular type of buoy for this purpose was deliberate. Q-83s had the longest life in the water of any buoys in the Navy's inventory at the time, up to sixty hours of continuous transmission. Once in the water, when its saltwater battery was activated and energized the buoy's radio transmitter, the emergency buoy could serve two purposes.

It could act as a locator beacon. An "on top position indicator" in the cockpit would then point the way to the buoy. As Gibbons reminded Elmendorf several times ("U.H.F. D.F. three four five decimal five"), aircraft with no OTPI and only a

UHF direction finding capability could find a channel 15 buoy on 345.5 megahertz.

For raft-to-aircraft communications. A floating microphone on a twenty-foot cord was attached to one end of the buoy. A downed aviator could speak into the mike and be heard on the receiver overhead. All P-3 SAR crews knew to tune their sonobuoy receivers to channel 15, 172.75 megahertz in the VHF band, in a rescue area.

In 1978, the same type of clips and nylon webbing lashed the buoy in place that held the rafts upright and in position, and Forshay could not get it free.

Finding of Fact. Airman Garcia inflated the starboard Mark-7 life raft. Lieutenant (junior grade) Gibbons swam after and inflated the Mark-12 life raft, which had rapidly begun to drift away from the aircraft when its tether either was cut or broke.

The Mark-12 got pushed out the hatch successfully, but its painter, sixty feet of 50–150 pound test line meant to keep the raft tied close to the aircraft during boarding, immediately parted and the raft started to float away. Gibbons swam after it, punching through a wave "as big as a house" to catch up with the raft and hanging on to slow its drifting until other crew members could join him.

If the crew were evenly distributed among them, two Mark-7 rafts would have been sufficient for fourteen men, and the loss of the Mark-12 would not necessarily have been a disaster. But the no. 1 Mark-7 wasn't available; it had already been abandoned and was going down with PD-2, still lashed firmly in its place. And so Gibbons's quick reaction to capture the Mark-12 saved several lives—likely those of Moore, Reynolds, and Ball—who would soon appear swimming one after the other around the tail of the aircraft in open water with nothing but their LPA life vests to support them and QD-1s to protect them.

Grigsby's tragic experience to come was a forecast of what almost certainly faced these three men, if they did not quickly make it into the relatively benign environment of a raft. Immobility, unconsciousness, and a mercifully quick death. Instead, all three of them would join Gibbons in the Mark-12, and live.

But Gibbon's recovery of the Mark-12 saved others, too. Had he been forced to join the nine in the remaining Mark-7, adding his five-foot-ten-inch, 177-pound bulk to its load, that leaking, terribly overloaded raft would have gone from providing marginal support to the men aboard to practically none at all. In this case it is doubtful that even one man would have survived the twelve hours between ditching and rescue.

Finding of Fact. Lieutenant (junior grade) Ball, Petty Officer Third Class Moore and Airman Reynolds, all of whom exited the port side of the aircraft and swam around the tail area, boarded the Mark-12 life raft with Lieutenant (junior grade) Gibbons.

Just before impact, Dave Reynolds leaned across the open center aisle toward Howard Moore and confidently promised, "We'll party when this is over." He was right. They would both survive to be guests at a three day reunion and party five months later in Fairbanks, joined there by the Air Force crew that would soon be circling overhead. Reynolds's and Moore's private celebration of life, however, got displaced and forgotten in the press of other events.[8]

When PD-2 jerked to a stop on its third bounce, more than fifty tons coming from nearly eighty knots to zero in the space of a football field, Moore released his safety harness, stood, spun around to face the nose, and quickly headed for the port side overwing escape hatch. He would go through that hatch, and step off the wing into the sea, despite the fact that there was no raft to receive him, and nothing in sight but the partly submerged wing, with its nacelles torn off, and huge rolling breakers out to the horizon. Reynolds was behind him pushing, Ball was still farther back. Their rush out the hatch was less a leap of faith than it seemed. To hesitate aboard PD-2 meant certain drowning, whereas the QD-1s and inflated lobes and collars of the LPAs provided some reassurance that they would have a chance to find a raft and enter it.

Petty Officer Miller never made it out of the aircraft and almost certainly not even out of his seat. He might have been killed where he sat by the breakup of the aft fuselage on impact, or he might have been injured and unable to extract himself from Station 21 as the plane went down. In either case, the end was very quick.

Finding of Fact. Lieutenant Caylor, Lieutenant (junior grade) Forshay, Ensign Wagner, Petty Officer Flow, Petty Officer Brooner, Airman Garcia, Airman Rodriguez, Master Chief Shepard and Petty Officer Hemmer boarded the Mark-7 life raft.

Rich Garcia arrived first at the starboard overwing hatch. He had already removed it by the time his crewmates began joining him in the tight, open space between the electrical load center and the sonobuoy storage rack that gave access to the emergency hatch.

Garcia quickly pushed the raft out and launched it. Meanwhile, John Wagner groped unsuccessfully for the fresh water bottle he knew was stowed on the deck, but he could not see or feel it in the flood of seawater pouring through the hatch and up through the floor. When Wagner gave up, the water in the cabin was already above the top of the hatch, and he had to dive down to get out, surfacing through a puddle of jet fuel. Once on the surface, he immediately threw up the apple he had bolted down during the last minutes of flight and then swam for the Mark-7, perhaps twenty feet away.

Garcia and Wagner were among the first, possibly the first two, to get into the Mark-7 raft and then turn to help others board. Like PO Gary Hemmer, Master Chief Garland Shepard went into the water, chose the closest raft and swam to it.[9] The two would sit next to each other near one end of the raft, with Shepard working diligently through the night to keep Hemmer alert and alive. Ed Flow probably arrived at about the same time, and he was helped aboard by the others already there.

Ed Caylor, behind Flow out the hatch, immediately slid the few feet into the water from the top of the fuselage and started a quick, scooping backstroke away from the sinking plane fearful that its suction might pull him under. (He thought the water would be very cold and was surprised at first by how warm it felt, until the adrenaline wore off.) Caylor stopped swimming only long enough to raise his middle finger at PD-2, a wordless gesture of frustration and anger at the airplane that had let them down.

Ed then noticed the Mark-7 behind his left shoulder, and began to swim toward it, still sculling on his back. He clambered aboard between Jim Brooner and John Wagner, but would soon slide over to make room for the navigator. Bruce Forshay was last to arrive at the Mark-7; he was the ninth to get in, crawling aboard between Ed Caylor and John Wagner. Wagner had watched him swim up, and noted that he seemed injured and was not swimming well.

Rodriguez must have arrived at the Mark-7 sometime before Forshay, but no one remembers when.

Finding of Fact. With the exception of Lieutenant (junior grade) Forshay, all personnel who boarded the life rafts were free of serious, physical injury. Lieutenant (junior grade) Forshay suffered a severe bruise of the right side of his back and upper right leg.

Afloat in the water behind the short stub of the starboard wing root, Bruce Forshay had a near perfect view of the length of the aircraft. He could see from the hole torn out of the skin at what had been his nav station forward, aft to a crack in the vertical stabilizer that presumably was responsible for the canted tail.

Once in the water, Forshay first swam for the Mark-7, saw that it was overloaded, and then made for the Mark-12. In his words, he "made absolutely no headway" toward it, so thinking quickly he turned again toward the Mark-7, where Caylor and Wagner helped pull him aboard between them. That quick decision saved his life. At the time, he knew there was something wrong with his back, but it did not bother him much.

Finding of Fact. Lieutenant Commander Grigsby, who was the last person to enter the water, did not board either life raft.

There is something vaguely Lincolnesque about the thin, full-bearded figure with a prominent nose staring out of the photograph in the First Baptist Church of San José's memorial program. The pose, before an unidentified waterfront, is slightly awkward. Both feet are pointed to the right, into the wind that pushes his trouser legs back against his shins. Grigsby's torso is turned 45 degrees, half toward the viewer, shoulders hunched. He is clasping a camera, waist-high, in what appear to be very large hands.

In the photo, Grigsby is in tropical white uniform, with that uniform's open collar, short sleeved-shirt, and black shoulder boards. It is possible that the picture was taken in Adak during the summer of 1978—there are no trees in sight and the estuary behind him could be one of many places on the island—possible but very improbable. Wearing tropical whites, the familiar, all-white "Good Humor man's uniform," would be unusual in Adak even in midsummer. More likely, the photo was taken sometime during the squadron's 1977 deployment to Okinawa, perhaps on Diego Garcia or the Cocos Islands during detachment operations in the Indian Ocean. The beard is unusual, too.[10] The vast majority of navy officers was clean-shaven then (and now). Facial hair was uncommon, restricted almost exclusively to an occasional carefully trimmed moustache, like Gibbons's or Wagner's.

Grigsby was last out of the cockpit. He went out through the overhead hatch behind Flow and Caylor, but apparently hesitated before going into the water. The two others did not. Grigsby responded to Caylor's shouted "Great job, Mr. Grigsby" from the water with a blank look. He probably did not hear it, but the accolade was well deserved. Grigsby had put them down perfectly.

Lieutenant (jg) Ball, who had followed Moore and Reynolds out of the port overwing hatch and along the fuselage, saw Grigsby on his hands and knees atop the fuselage, "looking as if he were counting heads," while Ball floated past the tail of the aircraft. Well clear of the tail, Ball just managed to intercept the drifting Mark-12, and was helped aboard by Airman Reynolds.

Ensign Wagner saw Grigsby atop the aircraft, too. He thought that Grigsby was in good shape and surveying the situation. If Grigsby were, in fact, surveying the situation, the sight in front of him would have appeared nightmarish. The aircraft he had been flying seconds before was now nose-down in the water, with its starboard wing gone. The nacelles on the port side were gone, too. Their departure point was marked by tall "mushroom-shaped" steam clouds rising abruptly into the sky about three-quarters of a mile beyond the tail, formed as the hot engines plowed into cold water and instantly vaporized it. The vertical stabilizer was cocked to one side, marking where the fuselage had broken aft during the last impact. Brown smoke leaked into the sky from the break.

What was left of PD-2 was now floating in a heavy chop, rolled side to side by a huge swell system that rocked the aircraft every fifteen seconds or so, while smaller waves broke regularly against the nose. A shine on the water marked the temporary slicks of tons of floating jet fuel, ejected from shattered tanks in the wings. The jet fuel would temporarily blind and gag several of the crewmembers.

Two yellow rafts bobbed uncertainly near where the starboard wing should have been, with waves breaking over them every few seconds. Everything else he could see would have been in shades of gray. Visibility from where he stood, at not more than ten feet height-of-eye, would have been practically nothing in the trough of the swell and probably not much more than a mile or two at its crest.

On the other hand, Lieutenant Commander Grigsby might not have seen a nightmare at all. He was raised a Baptist. In college, he was president of the Baptist Youth Fellowship. After college, he met his future wife during services while on a church-sponsored mission to Seattle. As an adult, as he had been as a child, Jerry Grigsby was a committed and devout Christian.

Standing atop PD-2, precariously legs astride in between the snapped high-frequency radio antenna cables draped into the water, the aircraft now more than half-awash and sinking fast, Grigsby might not have seen a catastrophe. Two of the three rafts floated below and before him in the water. The men of his crew were either inside them or successfully scrambling aboard, their white hard hats clearly visible against dark life vests and the gray sea. In the confusion of the escape from the aircraft, it would have been impossible for Grigsby to count each man individually and easy for him to assume that with so many heads visible, they all had made it. Easy for him to believe, as he must have hoped, that, with God's help, he had put AF 586 in the water so skillfully that they had all survived.

To Grigsby, the scene before him might not have looked like a disaster; it might have looked instead like a small miracle. And in a way, it was.

Gibbons, the first man to get in the Mark-12 raft with Ball, Reynolds, and Moore, watched Grigsby slide off the fuselage into the water, and begin to swim toward them. The inflated lobes of Grigsby's LPA life vest would have impeded the action of his arms, forcing his stroke into a vertical, climbing action rather than pulling him horizontally toward the raft, now drifting away rapidly with the wind. During one moment in his swim for life, Jerry Grigsby actually floated over the Mark-12's sea anchor, but, held on the surface by his life vest, he could not reach the anchor's tether to haul himself in. An attempt to throw the anchor (a cloth bag on a line) to him failed also, the wind merely carried it away like a kite.

Grigsby got close enough to the Mark-12 that Reynolds, watching from inside the raft, saw "a look of pain on his face" before Grigsby belatedly turned for the Mark-7. When the Mark-12's sea anchor drifted by out of reach, Grigsby turned in desperation toward the crowded Mark-7 raft, and began swimming toward it. Gibbons said he appeared to be uninjured and "swimming for his life."

The interference of the LPA probably accounted for the "frantic stroke" that Lieutenant (jg) Forshay observed from the Mark-7, where he was wedged in between Lieutenant Caylor and Ensign Wagner. Petty Officer Flow, on the same raft, saw it differently. Ed Flow spotted Grigsby about thirty feet from their raft, but thought that Grigsby was not making any real attempt to reach the raft.

Finding of Fact. Due to high winds and strong currents, the rafts could not be maneuvered into a position to pick up Lieutenant Commander Grigsby, nor was anything available of sufficient length to throw to him. He was alive, conscious and able to swim upon entering the water.

Several survivors on the Mark-7—Hemmer said two; Caylor was one of them, Rodriguez was almost certainly the other—bravely entered the water, trying to kick the Mark-7 raft toward their plane commander. Others aboard paddled in his direction with their cupped hands, trying to propel the raft upwind, while the injured Forshay yelled steering instructions to the men in the water.

Ed Caylor and Randy Rodriguez spent five to ten minutes, by Ed's estimate, back in the water after they had once boarded the Mark-7 raft, trying to move the raft toward Jerry Grigsby, who was bobbing helplessly. An effort to tow a small raft into the wind with seven men aboard would be a challenge in warm, calm waters. Under the conditions they faced, it was completely futile. The Mark-7 made no progress against the waves or wind. The two swimmers, exhausted and chilled to the marrow by the cold water, eventually had to be helped back into the raft by Bruce Forshay. The others soon, reluctantly, gave up their ineffectual paddling.

The distance between the raft and Grigsby steadily increased. Caylor lost sight of Grigsby at an estimated ninety feet away, both hands held above his head but otherwise not moving. Flow says he watched Grigsby out to several hundred feet from the raft, where he last saw him floating motionless in the water.

Petty Officer Hemmer later thought that the exhausting effort to save Grigsby had consumed as much as an hour, but it was almost certainly shorter than that; Ed Caylor guessed the total effort may have lasted six minutes. It is possible that as little as an hour or two after shooting the best landing approach of his life, Jerry Grigsby was dead.

The four survivors in the Mark-12, out of sight of the smaller raft behind the waves and showers of the late afternoon, assumed once Grigsby disappeared from view that their plane commander had made it safely into the Mark-7. Not until the two groups got together for the first time since the ditching in *Sinyavin*'s whaleboat early the next morning did the roster of survivors, missing and dead, become clear.

Finding of Fact. The aircraft sank within a maximum time of four minutes after impact. Some of the crew estimates were as short as 90 seconds.

Settled in the Mark-12, under water from his ribs down, Matt Gibbons decided that it would be four or five hours before Garcia's radar surface contact would arrive at the rafts.

Pushed by the wind, the two rafts began to drift apart quickly even while PD-2 was still on the surface. At a few feet height-of-eye, the visual horizon would have been very close in the best of circumstances. Now, obscured by high seas, concealed by cold, horizontal rain and occasionally by fog, too, once the rafts spread several hundreds yards apart they were invisible to each other, even before night fell.

After PD-2 sank, the Mark-7 and -12 floated out of sight of each other, leaving behind what must have looked to the dazed men in each raft like an empty, boiling sea. Twelve hours later, the rafts would be two miles apart.

Chapter 6

Search

Still high on adrenaline at first, once the thirteen survivors were aboard the rafts and settled down, they looked around and counted themselves in pretty good shape.[1] It would take a little time for the razor-sharp cold to slice through clothing and skin, through fat and down to muscle and bone marrow.

Conditions were especially good, by local standards, in the Mark-12. There, atop the inflated, insulating bottom and under the collapsed canopy flapping wildly against the raft's doubled-decked inflation chambers—the rib assembly that would have held the canopy erect was not in the raft's equipment kit, it had been removed during routine inspection—each man had almost ten square feet of watery space to himself.

Accommodations in the tiny, overcrowded Mark-7 were much less baronial. The nine in that raft had barely three square feet apiece.[2] Once aboard, Ed Flow's legs stretched the full width of the raft (later, he would lock his knees to keep the two sidewalls from closing in on them). The other eight, all shorter, had scarcely more room in the narrow float. Beneath their legs, in the center of the narrow raft, lay a tangled web of wet nylon shroudlines that kept survival equipment securely tethered to the floor. And no cover; Mark-7s were not equipped with them. The Mark-7 was completely open to the sea, the spray, the wind, and the rain: something to take to the beach, nothing with which to challenge the stormy North Pacific Ocean as winter approached.

They were alive. But the crew's initial euphoria, fueled by adrenaline and by their successful escape into the rafts, gave way quickly to reality.

AF 586 hit the water with its big fuselage fuel tank (seventeen thousand pounds capacity) empty. But there was as much as twenty tons of JP-4 jet fuel, kerosene, in its nearly full wing tanks, roughly equally divided among the four. In flight, after engine no. 1 was shut down for loiter and at least until the first fire warning, the flight engineer would have been cross-feeding fuel from no. 1's feed tank to engines 2, 3, and 4, to keep the aircraft balanced and to ease the load on the pilot flying. The no. 3 and 4 tanks, on the starboard side, would have been breached instantly when that wing tore off near the root with the final impact. Tanks 1 and 2, on the port side, almost certainly would have spilled their contents then too, if not before when the nacelles were wrenched from the wing. JP-4 is significantly less dense than cold seawater, and so the tanks' contents would have floated in long, greasy streaks on the surface until dissipated by rain, waves and evaporation. Thin tendrils of fuel were still visible on the deeply corrugated surface of the sea when X-ray Foxtrot 675 arrived on station more than two hours later.

Several among the crew were temporarily blinded by JP-4 in their eyes or sickened by swallowing it. Caylor had his face pushed into jet fuel pooled in the bottom of the raft while climbing aboard. The raw kerosene filled his eyes, mouth, and ears, briefly blinding and, curiously, deafening him, and making him violently nauseous. Moore, who also must have swallowed more kerosene than most during his swim around the tail, retched for hours in the Mark-12, unable to help with the bailing or with anything else. Wagner drank some unwittingly when he surfaced near the Mark-7, and Gibbons did too, on his way to capture the drifting Mark-12. Gibbons, "puking like a dog," worried for the next few hours that each upheaval was costing him precious body heat.

Every passing swell broke on top of them, showering the rafts with seawater and forcing constant, ineffective bailing. Rain, a cold horizontal torrent, drenched them when the waves did not. Snow flakes, or maybe it was sleet, speckled the rain. The rafts pitched violently in the enormous seas, in huge, swooping motions that raised or dropped them several times a minute twenty to thirty feet at a time, mixing seasickness with poisoning by ingested or inhaled jet fuel. The Mark-12's limp cover was blown about by the wind, admitting water and affording little real protection. Almost everyone in Caylor's Mark-7 would soon be seasick, heaving violently as the raft was tossed around by the waves. Caylor, remarkably, would recover from his nausea even as the others got worse.

They all were exhausted, wet, and terribly cold. Inside the rafts the Pacific Ocean was waist deep, its waters here stained a bright, school bus–yellow by concentrated, leaking dye markers. Its appearance had the men sitting up to their hips in some strange, foam-flecked broth. (Once the dye was bailed out of the rafts, the diluted, colored water would fade to the usual fluorescent chartreuse before losing its tint completely.) Some survivors in the Mark-7 used the space blanket from the raft's equipment kit to sluice out the seawater in the raft's bilges. The effort to bail was exhausting and futile. They soon quit trying. Later they would try to use the blanket as a windbreak, and later still as shelter for the dying Brooner from the rain and breaking whitecaps.

Seawater had begun to leak into the anti-exposure suits. Forshay and Rodriguez had large rips in their suits, Forshay in the left arm and Rodriguez in the right leg from hip to thigh, and the seawater flowed freely into them, drenching the men inside. Most of the intact suits, however, eventually admitted water through leaking zippers and seals.[3]

Finding of Fact. At 1432, X-ray Foxtrot 675, P-3C Ready Alert launched from Adak and was cleared direct to ditch coordinates.

Lt. Patrick Conway, twenty-six, Crew 11's tactical coordinator, was the mission commander of the Ready Alert crew. Eight years earlier, Pat Conway's low draft lottery number (thirty-two, even lower than Ed Flow's) had propelled him into the Navy Reserve Officers Training Corps Unit at Rice University; he had sampled enough of Army life in military high school in Kerrville, Texas.[4] In the late summer of 1974 he started training to become a naval flight officer.

In October 1978, Conway was coming to the end of his three-year tour in Patrol Squadron 9. He had been through the transition from P-3Bs to the new P-3Cs, completed two deployments to Okinawa, Japan, and spent time on Diego Garcia in the Indian Ocean. This was his second trip to Adak. (During his first detachment to the island in midsummer, he had gotten married. His bride, a Navy Supply Corps officer, had flown up from Oakland, California, for the ceremony and returned south a few days later to wait for him.)

Lt. Ronald Price, twenty-seven, was its plane commander. Tall, blond, and good looking, with the wavy hair of a TV anchorman, Price had been a walk-on basketball player as a midshipman second class (junior) at the Naval Academy. Later he would play on all-Navy softball and basketball teams. Price left Annapolis one year ahead of Ed Caylor, for whom he would be searching today. The two men were close friends; they had been in the 10th Company together through three overlapping years at the boat school. Price would leave the Navy in 1979 after his first squadron tour, one year ahead of Caylor, and go to fly for the airlines. Eastern got an excellent pilot, evidenced by the fact that Price had been Patrol Squadron 9's check airman, responsible for pilot training standardization. It was Price's tight, illegible signature at the bottom of Jerry Grigsby's most recent flight evaluation.

Beginning at 9:00 A.M. on the twenty-sixth and for the next twenty-four hours that Crew 11 would have the Ready Duty, Pat Conway's and Ron Price's obligation was to get the alert aircraft, PD-9 (Buno. 159890), off Adak and into the air within one hour of an order to fly.

Crew 11 at Adak was one of a number of Ready One P-3 alert crews scattered throughout the world, everywhere there was a maritime patrol squadron or detachment. In their assigned operating areas, these crews were the Navy task group commander's first response to anything unexpected on or under the surface. Other aircraft and crews would back up the urgent response for as long as necessary.

On Adak, and at other remote stations, the Ready One often doubled as the local medical evacuation aircraft, too. Injury or ill health could easily outstrip the medical resources of small dispensaries characteristic of these outposts, and speeding someone to a full service hospital could literally mean the difference between life and death. With two bunk beds in the back, and able to maintain sea level cabin pressure almost to fifteen thousand feet flight altitude, the P-3 made a good (if somewhat slow) air ambulance.

The small Adak detachment could not sustain an aircraft on station for long, even if the det were at full strength. Adak's was not, but thanks to the P-3's long legs and Ready One crews elsewhere, Adak could be rapidly augmented from Moffett Field or Barbers Point, or even Misawa, Japan (if the Seventh Fleet commander first agreed to transfer some of his assets back to the Third Fleet).

Augmentation would quickly become necessary. When X-ray Foxtrot 675's inertials aligned and the aircraft taxied out toward Runway 23 to join AF 586 west of Shemya, the detachment's flight line became deserted. The third aircraft, PD-8, was at Naval Air Station Barbers Point, Hawaii, completing a training torpedo weapons load with Lt. Cdr. Jim Dvorak's Crew 12.[5]

Today, Conway and Price would get XF 675 off the ground in only twenty-six minutes, a performance made possible by the decision to brief on the aircraft, and hastened by obvious urgency. Seconds after he had run onto the aircraft and tuned his high-frequency, long-haul communications radios, Denny Mette heard AF 586's Mayday call to Elmendorf. The remaining ten minutes of preparations to launch PD-9 were against the soundtrack of Bruce Forshay's and Matt Gibbons's cool reports of the deteriorating situation over HF frequency 11,176 KHz.

Hundreds of miles away, the enlisted crewmen in AF 586 were listening to the end of same soundtrack. Gibbons had patched their HF radio communications with Elmendorf into the cabin's intercom speakers, thinking that morale would be strengthened if everyone in the tube could hear what was going on and knew that help was on the way. Each time Moore heard Gibbons tell Elmendorf they were now ditching, his heart would stop; each time they did not go down, it would start pounding again.

After takeoff, XF 675 climbed quickly to flight level 180 heading west, on course for 52°40′ N, 167°25′ E, the coordinates Denny had copied from Matt from the HF. Mette estimated it would take Crew 11 just under two hours to get there. Before they got back on the ground at Adak early the next morning, they would have spent ten and a half hours in the air.

In an effort to encourage his squadronmates to hang on, Mette had told Gibbons that XF 675 would be overhead at 4:00 P.M. In fact, Crew 11 would sight the Mark-7 at 4:45, and spot the Mark-12, a quarter mile away, seconds later. By then, the Air Force had been in the area for almost thirty minutes.

Finding of Fact. At 1446 an Air Force C-135, call sign Scone 92, took off from Shemya and was diverted to the area of the ditch.

Unlike the patrol squadron detachment on Adak, 350 nautical miles to the east, Detachment 1 of the 6th Strategic Reconnaissance Wing, on Shemya, did not publish a daily flight schedule. Instead, the flight crews and their two RC-135S aircraft (serial numbers 612663 and 612664) from Eielson's 24th Strategic Reconnaissance Squadron sat on the Rock, cocked and ready to go, waiting for a braying klaxon horn that, like a starter's gun, would release them from the air base to sprint downrange at military power.

Once aloft and in position over the Bering Sea, the crews would spy with some of the world's most sophisticated sensors on Soviet submarine and intercontinental ballistic missile tests. Their targets were warheads and decoys plunging down into the Klyuchi impact area, midway up the Kamchatka Peninsula, from distant launch sites in the White Sea and at Tyuratam, in Kazakhstan. The forty tons of infrared telescopes and signals intelligence sensors packed into the RC-135S's commodious cabin were designed to capture data on the performance of the business end of the USSR's missiles undergoing flight test. This was the super-secret Cobra Ball mission. One goal was to measure Soviet compliance with accords reached at the bilateral Strategic Arms Limitations Talks.

But "the Ball" was more than that. That afternoon, thanks to their aircraft's unique systems, the crew in the back of Scone 92 would have better information about rescue efforts swirling about the rafts in the water below them than anyone else within thousands of miles. How much of that information could be used without breaching operations security, and how, were questions the first pilot, tactical commander, and airborne mission supervisor would have to answer.

The five Cobra Ball aircraft in the Air Force's inventory were a precious national intelligence asset, so important that supposedly the five had a higher priority for common parts than did Air Force One, the president's aircraft at Andrews AFB, near Washington, D.C. The loss of one Cobra Ball aircraft out of Shemya in 1969—with only a single, strangled radio distress call about fuselage vibrations and going on oxygen—was one of the Bering Sea's enduring mysteries. Thirty-nine men were lost. No sign of aircraft wreckage was ever found. A second RC-135S ran off Shemya's west runway the same year, no mystery there. In 1978, there were only three left in the fleet (and one of those, 664, would crash and burn landing east on Shemya in 1982, killing six).

In civilian clothes, Carter's RC-135S would have been a Boeing 707 commercial transport. It was big: fully sixty feet longer, forty-five feet wider, and more than twice as heavy as Grigsby's P-3. A 707 stuffed full of the best reconnaissance, navigation, and communications technology in America.

Flight crews deployed to Shemya from near Fairbanks, in central Alaska, for two weeks at a time. Cobra Ball crews loved it on the front lines of the cold war. Their conceit was that everyone else in uniform was practicing, but everything the Ball did was for real. Despite the monkish living conditions (crews slept in a bunkroom in the hangar and cooked their own meals) and miserable flying weather around Shemya, the 24th SRS boasted some of the highest personnel retention rates in the U.S. Air Force.

The Shemya alert hangars stood on a low hill overlooking the runway, separated from it by a taxiway with two 90-degree turns. During the island's long winter, those two sharp, downhill turns were sometimes glazed with ice, slick as an Olympic luge run. Easing the ponderous RC-135S gingerly through the turns while preparing for takeoff, feeling the three-hundred-thousand-pound aircraft drift sideways through first one and then the other, brought anxious moments to the cockpit before the flight had even begun.

No problem on 26 October. The klaxon sounded at approximately 2:35 P.M., signaling a "higher headquarters mission." The taxiway was wet, but traction was good, and the crew got their aircraft, Scone 92, towed out of the hangar and accelerating down the runway approximately eleven minutes after the horn went off, about an average response. In the cabin behind the cockpit crew, twelve men— the tactical commander, two navigators, electronic warfare officers, a photographer, an electronics technician, and special signals operators—sat in their seats bringing up their gear and thinking about Ivan.[6] Today, however, Scone 92's sophisticated equipment would be used on a not-to-interfere basis during a search and rescue mission.

Capt. Cliff Carter, USAF, hauled Scone 92 off Shemya AFB at 2:46 P.M. He turned northwest and almost immediately flew up into the cloud bands trailing down from the atmospheric low, now roughly two hundred miles north of the island and centered not far from where he was heading. During the next few days, the Aleutian low's quick easterly movement would progressively close island airfields to aircraft operations, forcing diversions and cancellations and complicating and impeding rescue operations for days. By early next morning, not long after Scone 92 returned to base, crosswinds would close Shemya a second time.

Carter was a second-generation Air Force pilot. His father had flown C-54s in the storied Berlin Airlift. The experience made him practically a charter member of the cold war. Carter senior ultimately retired as a Military Airlift Transport Service command pilot in 1961. The son's career in the same uniform began in 1972 and would be much shorter: an Air Force ROTC commission from Southwest Texas State University, flight training in Del Rio, Texas, followed by tours with the

82d and 24th Strategic Reconnaissance Squadrons in the Pacific. By January 1980, Cliff Carter would be back home in Texas, in civvies, looking for an airline job.

On 26 October 1978, Carter's aircraft and crew followed the familiar operational profile for only the first thirty-six minutes of their flight. After takeoff, Scone 92 sped for an orbit position off Kamchatka, where in the back of the aircraft Capt. Alan Feldkamp, the tactical commander, and his electronic warfare officers would ordinarily wait for "an event" to record.

Alan Feldkamp was another of the sons of small-town America who would congregate unexpectedly in the air west of Attu that afternoon. He was a farm boy from Seneca, in northeastern Kansas, hard by the Nebraska line. Like Carter, Feldkamp was an AFROTC graduate from a state university, Kansas State. Unlike Carter, his tour with the 24th SRS in Alaska was not his last in uniform. Feldkamp would spend twenty-two years in the Air Force, retiring in 1993 as a colonel.

At the top of the climb, one of Captain Feldkamp's EWOs in the back picked up a radio beacon on 8,364 KHz, the marine band emergency frequency. Minutes later, at 3:11 P.M., Lt. Col. Edgar Winklemann, the Det. 1 commander in mission control on Shemya, told the RC-135S crew that a Navy P-3 had ditched west of the island. At 3:22 Winklemann instructed Carter to abort his high-profile mission and diverted Scone 92 to the crash coordinates.[7] Winklemann's decision to send Carter looking for the Navy crew in distress was immediately endorsed by the parent squadron's commanding officer, Maj. Larry Mitchell, at Eielson AFB. The Soviets would unknowingly get away with a nearly free shot.

Scone 92 was not carrying out-of-area aeronautical charts, so Carter's two navigators, Capts. Bruce Salvaglio and Gordy Alder, quickly improvised new ones with the required coverage west of the Aleutians. Their route carefully boxed around the two Soviet-owned Komondorski Islands, lying directly between them and the ditching coordinates. After rounding the 25-mile buffer that surrounded the Komondorskis, Scone 92 had a straight shot to the coordinates, 110 miles away. Carter started his descent a short distance down track, to be below the undercast by the time they crossed the ditching coordinates. The "Raven," signals intelligence, crew in the back of the RC-135S had no direction finding capability on the distress frequency they were monitoring, but by switching between left and right receiver antennas they could make crude guesses about direction. Still improvising feverishly, Scone 92 homed in on AF 586's emergency beacon as the aircraft dropped down through the cloud layers toward the surface.

The RC-135S would be the first to arrive at the SAR scene and the biggest thing in the air overhead Crew 6's rafts. After less than two hours in the water, the unexpected sight of a Boeing in Air Force markings orbiting their rafts at low altitude, beneath the first ragged cloud layer at thirteen hundred feet, was a powerful morale booster to the Navy men afloat below.

At 2:54, coincidentally just minutes after Scone 92 took off, the Adak TSC sent out an OPREP-3 PINNACLE message by flash precedence, reporting that

AF 586 was down off Shemya and describing the malfunction incorrectly.[8] An OPREP-3 is the preformatted "operational report" used to report significant events or incidents involving U.S. military forces worldwide. "Flash" precedence gave this message priority above all other traffic in the Department of Defense communications system at the time, ringing attention-getting bells at command center teleprinters worldwide. Literally an instant after the message was sent, the news was in the hands of duty officers on watch:

> **Incident.** Aircraft emergency ditching.
>
> **Commander's estimate.** Aircraft on PARPRO mission had a massive electrical/hydraulic failure and had a controlled ditch. . . .
>
> **Details.** Time. 270029Z. Location. 5240N/16725E. Narrative. Crew had a controlled ditch near a poss[ible] Soviet ship in area. Crew status unknown. . . . Remarks. Aircraft ditched alongside surface vessel, possibly Soviet. 15 souls on board. 3 liferafts.

Eighteen minutes later, the Joint Chiefs of Staff message center readdressed Adak's OPREP-3 to the White House, the National Security Agency, the CIA, and the State Department's Operations Control Center.

The flag word "Pinnacle" in this message's subject line reflected that Adak thought the loss of the aircraft and crew would have national-level political, military, and media attention. "Pinnacle" sent the message to the top: on receipt it would have been delivered to the Joint Reconnaissance Center in the NMCC. The JRC watch team would automatically relay it to the secretary of defense and the White House Situation Room. The State Department's liaison officer on the JRC team could have quickly copied it to his department's operations center on C Street, across the Potomac River. Washington's subsequent political involvement in this distant event would play an essential part in the rescue of the crew.

Finding of Fact. Both life rafts were equipped with PRT-5 emergency radios. Only the Mark-12 raft was equipped with a cover. It was not, however, equipped with the cover supports. As a result, both rafts had to be bailed constantly in the high seas.

There were three emergency signal radios stowed aboard AF 586, one in each of its rafts. The small, hand-held URT-33 transmitted only on 243.0 MHz, the UHF distress frequency routinely monitored ("guarded") by all U.S. military aircraft in flight. It went down with the no. 1 raft. The two, much larger PRT-5s in the second and third rafts transmitted on both UHF military and HF marine distress frequencies. The PRT-5s—replacements for the old World War II–technology, hand-cranked CRT-3A "Gibson girls"—had batteries good for at least three days under ideal conditions but much less in the cold.[9]

Each raft also contained a survival equipment kit and every man went into the water wearing a nylon survival vest. Together, the kits and the vests gave both rafts a lot of other signaling equipment—water-dye packets, pencil flares, strobe lights, day/night distress markers, a mirror—but not much else. For comfort, the kits contained sunburn ointment and a foil "blanket"; for sustenance, two small cans of drinking water and one "food" packet of coffee-flavored Charms sugar candies and Chiclets gum for each man. With gallons of seawater sloshing around in the rafts and more gallons washing in with every wave, the bailing sponge from the survival equipment kits proved to be no more useful than the sunburn ointment packs. Without a functional canopy to keep the ocean out, even bailing buckets would have been inadequate, and they were not to be had.

Paddles, once a part of the kits, had long since been removed on the reasonable basis that in the open ocean no one would have the stamina to paddle anywhere, which fact made the pocket compass in the kit of doubtful utility, too.

As Jerry Grigsby had approached the Mark-7 in his desperate last attempt at salvation, he had yelled, "Throw the rope." Ed Flow searched frantically for the heaving line, imagining a long rope with a heavy "monkey's fist" knot at the end, and then yelled back Jerry Grigsby's death sentence, probably the last words Jerry ever heard. "We can't find it," Flow shouted.

There was no heaving line on the raft. An optional 50 foot nylon line might have been in a raft pocket, but it was unweighted and could not have been thrown successfully into the wind even if found.[10] Ed next tried to use their PRT-5 radio, a fifteen-pound packet attached to the raft by its own leash, as a substitute. The hope was Grigsby could grab the floating radio and be hauled in by crewmembers tugging on the line. Flow, kneeling awkwardly on the flexible bottom of the raft and swathed in his inflated life jacket and survival vest, hurled the radio towards Grigsby. It fell into the water five feet short and Grigsby made no attempt to reach out for it. Man and raft quickly floated sixty to seventy feet apart.

This unsuccessful cast from the Mark-7 was not the only use of an emergency radio. Gibbons and Ball in the Mark-12 managed to energize their PRT-5, too. One of the two radios was the source of the repeating SOS signal blanketing the North Pacific on 8,364 KHz that Scone 92 first heard.

U.S. Coast Guard communications stations and the service's smaller radio stations kept a receiver tuned around the clock to 8,364 KHz. (The frequency, which lay exactly in the middle of the 8 MHz calling band, was also widely guarded in the late 1970s by commercial stations scanning the band, because of its role as the International Lifeboat Frequency.)

When AF 586's SOS came up on 8,364 MHz, one of the Coast Guard Rescue Coordination Centers could have "tipped" operation of a Pacific-wide high-frequency direction finding (HFDF) net. The net would have fixed the position of the rafts by the intersection of lines of bearing from FAA- and Department of

Defense–operated shore stations picking up the emergency signal. HFDF had been perfected during World War II, when the target had been German U-boats on patrol, not mariners in distress, but the North Atlantic and Pacific were still ringed with the big "dinosaur cage" antenna sites because HF intercept and direction finding had an important cold war mission, too.

The net was not activated, however, evidently because AF 586's position was known. Instead, the Coast Guard's radio station on Adak and its larger communications station in Honolulu were instructed to transmit a distress broadcast on 500 and 2,182 kilohertz to all ships in range, telling them, "A Navy P-3 aircraft has ditched in position 57-42N 167-29E with 15 P.O.B. [persons on board]. Vessels in the vicinity are requested to assist if possible and contact nearest Coast Guard unit." The two sites were instructed to repeat the broadcasts every thirty minutes.

A life raft is a tiny object in the ocean, small and low in the water. The (often unsuccessful) search for rafts fills the literature of survival at sea. Thanks to the P-3's navigation system, to Matt's and Bruce's radio reports, and to the arsenal of flares on board the rafts, locating these survivors was not going to be a problem. The rescuers' challenge would lie not in finding the rafts, but in getting the survivors out of the water in the relatively few hours that spanned ditching and dying of exposure. That would take a ship.

Finding of Fact. Coast Guard Cutter *Jarvis*, after refueling at Adak, had gotten under way at 1538.

The Rescue Coordination Center at Juneau knew what was important. The survivors had to be plucked out of the water quickly, or they would die.

USCGC *Jarvis* was alongside the fuel pier at Sweeper Cove, Adak, on its mid-patrol break when Juneau directed the ship to proceed immediately west of Attu, to assist in the search for AF 586 and its crew. When *Jarvis* was ordered back to sea, AF 586's first Mayday call to Elmendorf was only eighteen minutes old. The cutter's commanding officer, Capt. Axel Hagstrom, the team at Adak's fuel piers, and the crew of YTB-783 (*Redwing,* a Navy harbor tugboat in the cove) would have the ship refueled and under way, with its amphibious HH-52 helicopter back aboard, in less than ninety minutes. It took special courage to fly the single-engined Sikorsky helicopter in the Aleutians, but as it turned out *Jarvis*'s aircraft would not participate in the rescue.[11]

Twenty minutes before AF 586 hit the water, the SAR coordinator at Adak had already asked the AMVER computer in Washington for any vessel in the area of 52°27' N, 166°00' E.[12] Soon, this would be refined to a request for information on all ships within three hundred miles of AF 578's impact point. After a few tries (the initial queries drew blanks), the Coast Guard had a list of fourteen vessels, with an estimated position, course, and speed for each. The closest was *Mikasa*, supposedly only fifty-seven miles away; the most distant inside of the three-hundred-mile search criterion were *Kapitan Bondarenko* and *Asia Maru*, both just off the Siberian Coast and a few miles apart. A Soviet fishing vessel, *Mys Sinyavin*, was inside the circle, but its last position, almost exactly twenty-four hours old when AF 586 ditched, was 20 miles west of Attu and 190 miles away from AF 586's splash point. Perhaps for that reason, *Sinyavin* attracted no special attention from Juneau.[13] At about the same time, the commander of the U.S. Third Fleet advised that he had no ships in the area.

By U.S. Coast Guard standards, and the standards of most navies of the world then (and now) *Jarvis* was a big, new ship: 378 feet long with a crew of 21 officers and nearly 160 enlisted men. It, like its eleven sister ships in the *Hamilton*-class of high-endurance cutters, was among the capital ships of the U.S. Coast Guard. Aptly in view of the Alaska patrol mission, its namesake was Capt. David H. Jarvis, USCG, who had spent much of his career in the Bering Sea.[14]

The *Jarvis* was barely six years old when it was called out for this rescue mission. It had been commissioned in August 1972, the first Coast Guard vessel to enter into active service from the Hawaiian Islands. (That distinction carried with it no special luck. Three months later, *Jarvis* ran aground with its commissioning crew and suffered major damage. It was the only grounding among the five Coast Guard cutter accidents that year.)

Under good conditions, *Jarvis*'s two 18,000-horsepower gas turbine engines could push the ship along at a sustained speed of about twenty-nine knots, but during the last few days of October 1978, conditions were terrible. In pounding seas and low visibility, at times *Jarvis* would make less than four knots toward the ditching coordinates, no faster than the speed of a short man jogging.

Approaching Buldir Island (52°21' N, 175°57' E), roughly halfway from Adak to the ditch site, *Jarvis* had already pushed through forty-foot seas for half a day, in the face of sustained fifty-knot winds.[15] Now, abeam Buldir, *Jarvis* would report seas fifty feet high and wind gusts as high as seventy-five knots in its fifth progress report to Juneau. In such monstrous seas, hull down in the trough between two waves, *Jarvis*'s bridge on the 03 level (three decks above the main deck) would have been almost level with the crest of the foaming rollers breaking to either side.

The cutter would not arrive at the SAR site until more than two days had passed. In view of the time-late on station and the departure of *Sinyavin*, the deployment of *Jarvis* to the site turned out to be more of a gesture than a real contribution to the search and rescue effort. Without a raft, survival in an anti-exposure suit supported by only a life preserver probably would have been possible only for a few hours. Even in a raft, eighteen hours would have been a very long time to endure the killing cold.

Finding of Fact. At 1540, Scone 92 established communications with X-ray Foxtrot 675 on Shemya Tower frequency and coordinated search intentions. Scone 92 was monitoring the emergency beacon (frequency 8,364), but had no direction finding capabilities.

A little over an hour into XF 675's sprint to the SAR scene, Denny Mette refined his arrival estimate: Crew II would get to AF 586's ditching coordinates at 4:24. At cruise altitude, moving fast and more than halfway there, Mette overheard Scone 92 reporting an estimate of 4:10 into the area. The P-3 would be entering the scene from the east, the RC-135S more from the north.

His cockpit promptly passed UHF direction finding information to the Air Force crew, thinking wrongly that PD-2's Channel 15 emergency buoy had made it out of the aircraft and was in the water marking the rescue datum. No matter. Scone 92 did not have a receiver aboard that could home on 345.5 MHz.

Finding of Fact. At 1610 Scone 92 arrived in the S.A.R. area and commenced a rectangular search pattern at 1,200–1,800 feet, remaining below clouds.

In similar circumstances, overhead an SAR datum in the open ocean, a World War II flight crew would have resorted to an expanding square search, with the first leg into the wind, everyone aboard peering out at the turbulent water passing swiftly beneath him while the aircraft flew a pattern that loosely resembled a Greek key.

Scone 92, the last word in operational signals intelligence and electro-optics technology of the late 1970s, did something similar.

Bruce Savaglio had once attended a seminar on search and rescue at Mather AFB, and his recollections were all anyone aboard knew about the subject. Coached by Savaglio, at the nav I station just behind the copilot, Carter rolled into a circular visual search pattern, a slowly opening clockwise spiral centered on where AF 586 went down. In the cockpit Carter and his copilot had to work hard at this unfamiliar altitude: the RC-135S's right hydraulic system had failed during their flight, eliminating power boost to the rudder, so they hand tooled the aircraft. At 220–230 knots, flaps up, whipping around over the waves like a pylon racer in some x-games airshow. In the back, the tactical crew, clustered on the starboard side of the aircraft, stared out the three side windows, searching for survivors.[16]

Finding of Fact. At 1617, Scone 92 sighted a flare and identified a raft at position 52°34' North 167°31' East. On succeeding passes, they identified the second life raft, and passed this information on to X-ray Foxtrot 675, that was still en route to the area. No aircraft or visual wreckage was sighted at any time.

Only seven minutes after starting to look, Scone 92 found the rafts. Carter's copilot, Capt. Bob Rivas, was first to see a flare rising from the water just to the right of the nose, two miles away. Rivas, famously quiet and unassuming, did not break out of character. His announcement, "There it is," meaning the survivors' raft, was almost inaudible. Soon, green smoke rising from one of the rafts acknowledged that the aircraft had been seen, too. During the next twenty minutes, they would spot each raft two more times, losing sight of it on each pass and regaining it on the next.

In Scone 92's cockpit, Rivas took everything he was seeing in stride, but one of the Ravens in the back did not. Capt. Greg Cummins, a graduate of the Air Force Academy and jump school, bravely—recklessly—proposed to put on a chute and drop into the water to help the men in the rafts. If Cummins had gotten out of the aircraft alive, he would have almost certainly drowned on water entry, entangled in shroud lines or dragged by the canopy, or died of exposure soon thereafter. Happily a cooler head, Feldkamp, restrained him.

In the rafts, the sight of the RC-135S overhead was like a tonic, a powerful stimulant. Ball, in the Mark-12, grinned at Gibbons and started chanting "Sky King, Sky King." Everyone now optimistically looked forward to pickup.

Finding of Fact. At approximately 1640, X-ray Foxtrot 675 relieved Scone 92 as primary S.A.R. aircraft over the survivors. X-ray Foxtrot 675 descended to 500 feet and Scone 92 climbed to 34,000 feet to assume a radio relay role.

Boeing's 707 transport was designed for economical, high-speed cruising in the lean atmosphere above thirty thousand feet. High altitude was the RC-135S's natural element, too. With the aircraft down under thirteen hundred feet, and often as low as five hundred, and maneuvering hard, Scone 92's four Pratt and Whitney TF-33 turbofan engines were sucking down fuel greedily while they hauled the big aircraft in tight circles around the two rafts at 220 knots.

Just after 4:30, Carter told the inbound Navy aircraft that he was getting low on fuel and needed to climb. (The two had started talking to each other at 3:40, after XF 675 crossed the midpoint on the way to the SAR scene and while Scone 92 was still en route to the site.) The first attempted altitude swap was aborted as they closed on each other in the clouds. When XF 675 marked overhead the survivors a few minutes later and actually got a glimpse through the cloud layers of the RC-135S heading the other way, Scone 92 began his climb to 34,000 feet and XF 675 continued his descent. Level at five hundred feet, XF 675 took over as the on-scene commander for the rescue that was now beginning its third hour.

The survivors' elation at having been found so quickly did not last long. Conditions in the rafts were too grim to support lighthearted optimism. In the Mark-7, Forshay noticed depression settling back down upon them soon after

Scone 92 appeared. Their mood was not even lightened when PD-9 suddenly materialized beneath the clouds accompanied by the familiar growl of its T-56 turboprop engines, to replace the RC-135S overhead.

For the next three hours, Carter and his crew would remain at altitude, relaying communications between Elmendorf and Yokota, XF 675 on station, and the aircraft coming to join him. The aircraft's prototype UHF satellite communications suite at the tactical commander's station, a one-of-a-kind UYA 7 system, meant that Scone 92's comms had even greater reach than the old technology, high-frequency radios on board either XF 675 or CG 1500. From high overhead, Capt. Alan Feldkamp, the Air Force crew's tactical commander, could describe the events below him in a blow-by-blow radio teletype commentary reaching far beyond Shemya. Beyond SAC's Strategic Reconnaissance Center in Omaha, and all the way to the Joint Reconnaissance Center and the National Security Agency, in Washington, more than five thousand miles away. To any headquarters that had the equipment to eavesdrop on Feldkamp's messages to Winkleman. Back on the same circuit came a question from the Chairman of the Joint Chiefs of Staff. "Is the aircraft still afloat?" General Jones himself wanted to know.[17] "No," Feldkamp typed in, "it's not."

Later, Carter would break away hurriedly to refuel from Scone 93, a KC-135 tanker launched off strip alert at Eielson to support him, and then return to the area for another two hours of communications relay before heading back to Shemya and a landing at 10:00 P.M. Theirs had been a great flight. Carter's and Feldkamp's postflight report to the parent squadron and wing concluded, "The sense of kinship with the downed crew members and exhilaration of that first flare was felt by every man on board and was the greatest 'gaslight' we will ever call."[18]

In early April 1980, every man aboard Scone 92 was awarded the Air Medal for "meritorious achievement while participating in aerial flight" on 26 October 1978. Cobra Ball crews got many such medals. The award was Carter's second and Feldkamp's fourth.

Finding of Fact. At approximately 1645, X-ray Foxtrot 675 sighted both rafts, one with an estimated six survivors and the second with one visible survivor. The crew dropped smoke markers and sonobuoys to mark the rafts. Wind conditions, high sea state and poor visibility made it extremely difficult to keep the rafts continually in sight, much less to accurately determine the correct number of personnel aboard.

The wind had died down slightly. It was still out of the southwest, but now blowing around thirty knots, occasionally gusting higher. Conway had quickly abandoned the use of smoke markers. The spume blowing across the tops of the waves was so heavy that the markers' dense, white plumes of smoke quickly became invisible against the background foam or lost in the rain. Sonobuoys made better placeholders. As the wind pushed the rafts away from one buoy, another buoy would be dropped, and tracked with the on top position indicator, until that buoy, too, had to be replaced.

During the next four hours, Price and the cockpit crew drove XF 675 around a racetrack pattern less than five hundred feet above the two rafts, trying to keep both of them in sight on each pass. The rafts continue to drift apart, and on some passes the crew lost sight of one or the other.

Pinned to this pattern by fear of losing sight of the rafts, the crew aboard XF 675 knew that they were not providing real help to the desperate men passing beneath their wing every few minutes.

Finding of Fact. At 1713, Coast Guard 1500, the C-130, landed at Naval Station Adak for refueling and briefing.

Eight hours after he had left, Bill Porter was back on the ground at Adak, parking Coast Guard 1500 alongside a fuel truck. His crew was there just long enough to brief, refuel, and pick up some food. They were not even halfway through what would eventually become a twenty-three-hour duty day, during which they would log 17.3 hours of flight time.

Naval Station Adak was familiar to anyone from Kodiak, but Porter was more at home with the Navy than most Coast Guardsmen. He had spent six years in the service. In the 1960s and 1970s, Coast Guard aviators got their pilot's wings the same place Navy and Marine Corps officers did, at Navy flight training facilities in Florida and Texas, but Porter had gone through pilot training as a Navy Aviation Officer Candidate. After he got his wings in October 1969, Porter had two tours of duty as a Navy officer.

The first was flying Guam-based C-130Qs, towing a long antenna out the back of the aircraft. Their important, deadly dull mission was providing emergency "connectivity" (communications in the form of emergency action messages, EAMs) to ballistic missile submarines on patrol in the Pacific. Flying the 130Qs in a tight orbit, such that the mile or more of antenna they streamed stood vertically took a nice touch on the controls, airmanship that was never recognized by aviators whose business was shooting things down or blowing them up.

His next tour was as a multiengine flight instructor in Corpus Christi, Texas, flying two students at a time in antiquated Grumman TS-2 "Trackers." Porter left the Navy as a lieutenant in 1974. Two years later, he was back in uniform and a Coast Guard lieutenant (junior grade), flying C-130s out of Coast Guard Air Station Kodiak, Alaska. At the end of October 1978, Porter had almost two thousand pilot hours in the C-130 and nearly fifteen hundred in other types of aircraft.

Lt. (jg) Rick Holzshu, his copilot, had a similar history. Holzshu had been an Air Force C-130 pilot before accepting a commission in the Coast Guard. Between them, the two Coast Guard jaygees had years of experience in the boxy airplane they would drive to the SAR datum that evening.

Finding of Fact. Personnel in both rafts assisted the S.A.R. aircraft by utilizing all signaling devices on a regular, continual basis.

Every man's survival vest contained a pencil flare gun and seven signal cartridges, and each vest also carried two double-ended "marine smoke and illumination" signals. Extras were stowed in the rafts' equipment kits. The flare gun, a pen-sized "Saturday night special" with a spring-loaded firing pin, fired a tracer round into the air. The longer lasting signal had a twenty-second flare at one end, for night use, and a twenty-second smoke at the other for use in the day.

Soon after Crew 6 went into the water, the men's metabolic fires began quite literally to cool from the normal 37 degrees C (98.6 degrees F). Basted in cold water and blown by a cold wind, even beneath the temporary protection of their anti-exposure suits, body temperatures began slowly to creep down. One of the first effects of the chilling was the loss of fine motor coordination as vasoconstriction reduced blood flow to their bodies' periphery by up to 90 percent. This first, automatic process of heat conservation gave up exactly the sort of manipulation necessary to fire pencil flares and ignite the larger day-night signal markers. Pencil flare cartridges had to be screwed into position one at a time with the firing pin cocked. The signals were fired by working a pull ring akin to a drink can's pop top.

Forshay found it very difficult to get to his signals because of numb hands and the small zippers on the vest. A few feet away, John Wagner took ten to fifteen minutes to pry his strobe light (a cigarette pack–sized light that flashes forty to sixty times per minute, with an eight-hour life) out of his vest for the same reason. The others had similar experiences.

The four in the Mark-12 raft alternated duties between constant bailing and occasional signaling. John Ball remembered the numbing sequence as "bail for a while, wave at the aircraft for a while." Eventually, Gibbons's hands grew so cold that he loaded the pencil flare gun by holding the small cartridges in his mouth and spinning the projector between his stiff hands onto their screw-in bases. In the Mark-7, Shepard was doing the same thing. Shepard had given one mitten away, but both his hands were equally stiff, like fins or flippers. Forshay did it, too. Caylor reloaded his flare gun once the same way also, screwing the live round between his teeth slowly into the cocked launcher as the others were doing, risking firing a tracer round through his mouth and into the back of his head.

Finding of Fact. Misunderstanding concerning the employment of Scone 92 developed at Adak. It was believed that Scone 92 was searching the area for ships, when, in fact, he was at high altitude due to fuel considerations.

Once XF 675 assumed the role of on-scene SAR coordinator, Pat Conway asked Scone 92, then probably well into its climb, to attempt to locate a surface ship, but he was told that they could not. (Det. 1's postflight report told their parent wing that Scone 92's navigation radar had been malfunctioning, so a radar search could not be done.) Somehow, this negative response was misunderstood by XF 675 and the Adak TSC, where the logbook has Scone 92 refueled and looking for surface ships. In fact, there were only two American aircraft in the area and neither one was looking for a surface ship.

Despite Crew 6's care to ditch near one, and Gibbon's notice to Elmendorf ("preparing to ditch at this time, this position. We're about ten miles from a ship") it would be five hours after the ditching before a rescue aircraft deliberately went to find a ship.

In the meanwhile, scouring local waters for help, Juneau asked four vessels, by name, to assist. These four included a South Korean fishing vessel, the motor vessel *Hanwoo*, the now-familiar tanker *Mikasa*, and two Soviet naval auxiliaries. The two, *Sadir* and *Sakhalin*, were not in the AMVER database but thought to be somewhere in the area by intelligence officers at U.S. Third Fleet headquarters.

Hanwoo declined repeated requests to help, saying that it had insufficient fuel. The 17th Coast Guard District immediately reported the ship's refusal—a violation of the international law of the sea that requires assistance to mariners in distress—to the Coast Guard commandant.[19] The delinquency report was also passed to the Department of State. *Mikasa* proved to be too far away, and the presence and positions of *Sadir* and *Sakhalin* were never confirmed.

Nothing would come from thirteen of the fourteen AMVER contacts.

Finding of Fact. At 1810, Coast Guard 1500 departed Naval Station Adak for the S.A.R. site.

Bill Porter and his crew were off Adak after less than an hour on the ground and just nine hours after they had first left the same place that morning. With full wing and external tanks, loaded with almost sixty-three thousand pounds of jet fuel, their aircraft was good for another fourteen hours in the air. The crew had already put in one full working day. There was no telling how much more they were good for.

Finding of Fact. At approximately 1915, X-ray Foxtrot 675 dropped the S.A.R. kit (consisting of two rafts and an equipment package) to the upwind raft, the Mark-12. The drop was extremely accurate, landing very close to the raft. The survivors were observed to have the ropes holding the rafts to the equipment container. The S.A.R. kit was dropped upwind of both rafts so that if the first raft could not pick it up, perhaps the second could.

The drop had to be "extremely accurate." Under these sea conditions, even a very small error would have meant that the kit would fall away, forever out of reach. Crew 11 reviewed and rehearsed SAR kit drop procedures several times during their high-speed transit from Adak. The unusual procedure, which requires slow flight at low altitude with three crewmembers clustered around an open main cabin door, fills its own part in Section IX ("Flight Crew Coordination") of the flight manual. On station, Price flew several bumpy practice passes at low altitude. The powerful winds at flight level prompted him to add thirty knots to the flight manual's kit drop airspeed.

The tempest blowing past PD-9's open cabin door, into which they would launch the kit, would be moving at 160 knots (185 mph), the equivalent of a very powerful category 5 hurricane. The procedure, a slow crosswind pass overhead the survivors followed by a right 90-degree, left 270-degree turn for the drop, is designed to put the kit down 50–150 feet directly upwind of the men in the water, without risking the two crew members who will push it out the door or the drop master who will supervise and coordinate with the cockpit.[20] Few crews practice the procedure and fewer still have ever performed it.

Three hours after Crew 11 first spotted the Mark-7, Mette at the nav/comm station got a call from Yokota on HF. Someone at Headquarters, U.S. Forces Japan, had done some research, and thought there were two South Korean vessels in their area. Yokota helpfully passed the crew their international radio call signs (6MBT and 6NLX) and the radio frequency to raise them on, 2,183 KHz. Mette acknowledged and called the ships. No response. Less helpfully, Yokota now suggested to the crew of a Navy patrol plane that they fly their aircraft across the bow of any ship they find, to direct them to the search area. Not done yet, the headquarters wanted to be kept informed. Yokota's repeated, insistent radio requests for "status" information during the night finally provoked the crew to stop answering their calls.[21]

Conway and Price decided to drop the SAR kit before dark, reasoning correctly that it would be unconscionable to return to Adak with it and impossible to drop it accurately after nightfall. Conway acted as the drop master with a salty chief petty officer standing by, survival knife unsheathed, to cut someone loose in case any lines tangled on the way out the door.

Their target was the Mark-12, where no visible signs of life suggested that this group of survivors was worse off than the crew of the Mark-7.

Finding of Fact. The S.A.R. equipment package could not be taken into the Mark-12 raft because it was too heavy to lift. It, along with one of the S.A.R. kit rafts, was tied alongside the Mark 12 raft.

Crew 11's SAR kit drop was perfect, so close as to have frightened some of the men in the target raft. The kit's two rafts drifted downwind—"blowing around like kites," Reynolds said—to straddle Matt Gibbons's Mark-12 with the equipment package in between them. Sadly, the men in the Mark-12 could not exploit XF 675's perfect drop of their SAR kit. Matt Gibbons said they could not get the package into their raft because "of its weight and their weakened condition." Instead, they tied the kit alongside "for possible future use." Their condition would have progressively grown worse and it is unlikely that the kit would have ever been used.

One mile or so downwind, a few of the men in the Mark-7 raft saw the kit fall away from PD-9, knowing that they needed it more than the men in the Mark-12. Later, CG 1500 would make an equipment drop of its own, in the dark from two hundred feet on a light in the water. PO Darryl Horning, squatting in the back of the aircraft beside the C-130's huge, open cargo ramp, would be the drop master. He pushed out a complete MA-2 kit, which included two twenty-man rafts and miscellaneous survival equipment, all roped together.[22] The equipment kit plunged into the dark ocean, drifted off and eventually sank unseen, taking a valuable two-way radio down with it.

Scone 92 would be the only aircraft overhead that did not drop survival equipment to the crew. The Boeing had flares and rafts on board, which contained two-way radios, but nothing was dropped during the relatively brief period the aircraft was alone at low altitude. Under these weather conditions, precision bombing with a raft by an RC-135S could not have been successful. Moreover, dropping a raft from a –135 had never been done before, and there was some concern that a raft coming out the aircraft escape chute would wipe out the horizontal stabilizer on its way down.

Finding of Fact. X-ray Foxtrot 675 refused to leave the S.A.R. datum to search for possible rescue vessels until relieved by Coast Guard 1500. The crew was fearful of permanently losing sight of the survivors because of the sea state and poor visibility.

Once the SAR kit was dropped, Price eased PD-9 back up a few hundred feet and pushed the power levers up for maneuver airspeed, around 190 knots with wing flaps partially extended.

At very low altitude and often in tight turns and a high bank angle, XF 675's radar had a tiny horizon. Most of Sensor Station 3's scope was flooded out by the bright, fluorescent bloom of sea return, radar energy returning to the receiver from the faces of waves below. The P-3 is designed to search areas of thousands of square miles. But right then, Crew 11 did not know what was ten miles away, or if there was anything there at all.

Finding of Fact. At 1938, Coast Guard 1500 arrived on scene and assumed on station commander. X-ray Foxtrot 675 climbed off station to commence search for a rescue vessel.

Coast Guard 1500 arrived on station after sunset. Down in the Mark-7, Garland Shepard could occasionally see a silvery fluorescence in the water, as tiny glowing marine organisms were raised by the wave crests and dashed into the raft.

The two aircraft carefully coordinated their swap. In poor weather and low visibility, with two aircraft intently focused on a set of coordinates, there is a real danger of midair collision. It has happened.[23] Normally aircraft swap procedures, replacing one crew at a datum by another, are carefully defined in exercise operation orders. In this case, obviously, there was no operation order. Price and Porter did not expect to be meeting at 52°40' N, 167°25' E after dark and had not planned on it. Everything was ad hoc. Cockpit chatter resulted in a quickly improvised procedure to keep their aircraft safely apart.

Three hours ago, XF 675 had asked Scone 92 for a radar surface search, and been informed that one could not be done. Bill Porter's arrival and assumption of the responsibility of on-scene commander freed Price from his frustrating tail chase, and released XF 675 to climb for increased radar range and conduct its own search for a vessel.

Finding of Fact. At 1955, XF 675 held a surface ship in radar contact approximately 30 nautical miles southwest of the liferafts.

There would be no survivors if the men in the rafts were not soon removed from the sea. Even if the abortive equipment drops were completely successful, their effect on longevity would likely have been very small, unlikely to extend anyone's life past the end of the next day, 27 October. As it was, in the early night hours Ed Caylor would reconsider his private estimate of survival time. His goal had been noon, Friday; now he just hoped to hold on until dawn. Afloat in the other raft, with an estimated gallon of cold water filling each leg of his suit, Gibbons thought that he might make it to morning but no longer. It is likely that all the other survivors saw sunrise as a milestone, too. (In an October 1996 letter to *Aviation Week & Space Technology,* Caylor wrote he could have survived for only another hour past their rescue.)

Approaching six hours in the water, and now in complete darkness, the men were just a few hours away from starting to slip individually over the edge of a biological cliff, body core temperatures below 30 degrees C. No aircraft on station could do anything about that, but one preparing to come could. Air Force Rescue 65825, an HC-130 aircraft from the 71st Air Rescue and Recovery Squadron, will leave Elmendorf AFB at 8:44 P.M. with two H-3 helicopters in trail, heading west.[24]

His twin-engine H-3 helicopters, call signs Rescue 804 and 805, are the answer. The two powerful Sikorskys carry famously hardy pararescue jumpers aboard, "PJs," men who will drop into the open ocean even under these conditions and get Crew 6 hoisted up, flown out, and delivered to medical attention.

Unrefueled, the H-3 helicopters cannot get much more than two hundred miles from shore, less probably in today's weather conditions, but with the HC-130's tanker support, the mission out to the ditch site and back becomes possible. The plan is that the flight will proceed first to Dutch Harbor, halfway out the Aleutians on Unalaska Island, and then on to Shemya, the stage for the rescue leg of the long flight.

But the big mother ship (the same type as CG 1500 and 1600) and its helicopters never actually get to the SAR area that night. Between 7:30 and 9:10 P.M., Rescue 65825 talks to Scone 92 on HF, getting information on the status of the search while heading west. The next time Rescue 65825 appears in a mission report, it will be 3:50 A.M., talking to Adak Tower. En route from a diversion at Shemya because of crosswinds, 65825 is now diverting from Adak to Cold Bay with his helos because of high winds and turbulence. When their night is over, the three aircraft will have shuttled from Anchorage to Shemya via Dutch Harbor, and back to Cold Bay, 170 miles east of Dutch Harbor, nearly two times the length of the island chain, to no purpose.[25] Juneau will release the two H-3s from this mission and back to Elmendorf and normal operations early Friday morning.

The sky and sea are dark now, a thick, velvety blackness that gives way reluctantly to the survivors' signals. At datum under layered cloud cover, a pencil flare occasionally arcs brightly into the sky, soliciting aircrew attention. The surface of the water around the rafts is speckled with a field of flickering lights, colored strobes, sonobuoy lights, and the glitter of a few marine flares that XF 675 has dropped. At one time or another, confused by what they see, observers in all three aircraft overhead will believe that there are not two but three rafts in the water. That erroneous count will be reported to Adak, Kodiak, and Coast Guard district headquarters in Juneau, and repeated in news media reports. Days later, *Jarvis* will come upon Gibbons's empty Mark-12, and it will be identified and reported to Juneau as the apocryphal "third raft."

Scone 92 calls, relaying a Sky King message. XF 675 and CG 1500 are instructed to light up their aircraft because of possible surface vessels in the area. The word from on high must have had a source in the Soviet Union, but no one on station knows that.

X-ray Foxtrot 675's blip on Sensor 3's radar display at 250°/thirty-seven miles is the downed crew's only hope.

When XF 675 gets his radar surface contact, Coast Guard Cutter *Jarvis* has been under way only four hours; it is estimating another forty-three hours en route and, in fact, will not arrive at the closest (northeast) edge of the SAR search area for another two full days.

Finding of Fact. At 2014, Coast Guard 1600 departed Elmendorf en route for Shemya to assist in the S.A.R. effort.

It is 1,266 miles from Elmendorf out the island chain to Shemya, about five hours into the wind at cruise speed for a C-130. No one at the Kodiak Rescue Coordination Center or at the Adak TSC knows how long he will need aircraft at the SAR scene. The Coast Guard has wisely begun repositioning relief aircraft and crews, to be able to sustain the effort underway west of Shemya indefinitely. The Navy has, too. Two P-3s will take off for Adak during the night and early morning from Barbers Point and Moffett Field. A second from Moffett Field will follow a few hours later.

CG 1600 has left Anchorage behind, heading west toward the end of the Aleutians and into the deteriorating weather. The aircraft takes off with two crews aboard. Lt. Cdr. John Power's flight crew will bring the aircraft in; the other crew, Lt. (jg) Al Delgarbino's, will be available to turn CG 1600 around and fly on a mission out of Shemya immediately. En route, hearing Shemya's current and forecast weather, CG 1600 diverts to Adak and lands at 3:09.

At Adak, a new Ready Alert aircrew has been patched together by the detachment and sent to barracks for crew rest. The crew will be in the TSC briefing at 2:09 A.M., 27 October, and will take off in PD-9 at 3:24 to replace XF 675 on station. Moments after they leave, Adak will set Storm Condition I and batten down for high winds.

CG 1600 will refuel and then sit chained to the deck at Adak for hours, waiting for better weather. Finally, at 7:38, CG 1600 will get the break its crew has been waiting for and take off, heading directly to the SAR station.

Finding of Fact. Between 2015 and 2036, XF 675 made numerous low fly-overs and fly-bys of the surface vessel (Mys Sinyavin) while signaling with their landing lights. They had no means of communicating via voice. They flashed the letters C-E-F in international Morse Code, which means "aircraft in the water—follow me." The Sinyavin did acknowledge their signal with a searchlight and turned toward the S.A.R. area.

The *Sinyavin* already had its powerful bridge searchlight on when XF 675 came upon it. Even under deck lights alone, the big trawler—nearly three hundred feet long, with its distinctive superstructure, cluttered deck, and tall kingposts aft supporting heavy trawl-handling gear—would have been easy to spot at the end of XF 675's radar run-in to the surface contact.

When XF 675 arrived on top of *Mys Sinyavin* at 8:15, the ship was already heading northeast, steaming as instructed for 52°40' N, 167°26' E, generally toward the rafts. One of the larger vessels on the fishing grounds, *Sinyavin* was seven years old at the time of the rescue. It had been built in distant Nikolayev, in the Ukraine on the Black Sea, in 1971.[26] Evidently, the plan was that *Sinyavin* would join the Pacific fishing fleet, because the vessel was named after a small cape on Sakhalin Island's southeast coast. In late 1978, the crew included twenty-seven officers, ninety men, and eleven women, who cooked and cleaned, a sort of floating household staff. Capt. Aleksandr Arbuzov, the ship's master, had been in command for the past four years.

The *Sinyavin* never saw AF 586 go down; it had been unknowingly opening the distance to the rafts since Grigsby hit the water more than five hours ago. Until contacted by radio from Vladivostok at around 7:00 P.M., Aleutian time, *Sinyavin* had been going in the other direction, for Korsakov, a port in the bight on the southern end of Sakhalin Island. It had finished fishing in the Bering Sea on Wednesday and was now heading in for repairs. An urgent call from the Far Eastern Fish Association in Vlad, relaying instructions from the parent ministry in Moscow for all ships to steam to the site and assist in the rescue effort, turned it about.

Ron Price switched on the landing lights under the P-3's wing, lighting up his aircraft, and repeatedly flew low on a racetrack over the ship oriented northeast-southwest, pointing back toward the rafts, while trying unsuccessfully to talk to the radio operator below. The last passes were flown directly at the ship at six to eight hundred feet altitude, with the pilots flying and the flight engineer flashing Morse code on the lights.

"CEF" might have meant something to the Coast Guard, who suggested the procedure, but it is unclear if it was the blinking signal or the aircraft maneuvers that finally got through to *Sinyavin*. After the fifth or sixth pass, apparently now comprehending but still mute, *Sinyavin* headed directly toward the site.[27] Once it was clear that the Russians were on track, Price pushed up the power levers and put his aircraft into a climb, heading east toward Shemya's fuel trucks.

XF 675 has been on station at low altitude more than four hours. Price no longer has the minimum required fuel, twenty-three thousand pounds, to get back to Adak. As Crew 11 climbs out, CG 1500 tells them he can remain on station for five more hours.

CG 1500 came on station long after sunset, and now he is alone overhead the downed aircrew. No one aboard the C-130 has actually seen a raft in the water at any time. More than once during the hours to come Bill Porter was to wonder anxiously if they were orbiting in the right place.

Finding of Fact. At 2036, XF 675 departed the area for Shemya after passing information about Mys Sinyavin to Coast Guard 1500.

XF 675 landed at Shemya AFB an hour and twenty minutes later, the beneficiary of the strong, gusty westerly that had been blowing all day, for fuel. There were less than six thousand pounds of usable fuel aboard at touchdown, enough for perhaps ninety more minutes of flight and well below Aleutian requirements. The goal was a quick turnaround for Adak, to return the aircraft for its next SAR mission.

Refueled, Price taxied toward the runway, to hear the control tower calling him with the information that Shemya weather was now below ceiling and visibility minimums, and the airfield was closed. Without a special instrument card that would grant him flight clearance authority under just these conditions, Price was required to return and wait out the weather. He did not. Ignoring the tower's strident repetitions of its bad news into his earphones, Price rolled PD-9 into takeoff position, confirmed with Conway they would exercise emergency authority to go anyway, and called for "max. power." XF 675 was off Shemya for Adak at 11:51 P.M.

On the flight home, Conway's crew was quiet, tired and depressed. Despite Scone 92's good work, they were pissed off at the joint service headquarters in Yakota, which had harassed them on station, and by their sister service that had tried to delay their return to Adak. They knew only that at least nine men from the crew of AF 586 appeared alive at the outset, but perhaps fewer were alive now. Even with *Sinyavin* on the way, no one aboard PD-9 could be confident that this would end other than in tragedy.

Someone who had the bigger picture in mind must have quietly squashed the FAA flight violation that was immediately filed by Shemya's tower supervisor against Ron Price, the pilot in command, as it moved up the line. Price never heard anything more about it.

Finding of Fact. By 2200, Coast Guard 1500 had communicated with Mys Sinyavin and had ascertained that her estimate to the scene was 2400. Her position was 52°34'N, 166°52'E.

Porter marked the position of the rafts with an electronic datum marker buoy and by flares. The expectation was that the marker buoy would drift on the surface along with the rafts, signaling their position to the C-130. Later, Porter headed over to the surface contact, a few minutes' flight time away.

The sudden appearance of another American aircraft overhead might have confused the crew of *Mys Sinyavin,* then at top speed but making very slow progress heading east northeast, downwind and across high seas, roughly in the direction indicated by the U.S. Navy aircraft some time ago. The seas were hitting the ship on its stern quarter, lifting it high from behind with each crest in a wrenching, corkscrew roll that ended when the bow slapped down into the following trough, and the cycle began again with the stern heaving up and *Sinyavin*'s screw chewing air. The wind had freshened, too. Beneath the clouds, the sea was lit only by *Sinyavin*'s deck and bridge lights leaking weakly out across the water through the rain and snow, and by its powerful searchlights on the bridge, spearing the sky ahead crazily as the ship pitched and rolled.

Rick Holzshu finally managed to gain contact with *Sinyavin*'s radioman, a sailor named Makhov, on VHF FM channel 16.[28] When a second voice replaced the first, Bill Porter was able to explain that others, not they, were in distress. "No, no," Porter clarified, speaking slowly, "men in the water. Course 090 at 25 miles. Please go." They exchanged names. "Maslov" was the name of the Russian on the radio. He was not a radioman, but he spoke English and Makhov did not.

"Bill," the Russian replied, "Bill, we go. Who in water?"

Unaware of the communications that had already snapped back and forth between Washington and Moscow, Porter's reaction was to be coy, cautious. He could not be certain if *Sinyavin* would risk its own crew to attempt a hazardous rescue of downed American servicemen. He did not know that the Defense Ministry had already informed nearby Soviet Navy, border guard, and fisheries vessels about the drama onstage more than three hundred miles east of Petropavlovsk-Kamchatski.

"Maslov, friends in the water. Please go."

"I understand, Bill."

Sinyavin was making good less than ten knots. Porter was flying back and forth, between the Soviet ship and the rafts. He renewed the flares in the water each mark overhead where he thought the rafts were, and laid a string of flares to guide the ship, route markers across an otherwise featureless sea. Arbuzov later confirmed that CG 1500 led him to the rafts, constantly correcting their course through the high seas.

"Maslov, you speak good English."

"Thank you Bill. Bill, how far?"

"Course 090° at 12 miles."

"Bill . . . you speak good English, too." Porter's crew erupted in laughter.

High overhead, Scone 92 heard the exchange. He relayed the news to XF 675 and Shemya Tower that the Russian fisherman was *Mys Sinyavin,* international call sign UONW. Alan Feldkamp felt the pressure come off. He knew that the ship had been slightly off course heading for the Americans. Now that was being corrected.

Finding of Fact. During this timeframe, the conditions of the survivors reflected the effects of exposure to the elements. Petty Officer Brooner, Airmen Rodriguez and Garcia, and Petty Officer Hemmer became lethargic and required a great deal of attention from the other survivors. They had to be kept continually propped up in the raft, talked to, and even slapped, to keep them awake.

Shepard thought that everyone had to stay awake to survive. Falling asleep, he believed, was the first step in the progression through unconsciousness to death. Bailing, signaling, singing, and talking were all part of the campaign against dozing off, and heading down that one-way path. Aboard the Mark-12, the afternoon had begun with John Ball telling stories about wild coeds and toga parties at Ohio State, his wife's alma mater, and Matt Gibbons singing snippets of half-remembered rock lyrics. Now everyone was just trying to conserve heat and stay alive.

Dying of exposure is less an event than a process. Depending on conditions, that process can be quite swift, only minutes long in extreme cases. In other circumstances, on tropical seas and with an occasional supply of rainwater, it can take weeks, and finally come in the forms of fatal desiccation or, more slowly, death by starvation.[29]

In the early 1940s, three German doctors conducted a series of sadistic medical "experiments" on human subjects, victims selected from the population of Jews and Russian POWs in Nazi prison camps. The lead and most enthusiastic researcher was one Dr. Sigmund Rascher, variously identified as a Luftwaffe captain or SS hauptsturmfuehrer. The others, Doctor Finke and Professor Holzloehrer, assisted Rascher in his horrible experiments on freezing and rewarming living humans. Ostensibly, the data collected were to form the scientific basis for the prevention and treatment of hypothermia experienced by Luftwaffe aircrews bailing out into the North Sea, who often survived immersion for only an hour or two. At least three hundred prisoners were used in the experiments, one-third of whom died immediately.[30]

Rascher's data on severe hypothermia (which he induced by submerging some prisoners in tanks of ice water and by exposing others naked to winter conditions at Dachau and Auschwitz) are unique. Data from volunteers, for obvious reasons, stop at approximately 35 degrees C (95 degrees F) core temperature, and animals and humans exhibit very different physiological responses to cold. Among other things, the Rascher data produced a curve, matching hypothermia symptoms to core temperature. He found that death was inevitable at a core temperature of 28 degrees C.

In their rafts, Crew 6's survivors would first move swiftly through the familiar discomfort of being chilled to an intense, bone-deep cold marked by furious shivering, vibrating continuously and uncontrollably. This passage would signal a two degree drop in core temperature, to 35 degrees C. The shivering would be ineffective in masking great pain from the cold. Next, the loss of two or three more degrees would be marked by long periods of "cold narcosis" (torpor) punctuated by short interludes of bare consciousness, and an ominous end to the shivering, as if the body had gone beyond trying to stay warm. In fact, shivering stops because muscle glucose has been exhausted.

Below 30 degrees C, blood pressure would already be almost undetectable and pulse and respiration would slow as if in hibernation. Then consciousness would be lost, and death would follow as core temperature sank below 27 degrees.

Crew 6's life vests, anti-exposure suits, and rafts postponed that quick progression to death, but now, huddled in their raft for about eight hours, the men in the Mark-7 raft were running out of time. And their raft was deflating.

The Mark-7 raft is nothing more than a scaled-up Mark-4, a four-man raft. It is a roughly rectangular tube with rounded corners above a rubberized sheet floor: no bow, no stern, no insulation from the cold water below. An inflatable thwart near one end holds the raft's sides apart and can serve as a seat. Compart-mentalization (two in the raft, one in the thwart) prevents a single puncture from sinking the float. The hull compartments inflate automatically, but the seat must be pumped up by hand. The nine had never pumped up the thwart. Then they discovered an air leak at one end. Wagner thought that an inflation valve inadvertently bumped during bailing caused the leak. The hand pump could not be made to seat on the valve, and air kept leaking out.

Jim Brooner had begun complaining to Ed Caylor about the cold almost immediately, as soon as he got into the raft, his short legs next to Bruce Forshay's on the other side. He said he was wet up to his thighs. Brooner, five feet nine inches tall and 150 pounds, strong and wiry, was a tough young man. He had been a rodeo competitor in high school, but nothing in a dusty show ring had prepared him for this. During the night, Brooner slumping in his place, dropped down even lower in the cold water that nearly filled the raft, and had to be lifted to a sitting position repeatedly. Sometime before midnight, he could no longer be forced to talk and sing. He first started mumbling incoherently and then, later, fell silent.

Rodriguez, who had leapt bravely into the water with Caylor as part of the attempt to save Grigsby, must have been terribly cold from the outset, too. When his body and survival equipment were returned to the United States a week later, the suit exhibited a long gash down one of the legs. Because of it, he had been largely unprotected from the cold, and the water pooling inside the suit around the large femoral arteries and veins in his legs must have accelerated the cooling process.

Finding of Fact. At approximately 2300, Airman Rodriguez succumbed to the elements.

Airman Randall Paul Rodriguez, from Denver, Colorado, was the first survivor to die in the Mark-7 raft, but not by long. He would be joined in death within the next two or three hours by the other two young, enlisted sensor operators on the crew, PO James Dennis Brooner and Airman Richard Martin Garcia.

Randy Rodriguez joined the Navy right after graduating from Lincoln High School in Denver. He died a few days short of his second anniversary in the service. The months-long training program for air antisubmarine warfare techni-cians, and P-3 aircrew members meant that Rodriguez was very new in the squadron. He had checked into Patrol Squadron 9 just over three months earlier, on 20 July. At the time he died, Rodriguez, like Rich Garcia, was making $485 a month.

Within ten or fifteen minutes after the ditching, Airman Rodriguez's core temperature—the temperature of his brain, spinal cord, heart, and lungs—had begun to drop. His valiant attempt to help drag the Mark-7 closer to the floundering Lieutenant Commander Grigsby would have accelerated Rodriguez's loss of life-sustaining heat. That awkward effort, hanging on the crowded raft and kicking into the face of the wind or sea impeded by the lobes of his inflated life vest, must have been exhausting. Each slow and ineffectual kick would have pumped the thin layer of warmed water trapped between his body and the QD-1 out through the rip in the leg of the garment, and pushed warm "core" blood into his arms and legs, where it would cool more quickly than if he had remained in the raft. It would have been an effort to scramble back aboard, too.

At first, Master Chief Shepard, sitting on Rodriguez's right hand in the Mark-7 and near its deflating end, thought that the young sensor operator "appeared to be in decent shape physically." He thought that the others, Brooner and Garcia, looked OK then, too. But hours later, as darkness fell and into the night, Rodriguez began to fail rapidly.

The collapsing raft probably accelerated the process. They had only had a foot or so of freeboard to begin with, and as air leaked out of one end of the raft it sank progressively lower, forming a ramp that repeatedly eased the flagging Rodriguez into the water. He kept slipping down, and Shepard or Flow kept pulling Rodriguez back aboard between them and holding him up.

During one of his occasional alert moments after nightfall, Ed Caylor noticed that Randy Rodriguez was overboard. Caylor thought then that the young sailor might have gone into the water on purpose. Floating in the water, with just shoulders and head above the surface, Rodriguez would be partially protected from the biting, piercing wind. The immediate effect would be to feel warmer, just as they had felt swimming toward Jerry Grigsby hours ago. If Rodriguez had, in fact, reentered the water willingly, he had found a terrible refuge. The cold water would suck the little heat his body still held twenty-five times more efficiently than could the cold air.

It is possible, too, that Rodriguez entered the water actually seeking its cold. At around 29 degrees C core temperature, blood vessels near the skin's surface can suddenly dilate in response to a signal from the body's temperature regulation system, and be quickly flooded with still warm blood from the core.[31] This brief episode of vasodilation, sometimes called "hunter's" or "fisherman's response," is a regulatory mechanism to keep the tissues viable. In Rodriguez's stricken state, the sensation could have been felt as a quick flush of intense heat. On land, this same, imagined burning feeling can drive hypothermia victims to tear off their clothes (paradoxical undressing) for relief. It could have put Rodriguez into the water.

His end came unnoticed sometime later, just before Shepard looked up and saw Rodriguez floating face down in the water next to the raft, strands of mucous streaming from his nose and mouth. At the other end of the raft, only a few feet away, Ed Caylor drifted back to consciousness and saw the body, too. Rodriguez had a turn of the raft's rope around one hand, holding him in place close aboard, but now infinitely far away.

Crew 6 in front of PD-6 in September 1978 at Moffett Field. *Left to right:* PO 3d Class Howie Moore, PO 3d Class Gene Cummings, PO 3d Class Jim Smith, Lt. (jg) Bruce Forshay, PO 3d Class Greg Bush, PO 2d Class Ed Flow, Lt. (jg) Matt Gibbons, Lt. (jg) Steve Anderson, Ens. John Wagner, Airman Randy Rodriguez, and Lt. Cdr. Jerry Grigsby. The crew had just won the wing's monthly award for intelligence photography. MATT GIBBONS

Ensign Jerry Grigsby's official "after solo flight" photo at Saufley Field, Florida, in 1964. This training command publicity photo, like all others of its type, was taken in front of a picture of a T-34 trainer days before Grigsby's first flight in Training Squadron 1. He is wearing newly issued flight gear and a fake parachute harness. The gold hard hat he's holding is also a prop, as Navy flight helmets at the time were white. U.S. NAVY

Jerry Grigsby in the cockpit of his Patrol Squadron 50 Orion after completing a nonstop flight from the naval air facility in Atsugi, Japan, to Moffett Field. The grease penciled number on the tactical plotting board in front of him indicates that the aircraft used 51,375 pounds of fuel during the trip. LOREEN GIBBONS

PD-2 in flight over the Golden Gate Bridge, June 1978. The aircraft off the left wing is a Royal Air Force Nimrod. RICK BURGESS

The "Ball" landing at Majors Field, Greenville, Texas, on a clear day in 1977 or 1978. The same Air Force RC-135C, flying out of Shemya, was the first aircraft to spot the Navy rafts and circled both at very low altitude to mark their position. The two optical windows behind the rectangular sensor bay forward of the wing mark the positions of two camera systems. A third optical window is not visible behind the right wing. These and the cockpit windows gave the crew their only view of the water.

Later Capt. Cliff Carter would climb the big Boeing for fuel conservation, but it remained generally overhead the SAR site to relay communications between aircraft on station and headquarters in Alaska, the continental United States, and Japan. ALAN FELDKAMP

Coast Guard 1500 took off from Adak for Kodiak and home minutes after Alfa Foxtrot 586 left Adak on its PARPRO mission. The Coast Guard crew would spend more than seventeen hours in the air during the next twenty-four hours, many at low altitude at night and in bad weather atop the rafts. The crew *left to right:* Lt. (jg) Bill Porter (plane commander), PO 1st Class Barry Philippy (navigator), PO 3d Class Ray Demkowski (radio operator), PO 2d Class Ken Henry (loadmaster), PO 1st Class Darryl Horning (flight engineer), PO 3d Class Butch Miconi (scanner), and Lt. (jg) Rick Holzschu (copilot). (Seaman Dan Mallot not pictured.)
U.S. COAST GUARD

The USCGC *Jarvis* in good weather. The Hawaii-based Coast Guard cutter was deployed on the Alaska patrol when Navy Alfa Foxtrot 586 ditched off Shemya. Hundreds of miles from the splash point and on the opposite side of a powerful weather system, *Jarvis* was unable to get to the search and rescue site until days after the survivors had been picked up. U.S. COAST GUARD

Master Chief "Inu" Shepard (*center*) and PO 1st Class Gary Hemmer (*right,* in glasses) at the farewell luncheon in the border guards' hospital at Khabarovsk, USSR. Shepard is wearing his winter-weight flight suit. Hemmer is in a borrowed summer-weight suit. MATT GIBBONS

Air Force 59406 on the ramp at NAS Moffett Field on Saturday, 4 November, soon after landing. The squadron's air antisubmarine warfare technicians, shop mates of the three who died on board the Mark-7 raft the week before, have formed an honor cordon. A navy color guard is leading the three coffins off the aircraft. MATT GIBBONS

The survivors of AF 586 and Scone 92's crew met at Eielson AFB on 2 April 1979; sixteen of them are in this picture, posed in front of Patrol Squadron 9's PD-7. *Top row, left to right:* Col. Bill Perry, Lt. (jg) Bruce Forshay, Lt. Ed Caylor, PO 2d Class Ed Flow, Capt. Bob Carlson, 1st Lt. Rick Stotts, 1st Lt. Bruce Carson, Capt. Bud Irons, Capt. Bruce Salvaggio (in sun glasses), Capt. Gordie Adler, and Lt. (jg) John Ball. *Kneeling, left to right:* Lt. (jg) Matt Gibbons, Ens. John Wagner, Capt. Al Feldkamp, Capt. Hank Lees, Capt. Cliff Carter, Col. John Dale, and Airman Dave Reynolds. (Colonels Perry and Dale were wing officers, not members of Scone 92's crew.) ALAN FELDKAMP

On 30 April 1979, Rear Adm. Charles Prindle presented medals to Crews 6 and 11, the survivors of AF 586, and the crew of XF 675, in Patrol Squadron 9's hangar at Moffett Field. XF 675 was the first U.S. Navy aircraft on scene. Crew 11 was standing the one-hour alert at Adak when AF 586 went down. *Standing, left to right:* PO 1st Class Len Northrop (FE), Lt. Pat Conway (tacco), Lt. (jg) Denny Mette (nav/comm), Lt. (jg) Matt Gibbons, Lt. Ed Caylor, Lt. (jg) Randy Luecker (2P), Rear Admiral Prindle, PO 3d Class Pete Geldard (Sensor 1), Lt. (jg) Van Gamble (3P), PO 3d Class John Hample (Sensor 3), PO 1st Class Hugh Littlejohn (IFT), Airman Bill Ratteni (Sensor 2), PO 2d Class Ed Flow, and Lt. (jg) John Ball. *Kneeling, left to right:* Lt. (jg) Bruce Forshay, PO 3d Class Gene Cummings (Ord.), PO 3d Class Howard Moore, Ens. John Wagner, and Airman Dave Reynolds. (XF 675's plane commander, Lt. Ron Price, not pictured. XF 675 crew positions in parentheses.) U.S. NAVY

P3-C STARBOARD SIDE GENERAL ARRANGEMENT

This side of the aircraft holds four crew stations, the main electrical load center (from which electrical power is distributed throughout the aircraft), and spare sonobuoy storage and buoy launch tubes. The crew rest area, behind Stations 9 and 10, includes a head, galley, dinette and two bunk beds. No weapons were in PD-2's bomb bay on this flight.

1. Nosewheel Well
2. Copilot
3. Nav/Comm Station
4. Nonacoustic Operator Station
5. Main Electrical Load Center
6. Starboard Overwing Emergency Exit
7. Emergency Equipment
8. Sonobuoy Storage Rack
9. Observer Station
10. Head
11. Cabin Outflow Valve
12. Dinette Area
13. Bunks

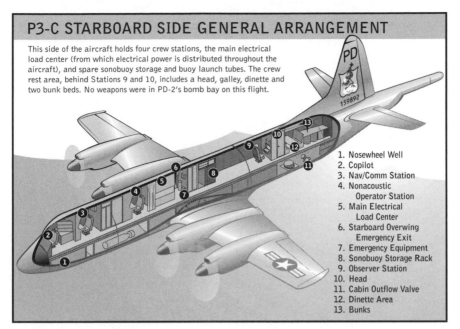

General arrangement diagram of the P-3, starboard side

P-3C PORT SIDE GENERAL ARRANGEMENT

The port side of the aircraft contains five crew stations (six including the flight engineer's centerline seat) and almost all of the floor-to-ceiling racks that house the aircraft's submarine-hunting electronic "black boxes." All of this equipment had electrical power on when PD-2 ditched. As water entered the racks, it created a shower of sparks and clouds of smoke.

1. Nose Radome
2. Pilot
3. Flight Engineer
4. Flight Station Auxiliary Emergency Exit Hatch
5. Flight Station Overhead Emergency Exit Hatch
6. Tacco Station
7. Bomb Bay
8. Fuselage Fuel Cells
9. Acoustic Operator Stations
10. Hydraulic Service Center
11. Emergency Equipment
12. Port Overwing Emergency Exit
13. Entrance Door Ladder
14. Main Cabin Entrance Door
15. Observer Station
16. Galley
17. Crash Location Radio Beacon

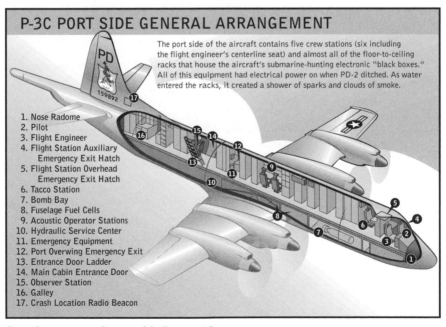

General arrangement diagram of the P-3, port side

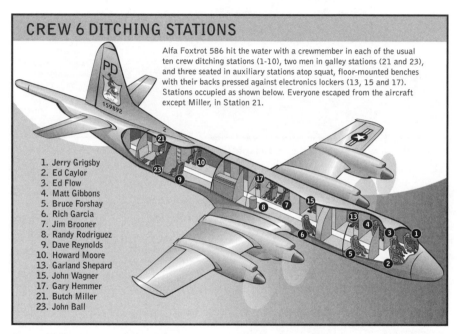

CREW 6 DITCHING STATIONS

Alfa Foxtrot 586 hit the water with a crewmember in each of the usual ten crew ditching stations (1-10), two men in galley stations (21 and 23), and three seated in auxiliary stations atop squat, floor-mounted benches with their backs pressed against electronics lockers (13, 15 and 17). Stations occupied as shown below. Everyone escaped from the aircraft except Miller, in Station 21.

1. Jerry Grigsby
2. Ed Caylor
3. Ed Flow
4. Matt Gibbons
5. Bruce Forshay
6. Rich Garcia
7. Jim Brooner
8. Randy Rodriguez
9. Dave Reynolds
10. Howard Moore
13. Garland Shepard
15. John Wagner
17. Gary Hemmer
21. Butch Miller
23. John Ball

Crew 6 ditching stations at splashdown

P-3 EMERGENCY EXITS

Although the P-3 has a total of five emergency exits, the majority of the crew used a single exit during evacuation. Eight crewmembers – Brooner, Garcia, Hemmer, Shepard, Wagner, Rodriguez, Gibbons and Forshay – escaped through the starboard side hatch [4], launching two life rafts on the way out. Moore, Reynolds and Ball abandoned the aircraft through the overwing hatch on the port side [2]. Flow, Caylor and Grigsby left through the overhead hatch in the cockpit [5].

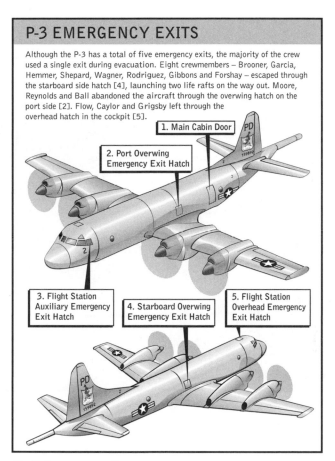

1. Main Cabin Door

2. Port Overwing Emergency Exit Hatch

3. Flight Station Auxiliary Emergency Exit Hatch

4. Starboard Overwing Emergency Exit Hatch

5. Flight Station Overhead Emergency Exit Hatch

The P-3's emergency exits

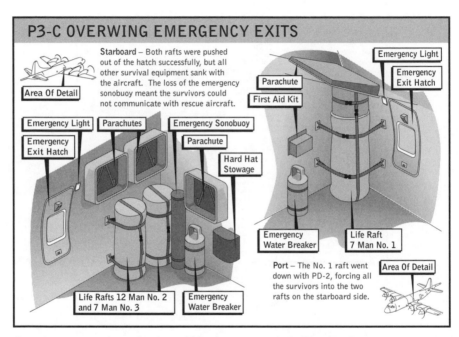

P3-C OVERWING EMERGENCY EXITS

Starboard – Both rafts were pushed out of the hatch successfully, but all other survival equipment sank with the aircraft. The loss of the emergency sonobuoy meant the survivors could not communicate with rescue aircraft.

Area Of Detail

Emergency Light

Emergency Exit Hatch

Parachutes

Emergency Sonobuoy

Parachute

Hard Hat Stowage

Emergency Light

Emergency Exit Hatch

Parachute

First Aid Kit

Life Rafts 12 Man No. 2 and 7 Man No. 3

Emergency Water Breaker

Emergency Water Breaker

Life Raft 7 Man No. 1

Port – The No. 1 raft went down with PD-2, forcing all the survivors into the two rafts on the starboard side.

Area Of Detail

Overwing emergency escape hatches and life raft stowage on the Lockheed P-3 Orion

Chapter 7

Washington and Moscow

Hours ago, Grigsby's aircraft had caromed off the top of one or two waves, hurtled on losing momentum for several hundred yards, perhaps as far as three-quarters of a mile, and then dropped heavily into the North Pacific between two swells. The aircraft burrowed to a stop, completely spent, almost atop the geographic seam between the two global superpowers of what, in 1978, was still a sharply divided, bipolar world. In two or three minutes PD-2 would sink, only eighty miles—fifteen minutes at normal cruising speed—closer to American-owned Attu than to Soviet Kamchatka.

When Crew 6 went down in PD-2 at 2:30 P.M. Thursday, Adak time, it was 4:30 P.M. in California and 7:30 P.M. in Washington. Moffett Field was approaching the end of its working day. Around the Washington beltway, traffic was already on the backside of the evening rush and the dinner hour was getting under way. In a city not then especially well known for fine dining, the first round of cocktails would have been segueing into a second in the elegant eateries lining K Street or in some of the better restaurants on Georgetown's Wisconsin Avenue. Only watch standers and workaholics were still in their offices on either side of the Potomac River.

Local time in Moscow was anomalous. Thanks to an uncorrected bureaucratic snafu sometime during Stalin's regime, the entire country had gone on daylight saving time one spring but never came off the following fall. From then on, every time zone in the USSR was effectively displaced one hour to the east. And so, in Moscow, across the International Dateline, it was 3:30 A.M. Friday when AF 586 ditched, about four hours before local sunrise, hours before government ministries would start the day's work at 9:00 in the morning. At this early hour, operations centers at the key ministries and Main Navy Staff headquarters were staffed and functioning, but all other government offices were empty and quiet. (At nearly 56° north latitude, Moscow's day would be short. Friday's late sunrise would be paired with an early evening sunset, and soon after 5:00 P.M. the city would once again become dark. In 1978, the Soviet capital remained on standard time—its standard—through the year. Washington would itself switch to standard time early Sunday morning, 29 October, increasing the time difference between the two cities by one hour. In later years, however, Moscow would observe seven months of "summer" time in common with other European capitals.)

Unlike Soviet government and foreign embassy offices in Moscow, the Yokota headquarters of the commander, U.S. Forces, Japan, was already fully manned for the working day, where it was 8:30, Friday morning.

Awareness of what was happening west of Shemya spread in concentric circles, like ripples on the surface of a pond, around the Aleutians. The first two such ripples, Matt Gibbons's report that AF 586 was aborting its PARPRO mission and, soon thereafter, his declaration of an emergency, quickly reached the intelligence specialists who would shut down the elaborate mission support system that tracked AF 586's progress, the coastguardsmen who would launch and manage the SAR effort, and patrol wing headquarters at Moffett Field and Barbers Point.

TSC Adak's Flash precedence OPREP 3 message, reporting that AF 586 was down in the water, reached a much larger and more senior audience. Its readers included officers at fleet and joint service command headquarters, on Oahu, and civilians and military people outside of the Pacific theater whose responsibilities went well beyond the execution of a single mission (no matter how sensitive) or the conduct of the rescue. By 5:20 A.M., Moscow time, the message, readdressed twice, had reached the American embassy in the Soviet capital.

Scone 92's unique satellite communications system powered the fastest and most far-reaching ripples. Alan Feldkamp's contact report carried three bits of essential information—that there were survivors afloat in rafts, precisely where the rafts were, and that there was a Soviet ship in their vicinity—to detachment headquarters on Shemya and also straight to the Joint Reconnaissance Center, where his news flowed on secure landlines to the Departments of State and Defense and to the White House.

In two short hours late Thursday evening, "Washington," meaning senior officials of the Departments of State and Defense and staff members of the National Security Council, agreed on a course of action: the Soviets would be asked to help. President Carter would not be briefed on the situation until Friday morning, shortly before the rescue at sea. The decision to engage the Soviets had been made hours before, at a lower level than the president.

At 9:30 P.M. Eastern Daylight Time, Ambassador Marshall Shulman in the State Department sent Ambassador Malcolm Toon at the Moscow embassy a Flash precedence, personal message that began "Secretary [Vance] requests." The terse, four-sentence cable asked Toon to contact the Soviet Ministry of Defense and seek rescue assistance for downed "U.S.A.F. aircraft personnel."[1] Shulman told Toon that a Soviet vessel was understood to be in the vicinity and, sharpening the sense of urgency, added that less than three hours of daylight remained at the ditching site.

Toon's staff moved quickly. Given the early hour, the embassy's contacts must have been with ministry operations centers, where duty officers would have passed the American request up the line for the attention of their principals, almost certainly still at home in bed. Shulman had his answer from Moscow before midnight. The Ministries of Foreign Affairs and of Defense, Toon told him in reply, had been contacted at 5:30 A.M., Moscow time; the Soviet Navy had also been notified.

Capt. Tony Bracken, the U.S. naval attaché, had called the Soviet Navy's command center directly, bypassing the established diplomatic channels, to seek a duty officer's help. On Monday, a bureaucrat in the Ministry of Foreign Affairs called the embassy to complain about Bracken's impolitic end run. (The correct protocol would have been to pass his request through the liaison group at the defense ministry.) The spat blew over quickly, demonstrating that even in Moscow, if only sometimes, it was easier to get forgiveness than permission.

There was no good reason for the Americans to expect the Soviet Union to cooperate, and some reason to doubt that it would. AF 586's provocative mission could not have been unknown or a mystery to the Russian commanding general in charge of the Far Eastern air defense district or to his immediate superiors in Moscow. (Air defense forces had a separate chain of command direct to Moscow, and did not report to the local military district headquarters, in this case Vladivostok.) The United States had flown PARPRO missions off (and even over) the Russian Far East for years, beginning soon after the end of World War II, when the Strategic Air Command began planning its nuclear strike missions in earnest. By the early 1950s, such flights, featuring an assortment of aircraft varied enough for an aeronautical zoo, had become routine around the periphery of the USSR, provoking regular Soviet attempts to shoot down the more impudent missions and to file bitter diplomatic protests over the others.

For most of the twenty-five-year period following the Korean War, 1953–78, the Soviet Union had done all it could to disrupt these provocative intelligence-collection flights in any way possible, including taking them down. These were deliberate shoot-downs, not the inept Chinese airmanship that would nearly put an EP-3 into the water off Hainan in 2001.

Twenty-three years earlier, Patrol Squadron 9 had itself lost a PARPRO aircraft to Soviet fighters. On 23 June 1955, two Provideniya-based MiG-15s jumped one of the squadron's P-2V5s on a PARPRO mission in the Bering Sea. Before the MiGs broke off their attack, their 23-mm cannons had set the P-2's starboard engine afire. Lt. Richard Fischer, the pilot, managed to crash-land his aircraft on American-owned St. Lawrence Island, in the northern Bering Sea. He saved all eleven aboard, although ten of his crew were wounded by gunfire or injured in the crash. The burned hulk of Fischer's aircraft, CB-3 (Buno. 131515), is still visible on the island's northwest cape.[2]

Although everyone had seemingly mellowed over time—the last Russian attempt to shoot down an American reconnaissance aircraft was in late 1970 over the Kara Sea—as the intelligence collection rivalry shifted to space, there was no reason for the Soviets to suddenly turn into good Samaritans. U.S. PARPRO flights had become less provocative over time, but they were no less audacious. Witness the marathon Rivet Joint intelligence collection flights during the 1970s, droning across the frozen top of Asia, from Elmendorf, Alaska, to Mildenhall, England, and return.

But now the Soviets were being asked to help save the lives of a crew that hours ago had flown just such a mission. Perhaps the United States was relying on the residual good will generated by a U.S. Navy rescue of Soviet seamen after two months adrift a few years before, testing to see if the half-life of Soviet gratitude was long enough to cover this event. Offhand comments in Moscow later indicated that the Soviets had remembered the earlier incident, even if the Americans had not.

Whatever their motives, the key Soviet ministries (Foreign Affairs on Smolenskaya Square, Defense on the Arbat, and Fisheries north of the Kremlin on Rozdestvenski Boulevard) moved very fast. The fact that military, air, and naval units in the area were alerted quickly is not surprising. Presumably Moscow was able to contact any of its commanders in the Pacific in a matter of minutes, perhaps much faster. More impressive and more surprising is the speed with which the less prominent Ministry of Fisheries (Ministerstvo Rybnogo Khozyaistva) found its ships at sea closest to the site, made radio contact with them, and passed the appropriate orders to trigger the rescue attempt.

The next news from the USSR came at 9:30 in the morning, Moscow time, 1:30 A.M. in Washington. (At the same time on the other side of the world, CG 1500 was tethered overhead the rafts in the dark, while approximately thirty miles to the southwest, XF 675 orbited *Mys Sinyavin,* desperately trying to communicate with the ship. In a few minutes, XF 675 would have to depart for Shemya.) The embassy was able to report to the department that the nearest Soviet ship, an unnamed trawler, was now en route to the crash site but still ten or eleven hours away. Three other "rescue" ships had also been dispatched to the scene. These would take a full twenty-four hours to arrive. Meanwhile, Soviet aircraft were in the air and searching for survivors.

The Americans had achieved their first and most urgent goal, to get nearby Soviet ships to participate in the search and rescue effort. Given the *Jarvis*'s estimate on station, and despite the possibility that the U.S. Air Force could get Rescue 804 and 805 (the Elmendorf-based H-3 rescue helicopters and their parajumpers) overhead the rafts in the nearly empty sea off Shemya, a Soviet vessel was the best chance to get the crew out of the water before they all died of exposure.

More news came a few hours later, just after noon Moscow time, when the Ministry of Defense told the embassy that "the Soviet Main Navy Staff has been given all information and all possible measures are being taken," further confirmation that the Soviets were acting on the American request. The first ship, the Russians now said, would arrive at the coordinates at 6:00 P.M. (Moscow time), and five others were in transit. Washington was immediately informed.

The Department of State's quick response to this information was to urge the Soviets to continue with their efforts, saying that the closest U.S. ship (*Jarvis*) would not get to the scene for another thirty-four hours and that at least eight men had survived the ditching and were now afloat in three rafts. The same cable passed Secretary Vance's personal appreciation to Foreign Minister Gromyko for the prompt Soviet response to the American request.[3]

The updated coordinates passed to the Soviets were 52° 39' N, 167° 30' E, four miles east of the position Matt Gibbons had reported in his last transmission to Elmendorf, and almost certainly taken from Scone 92's navigation system, logged by Feldkamp as he marked on top of the rafts.

Far away at sea, *Mys Sinyavin, Mys Belkina, Gorodok,* and the other Soviet vessels instructed to respond to the American appeal, turned to head for this position.

Chapter 8

Rescue

In the 1970s, aircrewmen joining Pacific Fleet aviation squadrons went through a mandatory two-week syllabus of land- and sea-survival training in southern California prior to reporting for duty. Training for survival on land (called SERE, and pronounced "sear," an acronym for "survival, evasion, resistance, and escape") was a vestige of the recent Vietnam experience, when the fleet's attack and fighter squadrons had reluctantly helped populate Hanoi's Hoa Lo Prison. SERE's climax was a period locked up in a replica prisoner of war camp the Navy had faithfully recreated in the high desert, near Warner Springs, that was so shockingly realistic it featured authentic torture, muttered confessions, and occasional broken limbs. (The sensation of drowning on the "water board" was especially vivid and terrifying.) A clinical psychologist acting as a safety observer, and probably scrutinizing the "war criminals" and their "guards" with equal professional interest, supervised everything covertly.

The effect of the few days of abuse in the camp was powerfully magnified by the fact that it came at the very end of both phases of survival training, during which entire time students had no food and little sleep. The experience was so miserable that graduates cached copies of their SERE course completion certificate in safe places, so that they could always prove they had been there and done that, and would never have to go to Warner Springs again.

SERE, especially the stumbling, forced marches with your head enshrouded in a bag that stank like wet fur or the hours spent squatting in a tiny, wooden crate alone with a sour-smelling urine pail and your thoughts, fixed an image into each crewmember's mind of what being held in any Communist bloc country would be like.[1] North Korean captivity would be the worst, a ferocious assault on your mind, body, and patriotism. Torture and merciless interrogation. Turnip soup to eat, or less. Compared to that or to a North Vietnamese standard, interrogation by the Russians might be less painful and more sophisticated, perhaps, but its goal would be the same: secrets, the yielding up of any classified knowledge each man might have. In terms the crew would have understood, after SERE, they were "safety wired in the resist position," trained to expect the worst and to deal with it.

Measured against the deliberate abusiveness of SERE, the at-sea phase of aircrew survival training was positively benign. Happily so, it had to be repeated with every assignment to a squadron, paired with an ascent to thirty thousand feet in a low-pressure chamber to experience befuddling hypoxia and a flight physiology/night-vision update.

Survival at sea training (DWEST, deep water survival training) comprised beachcombing with paratepee-building ashore, and a parachute harness drag, raft cruise, and helicopter hoist at sea. ("Sea" was the San Diego Bay off the Naval Amphibious Base at Coronado. There the southbound California current, transporting water from the Gulf of Alaska, kept the surface temperature at a chilling 54 degrees F year around.) Everyone aboard AF 586, except Gary Hemmer, was a DWEST graduate.

Like the hyper-realistic SERE, DWEST was built entirely around the needs of aircraft carrier aviators: bailing out over water; getting out of the parachute's harness and into a one-man raft; being rescued quickly thereafter by a helicopter. A maritime patrol aircrew could expect none of this. While a bailout from an Orion was possible in theory (P-3s did carry a backpack parachute for each ditching station), it was strongly discouraged in the flight manual. "Thorough consideration should be given to the consequences of scattering flight crew members over a large area of ocean without benefit of life rafts," the manual intoned soberly, and then it continued: "The command 'Prepare to bail out' (when over water and a great distance from land or surface vessels) should be issued only after it is determined that ditching cannot be safely accomplished. Bailout should be conducted with the aircraft circling to avoid widespread separation of crewmembers."

Stringing the members of a crew out across the open ocean with nothing but each man's personal survival equipment was a near-certain death sentence for everyone. The P-3 did not carry one-man rafts, and practically never operated near helicopters. In short, DWEST did not include any training especially relevant to the crew of a multiengine aircraft that went down far from a friendly aircraft carrier battle group, its plane guard destroyers, and hoist-equipped helicopters. Nothing about lining up to abandon the aircraft, launching the rafts as the plane sank, and surviving the hours, or even days, that might pass before rescue. The squadrons tried to fill some of this gap with crew ditching drills, walk-throughs of the exit procedures outlined in Section V of the Flight Manual, but these were static, dry land exercises and lacked realism.

The Navy also offered a cold-weather survival training program, at the Canadian Forces Base at Comox, on Vancouver Island, British Columbia, but its subject was arctic survival techniques on land. No one had thought it necessary to combine cold-weather training with DWEST, even for volunteers. Realistic training for cold water survival would have been too close to the real thing, like practicing bleeding. It was assumed you could do it if you had to. Cynics thought they would never have to, that no one could survive a P-3's impact with the water.

The men in the rafts were enduring something they had never experienced before. Water does not have to be at or even near freezing temperature for whole body immersion to have a fatal effect, and death from exposure can come in warmer water and more quickly than is commonly understood. At a water temperature under 40 degrees F, most unprotected adults, meaning those wearing street clothes or less, will be helpless or unconscious in thirty minutes and dead in ninety. The U.S. Coast Guard publicizes two "Rules of 50" that dramatize the effects of 50-degree F water—still not warm, but fully 18 degrees above freezing—on the human body. First, an average adult has only an even chance of surviving a fifty-yard swim in fifty-degree water. Second, a fifty year old has only an even chance of surviving fifty minutes in fifty-degree water.

Every man aboard AF 586 was wearing a QD-1 anti-exposure suit over a Navy-issue flight suit and an assortment of underwear and civilian clothing, but only Master Chief Shepard was wearing the prescribed *winter* flight suit beneath his QD-1. This full ensemble, the Navy said, "is designed and has been shown in laboratory tests to provide adequate exposure protection for a minimum of six hours of immersion in 45–50° F water." Flight gear (crewmembers' jackets, flight suits, gloves, and sunglasses), however, was purchased out of the same fund allocation that paid for jet fuel, hydraulic fluid, and engine oil. Few squadrons purchased much winter gear, and it was not always available when ordered.[2]

Warmly dressed in a winter flight suit beneath his QD-1, Shepard fared reasonably well. Hemmer would almost certainly owe his life and his remaining twenty years to Shepard's careful choice of clothing that morning and to the other man's ministering care.

Only one man in the Mark-12 wore the inflatable hood accessory of the anti-exposure suit. The other twelve either did not know about the hoods or could not find theirs. When not using them to bail with, they continued to wear the white aviator's helmets they had put on when Condition V was first set forever ago. The helmets were a poor alternative to the hood. Because of the circulation pattern of blood in the body, approximately one-third of total heat lost is radiated from the head. The hard hat, specifically designed for good air circulation around the head, did not have the insulating qualities of the hood, but it was more familiar and its rigidity might have imparted a sense of security that the flexible hood could not.

Some had found the anti-exposure suit's accessory mittens, but other survivors were still wearing their thin, Nomex and leather flight gloves ("Gloves, Flyer's, Summer," in the curious, backwards nomenclature of the Navy's supply system). In between gut-churning heaves and soon after dark, Moore had marveled at the fluorescent glow of his wet gloves, doused by glowing marine organisms. These single-ply gloves were good for the intended purpose, flash fire protection, but when wet they were totally unsuited for retaining heat and preserving manual dexterity.[3]

Since turning for the SAR scene, *Sinyavin* had battered its way east for five hours at full speed, during the final miles following CG 1500's burning flares on the surface, beneath the airplane nervously chivying it along. It approached the area sometime after midnight, with CG 1500 still overhead, but now carrying only a few more hours of fuel on board.

Nearing the rafts, Porter asked the Russian to have all the ship's exterior lights turned on and to sound its foghorn. Maslov understood the request for the lights, but not for the horn.

"Maslov, horn please." The lights came on.

"Bill, Bill, I do not understand. Speak slowly."

Porter's response was quick and clear: "Honk, honk, honk." Laughter from the crew.

"OK, Bill. I understand."

Sinyavin's horn began to moan. Downwind, but with their hard hats on, it is doubtful the survivors heard the signal before they saw the ship.

Finding of Fact. At approximately 0145, crewmen from the Sinyavin picked up the first four survivors from the Mark-12 raft. The Sinyavin put a small boat in the water to execute the pick-up. Those picked up initially included Lieutenant (junior grade) Gibbons, Lieutenant (junior grade) Ball, Petty Officer Moore and Airman Reynolds.

Beginning not long after nightfall, Dave Reynolds thought that he saw the lights of a ship on the horizon. He was to think that for most of the night, but the "lights" remained fixed in place hour after hour, faint and just on the edge of vision. Gibbons later decided they must have been flares from the other raft, but the lights could have been imaginary, too.

When the survivors really did see *Sinyavin* approaching a mile or two away—first, the cyclopean searchlight probing toward them, then the rest of the ship—the men in the rafts "lit up the sky" with signals by one account. So much so, that Reynolds thought the constellation of smokes and flares on the water risked confusing the rescue crew. It did not. By then, after eleven-plus hours in the water, "lighting up the sky" could not have meant an especially impressive display. It was taking the men as long as fifteen minutes to load and fire a single pencil flare, and when *Mys Sinyavin* materialized out of the night, there were only four rounds left aboard Gibbons's raft.

In the air, a red flare ignited in front of CG 1500. It came from the Mark-12. "Bill, Bill," *Sinyavin* called, "we see."

On *Sinyavin*'s bridge, Captain Arbuzov carefully maneuvered his ship so as to form a protected lee in which his boat could do its dangerous work, and slowed to a near stop. In the incandescent beam of the "projector" on *Sinyavin*'s bridge, Arbuzov saw the Mark-12 and its entangled SAR kit, and thought that he was seeing two rafts. Then *Sinyavin* put one of its small boats in the water. The ship's senior navigator, V. N. Storchak, had been selected to be chief of the boat. He went over the side with V. N. Kushkin, the mechanic assigned, and they set out for the raft.[4]

Matt Gibbons's luck continued to hold out. *Sinyavin*'s motor whaleboat got to the Mark-12 raft first, and picked up the four men inside. In fairness, Gibbons, Ball, Moore, and Reynolds could be judged lucky only in comparison to those in the smaller raft. Despite the cover, they had been sitting in waist-deep water for hours. All were terribly cold. Moore, in particular, was in desperate condition. Hours before he had been shaking violently, followed by incoherent mumbling and then, ominously, he had become still and silent.[5]

Conditions in the larger raft were bad enough that its occupants would probably have survived the others only by a matter of hours, perhaps into daylight but almost certainly not through the day, Friday. A few weeks after the rescue, Matt Gibbons recalled that when the whaleboat pulled alongside, "we were far gone. We could talk, and we could see and we could hear, and a couple of us could move our hands, but that was about it."

Arbuzov had Storchak's first report, that three survivors (actually four) had been recovered, relayed to CG 1500, overhead. It was then that he learned from Porter there was another raft in the water, two miles north.

In Moscow, nine time zones east of Kamchatka, roughly twelve hours after Ambassador Toon was instructed to approach the Soviets for help, the Ministry of Defense called the embassy to report that four survivors were now aboard *Mys Sinyavin*. Those floating half-submerged in the Mark-7, living and dead, had to wait until the whaleboat picked them up forty-five minutes later.

Finding of Fact. At 0200 Coast Guard 1500 departed the scene due to low fuel. At that time, Mys Sinyavin was proceeding to the second raft.

At CG 1500's radio station behind the cockpit, PO Ray Demkowski had been copying weather reports for Shemya, Adak, and Cold Bay during the flight. Just as *Sinyavin* turned to head to the second raft, Lt. Cdr. John Powers, plane commander of CG 1600, called Porter to tell him they were diverting to Adak because of crosswinds at Shemya. The wind was now directly across Shemya's lone runway, and above the limit for safe landing. Until then, Porter's plan had been to land there, too.

The crew of Coast Guard 1500 had good reason to be proud of their performance as they left station. After a seven-hour Adak-to-Adak round trip, they had flown to the SAR area and in darkness and poor weather, dropped a radio and raft package, successfully kept in contact with the rafts for hours, guided a Russian trawler directly to the site, and been overhead to witness the start of the pickup of the survivors. Most of that at just a few hundred feet of altitude above the stormy ocean, at night. All of it with only two pilots and a single flight engineer.

Climbing away from *Sinyavin* and the rafts, and now heading for Adak an hour or so behind John Powers, Porter and his flight engineer, Darryl Horning, puzzled over the C-130 flight manual's maximum range tables. Elated by the rescue but exhausted by their long day, the two could not make any sense out of the close columns of numbers they were reading and simply pulled the power back to a setting they agreed must be "pretty close" to the correct one for maximum range, and headed east.[6]

Porter's departure meant that there would be no U.S. aircraft overhead the rafts and *Sinyavin* until Adak's second Ready Alert flight arrived on top. In the meanwhile, and with no direct contact with the Soviet trawler, Washington asked the embassy in Moscow to pass a request to the Soviets: "Appreciate rescue assistance of *Mys Sinyavin.* Please instruct *Sinyavin* to continue search and rescue until all fifteen (15) aircrewmen are recovered. U.S. Coast Guard Cutter *Jarvis* expected on scene [Saturday, midday] with medical assistance. Request transfer survivors to *Jarvis.*"[7]

A few hours later, now with aircraft overhead the trawler again, Juneau repeated the request through the radio station at Adak, adding the detail that *Jarvis* was proceeding at "best speed." The American objectives would remain the same throughout the SAR effort: to keep *Sinyavin* on station and searching for other survivors until *Jarvis* arrived and to gain custody of the men as soon as a transfer at sea could be done.

When Coast Guard 1500 neared Adak just after 4:00 A.M., Bill Porter could not follow Rescue 95825's example and head for better weather at Cold Bay. Porter had enough fuel for a couple of tries to get on the ground at the naval station in front of his nose, but not enough fuel to go anywhere else. Leaving the rafts two hours earlier, he had immediately decided on Adak as their destination when CG 1600 told them Shemya was closed because of crosswinds, and Adak it now had to be.

Bill Porter did fine. He flew a ground-controlled, precision radar approach to Runway 23—Adak's controller quietly reciting flight path and glide slope information over the radio as Bill eased CG 1500 down over Zeto Point—broke his approach off under the overcast when he had Adak's Runway 23 lights in sight, and banked right then left to land on Runway 18. One-eight was more nearly into the wind and just as long as 23, but it was not aligned with the precision radar that had brought Porter's C-130 in sight of the ground.

Porter later wrote that his GCA approach to Adak was "O.K.," and maybe it was, but tiny Adak can be a challenge to get into under ordinary conditions. At night under low clouds, banking hard to stay inside of Mount Moffett looming off the right wingtip, unseen but nearly four thousand feet high, in high winds and after a twenty-three-hour day, it had to have been hairy. Especially during that brief, disorienting moment after Runway 23's lights went out and before 18's lights went on. He taxied in to park next to CG 1600. Then Darryl Horning, thick moustache drooping as if in fatigue, chained their aircraft down facing south, props feathered and into the wind. Cans of beer in hand, the crew went to debrief.

Finding of Fact. Between 0100 and 0230, Petty Officer Brooner and Airman Garcia succumbed to exposure. Brooner and Garcia both became very quiet. When they did try to talk, their speech was indecipherable. Garcia slipped from the raft and or fell into the water and was observed floating face down in the water shortly before pick-up.

Assailed by the brutal cold, the survivors were shrinking inside themselves, fading in and out of consciousness, but still fighting back. At one end of the raft, Flow, Shepard, and Wagner took turns trying to keep Rich Garcia awake and out of the water. At the other end of the small raft, Caylor and Forshay were desperately trying to keep Jim Brooner between them alive the same way, trying to get him to talk, to stay awake, to sit up out of the water. For a time, in an effort to get him above and out of the water entirely, they stretched Brooner atop their legs, swaddled ineffectually in the equipment kit's single-ply Mylar "blanket." It is doubtful that the well-intentioned effort made any difference to Brooner, who by then was probably beyond any help his crewmates could offer.

Survivor accounts of the deaths of Brooner and Garcia early Friday morning are sketchy and fragmentary. Their observers were rapidly losing acuity. Gary Hemmer did not remember much after the RC-135S appeared and nothing at all after XF 675 dropped the SAR kit until Sinyavin's whaleboat came alongside. By the time the last two sensor operators died, the five others in the Mark-7 raft were close to death, too, and comprehending very little anymore. John Wagner, who had noticed before midnight that the two were moving less and less and that Brooner was sliding into the water and Garcia was slumping in the raft, only remembered not being "too concerned" hours later about either man.

At the end, nothing worked. Brooner, who regained just enough strength to grasp ineffectually for Wagner's strobe light in a last spasm of life, died with the lights of *Mys Sinyavin* in sight, with Forshay and Caylor still working on him. No one at the other end of the raft noticed. They were too busy with Garcia and Hemmer to see what had happened a few feet away. Gibbons would describe Caylor as in very bad shape when the pilot was finally brought aboard *Sinyavin*. Brooner's death so close to rescue had crushed him.

Jim Brooner was twenty-three when he died. Rich Garcia, twenty, was barely two years out of Oak Grove High School, in San José, California, when he died. Randy Rodriguez was younger by one year, just nineteen. Why did only the youngest men in the rafts die?

"The will to survive is often directly influenced by the ability to survive," noted the Pacific Fleet commander in his fifth endorsement to the investigation. "Whether a rescue situation is 5 minutes in length or 12 hours in duration, the energy and stamina required, as opposed to that available, can end up being the difference between life and death. Accordingly, Commander, Naval Safety Center is requested to insure that guidance on the importance of physical fitness is continuously emphasized to all concerned." What the commander had in mind in this homily on physical fitness is not completely clear. It is possible that the staff officer in fleet operations who drafted the letter simply could think of nothing much to say eight months after the ditching.

There was, in fact, nothing about the physical condition of the crew mentioned in the investigation or the four prior endorsements, but all crew members were required to pass Navy flight physicals and given that, and their relatively young age, it is probably reasonable to assume that they were in much better than average health and physical condition. The Safety Center's accident report does not add anything about physical condition beyond the height, weight, and certain body measurements of the crew.

Grigsby, thirty-six, was eleven years older than the crew average, but only two years older than both his passengers, who lived. The reports of his behavior once out of the aircraft are equivocal, and it is unclear why he, alone, did not make it into a raft. Perhaps the inflated lobes of his LPA made it impossible for Grigsby to swim to a raft as some others did, or perhaps his first choice to head for the less crowded but more distant Mark-12 set up the failure. By the time he gave up on the Mark-12, he apparently was too spent to make it to the drifting Mark-7. (Forshay had dithered in the same way, but in the end managed to join the crowd already in the small raft.)

The patrol plane commander is assigned to the no. 1 raft in the event of ditching, that is the Mark-7 raft on the port side that Rodriguez and Moore were unable to launch. It is possible that Jerry Grigsby might have survived had the no. 1 raft been launched, inflated, and lying close aboard the fuselage when he rose through the hatch out of the cockpit, the last man out.

Afloat, alone in an LPA life jacket and exposure suit, he should have been able to survive for as long as six hours—sadly, that would have made no difference in his fate. More likely, he was numb in minutes, unconscious not long thereafter, and dead a few hours later. Almost certainly he was gone before sunset. The relatively brief search that continued on Friday was almost reflexive, and could not have been done in the expectation of finding either Grigsby or Miller, and not alive.

The fact that only the three sensor operators died of exposure in the rafts led to a lot of speculation and at least to one bizarre theory. The most common thesis is hinted at in the Pacific Fleet endorsement quoted above: the will to live. None of the three was married. This condition led some to the easy conclusion that because these men were single, they "had nothing to live for" and, in the enervating conditions aboard the small raft, simply gave up and allowed themselves to die.

The same idea reappears in a letter from the Navy's Bureau of Medicine and Surgery to the squadron in late February 1979: "*Intangibles:* In going through the clothing of the three fatals they were at least, if not better, dressed than many who survived [*sic*]. They were small men, which would cause them to lose heat more rapidly. It was interesting that all three were wearing leather jackets.[8] I don't know if this was a factor in their death or not, but we do know that coat is not a very good thermal garment. Nothing I saw of their clothing and anti-exposure suits made me believe that they were less protected than the others. We do not know what constitutes 'the will to live' or how to teach it, but one must consider it a factor."

The bizarre theory goes like this. They were allowed to die by other members of the crew to ensure that the Soviets would not somehow extract from them their technical knowledge of antisubmarine warfare. This truly fantastic explanation neglects the inconvenient fact that Shepard, the most experienced antisubmarine warfare technician aboard, and Hemmer, who knew more about U.S. Navy ocean surveillance systems and their capabilities than anyone else, were "allowed" to live.[9]

An even darker rumor made the rounds of some squadron hangar decks at Moffett Field. AF 586's "Os" (officers), it was whispered, had pushed the three "Es" (enlisted men) overboard, in order to have more room in the raft for themselves.

A less conspiratorial explanation was sought in the condition of the anti-exposure suits. It was known that most suits had eventually leaked, even the seemingly intact ones. In *Sinyavin*'s galley and sickbay, the Russians had poured cold water out of each man's boots, a mixture of salt water, urine, and sweat.[10] Ed Flow estimated his boots held only one pint. Ed Caylor guessed up to half a gallon. Gibbons estimated a gallon.

In the wing commander's February 1979 endorsement to the investigation, the anti-exposure suits aboard PD-2 were described as "in very bad condition and leaked— most of these rubberized anti-exposure suits are eight-to-ten-year-old salvage items obtained from the Air Force and have begun to deteriorate." In fact, as a careful canvas of the survivors the next month revealed, this was an exaggeration.

All of the suits had been inspected and functionally tested in November 1977 and inspected again (without testing) in June 1978, as required. Before the ditching, crewmembers had the presence of mind (and the time) to inspect the suits as each was put on. None exhibited any defects prior to use, so it is likely that the rips found on Forshay's and Rodriguez's happened when both men exited the aircraft, an unfortunate but probably unpreventable event.

Twelve of Crew 6's QD-1s came back with the survivors. The nine Navy suits averaged nine years of age; the three ex–Air Force suits averaged six years. All of them were subjected to careful inspections, looking for design deficiencies, evidence of neglect and abuse before the ditching, and of material failure during the night in the water. The result of the inspections was anticlimactic: the suits had worked. Under the grim conditions off Shemya, however, they could not have been expected to work forever or even for long. Twelve to 18 hours appeared to be the maximum, better than the specification prescribed.[11]

Whatever lacking (or losing) the will to live might mean, as an explanation for the death of three healthy young men it sounds suspiciously like the discredited nineteenth-century medical notion that held "melancholy" was either the cause of fatal disease or the predisposition for it. In this antique view, depression, fear, and grief eventually had fatal consequences; conversely a "hopeful disposition" was "most unfavorable" to the development of disease.[12] The most likely explanation for the deaths of the three youngest men in the Mark-7 is probably the most obvious one. Slightly more susceptible to the cold than their crewmates for whatever reason—small size, light weight, and low body fat were likely factors—and in the least seaworthy raft by the luck of the draw, Rodriguez, Brooner, and Garcia died of exposure first.

The absence, or presence, of a "hopeful disposition," the will to live, probably had little to do with what happened in the rafts that night. Beginning with Hemmer and then the others on the Mark-7, and perhaps with Moore on the Mark-12, the remaining ten would probably have died sometime later on Friday had not *Sinyavin* emerged out of the night when it did. It is possible that Matt Gibbons, heated by some special strength, might have hung on until early Saturday, but even he did not think so.[13]

Finding of Fact. At approximately 0230, the small boat from Mys Sinyavin picked up the six remaining survivors, as well as the three dead. All were extremely weak and unable to effectively move or walk without assistance. All survivors were taken aboard Mys Sinyavin.

Porter had told *Sinyavin* that a second raft was two miles away. Once Storchak had Gibbons's group aboard his boat, he abandoned the now-empty Mark-12 and told Kushkin to steer north toward the other raft.

A line (probably the line to the sea anchor) trailing in the water from the Mark-7 fouled the rescue boat's propeller, delaying by a few, intolerable minutes the recovery of the desperate men on the second raft. By the time *Sinyavin*'s boat finally arrived alongside the Mark-7, the raft had deflated to the point that its two sides were closing in on each other, pulled together by the weight of the men and water. To the living men inside, it must have been as if the sea were almost finished swallowing them. No one in the small raft could move. With the last survivor aboard, before the Russian boat crew turned for *Sinyavin,* they watched the Mark-7 sink.[14]

All the men from the P-3 had to be lifted into the boat and, later, from the boat to the trawler's deck. Shepard remembered *Sinyavin*'s whaleboat as a small boat, sixteen to twenty feet, with three men aboard. That length would have made it no bigger, perhaps much smaller, than the waves its crew was challenging. In high seas, the whaleboat had to keep way on while its crew collected the desperate Americans. To stop dead in the water would have been to lose control of the small boat, and risk broaching and then capsizing. Forshay was fearful of being dropped into the water by the large Russian fisherman leaning over the bow to scoop him out of the raft. The boat might have been larger than Shepard remembers, because its crew probably totaled five, and all ten survivors and the bodies of the three who had died were taken to *Sinyavin* in a single trip.

Sitting in the boat next to Gibbons and Forshay as the three held a quick, groggy muster, Caylor realized for the first time that Butch Miller must not have escaped from the aircraft.

The recovery of *Sinyavin*'s whaleboat, now packed with dead and nearly dead Americans, aboard the mother ship demanded outstanding seamanship. Once alongside, the small boat was tossed up and down twenty feet at a time by the waves, while the crew wrestled with the rope falls hanging down from the ship's davits. A misstep could result in being crushed between the ship and its boat, battered by a swinging block, or being knocked over the side and into the water.

Just after 5:00 P.M. Moscow time, the Defense Ministry's 3:10 P.M. status report on survivors to the American embassy was amended: there were now ten men aboard the trawler, and *Mys Sinyavin* was continuing the search for the others. The condition of the survivors was unknown. (It would later develop that no one in Moscow knew if the trawler had a doctor aboard.)

A more complete report soon came from the deputy director of the USA Division at the foreign ministry. The "Soviet vessel has taken on board ten survivors of P-3 crash. Three dead crewmen have been found," he said, and the "remaining two crewmen are reported by American survivors to have been killed."

Finding of Fact. All survivors were immediately taken to either the ship's dispensary or the galley. They were taken out of wet clothing, given warm blankets, hot tea, hot baths, and were treated for exposure by the ship's doctor. They were then taken to bed and watched carefully over the next 24 hours. The care they received was excellent, in the opinion of all survivors.

The men of the Soviet fishing fleet off Kamchatka were all cold-water sailors, among the world's most experienced, and *Sinyavin*'s small medical staff was necessarily expert in the treatment of exposure. The immobile, barely animate Americans being carefully lifted aboard presented the ship's medical officer, A. Safronenko, with a familiar, albeit especially acute, problem. As they remember it, everyone was immediately brought below to the ship's sickbay or galley, stripped in a steam room, wrapped in warm blankets and given hot tea, then bread and jelly and hot baths.

"Core temperature" is the temperature of the heart, lungs, and brain, the vital center into which life retreats as the body progressively loses heat. Normal is 37 degrees C, 98.6 degrees F. Beginning at 35 degrees C, the cerebral metabolic rate begins to decline quickly, a survival mechanism protecting the brain from the reduction in oxygenated blood flow to the head. Below 35 degrees C, all other vital life processes are caught in a sort of biological entropy also. Everything slows and stiffens. At a core temperature of 34 degrees C, amnesia starts to drain the mind. With the loss of another degree or so, stupor sets in.[15] A few more, and hallucinations start. Even while the body cools, the muscles of the heart's ventricles (its high-pressure pumps) continue to contract, but at some low temperature, they beat spasmodically ("fibrillate"), effectively disrupting the organ's pumping action.

Based on descriptions of the survivors' symptoms, days later American doctors at Yokota believed that the survivors' core temperatures when they were lifted aboard *Sinyavin* early Friday morning were in the range 28–31 degrees C. If that is a reasonable estimate, then the survivors' first day's rehabilitation aboard *Sinyavin* was more complex and its outcome more uncertain than they knew or remembered. Their knowledge of what was happening to them, and memories of the experience, were victims of exposure, too.

Only Gary Hemmer's condition at the time of rescue did not have to be deduced later. He was carried aboard *Sinyavin* with a body core temperature of 28 degrees C, so one of the ship's crew would tell the American officers during the two days they were steaming towards Petropavlovsk. The ship's medics worked to revive Hemmer through the rest of the night in sickbay. Long after the others appeared out of immediate danger and had been removed to bunk beds in crew's quarters, Hemmer was still being carefully thawed back to life, a degree at a time.[16] The danger now was "rewarming shock," a fatal drop in blood pressure if blood is allowed to flow freely into suddenly reopened capillaries. Like the others, Hemmer had to be warmed from the inside out.

Midday Sunday in Moscow, a Ministry of Foreign Affairs officer would report to his American counterpart that "the condition of the survivors was very serious and all were on the verge of death at the time of rescue."

The *Sinyavin* left the crash site not long after daylight, heading almost due west. Needing repairs, full of fish, covered with barnacles below the waterline, and running across the seas, at times *Sinyavin* made good only eight knots. On the way, the ship's master, Captain Arbuzov, would explain to Moscow by radio that *Mys Sinyavin*'s progress to Petropavlovsk was being impeded by heavy weather and by ice floating on the surface of the sea. It would arrive in port late Saturday, 29 October, local time or very early Sunday morning.

Like Porter, Captain Arbuzov had reason to be proud of what his crew had done. In the understated words of TASS correspondent Mikhail Khanukh, Abruzov's sailors had "displayed courage and self-sacrifice under difficult conditions. . . . Ten Americans owe their lives to the speedy and bold actions of the Soviet seamen."

Two other Soviet fishing vessels, the *Mys Belkina* and *Gorodok,* would come from the Bering Sea to join the search at the datum, and look for the still-missing crewmembers. At 5:25 A.M., the second Patrol Squadron 9 P-3, Delta Foxtrot 704, would arrive on station to resume the rescue effort. Several Soviet military aircraft would appear in the area, too. Their presence would be reported to the Rescue Coordination Center as "not hampering search efforts" by the Americans. The immediate sense of relief that Russians and not North Koreans had rescued the crew gave way quickly to the realization they must be headed to the Soviet Union.

The survivors were assigned to two compartments for the cruise into port. Caylor's bunkroom was loud and bright around the clock, with a radio on continuously and Russians coming and going seemingly at random. Despite his exhaustion, he found it difficult to rest. Caylor thought the noise and lights were part of a diabolical Soviet program to disorient him before interrogation; he had heard of the technique at SERE school and thought he recognized it here. Only later did Caylor realize that he was sharing the berthing space with some of *Sinyavin*'s sailors, who had work to do and watches to stand. On reflection, Caylor would later describe his time on *Sinyavin* as "great," and considering the alternative, it certainly was.

Bruised a rich purple the color of eggplant from the nape of his neck to the base of his spine, Bruce Forshay lay in an upper bunk of the other bunkroom for most of two days, grateful to be alive and emerging only to go to the head.[17] The others, excepting Hemmer, regained mobility fairly rapidly and by the second day were moving more or less freely in a small area belowdecks, through the passageways connecting the neighboring berthing and messing spaces of the ship. Gibbons and Moore roamed the ship, sightseeing as much as they could.

The men and women of *Sinyavin*'s crew—the eleven women were aboard as laundry and scullery maids, and as cooks and "girlfriends"—showed a friendly curiosity toward their passengers. (The unfamiliar Velcro fasteners on the Americans' flight suits, a technology evidently not yet available on Sakhalin, attracted special attention.) At least one American thought that he was offered female company for a night. The officers were invisible. Only one, assumed to be the political officer, ever made an appearance. They never saw the ship's master, Captain Arbuzov.

No one told them anything, but everyone on the aircrew understood that the few days on board the trawler might be a brief interlude between their ordeal on the rafts and a very different ordeal in the hands of their surprise hosts.

Before they disembarked, most were strong enough to down *Sinyavin*'s regular ration of borscht, salted meat, cabbage, sour cream, and sweet tea several times. Several remember the permanent tureen of hot *kvass,* a mildly alcoholic cider, in the crew's lounge as having special restorative powers.

Chapter 9

The Search Continues

There were two other aircraft parked on the ramp at Adak early Friday morning when CG 1500 finally taxied up, a P-3 from Moffett Field and John Powers's C-130 from Coast Guard Air Station Kodiak, just in on a one cushion bank shot off Shemya with Al Delgarbino's spare crew in the cabin. Both crews, Powers's and Delgarbino's, would fly later in the day.

Jerry Grigsby had not been found, nor had Butch Miller, but there had been no deliberate daylight search yet for the last two men. Although an early Friday report by radio—Ed Caylor's message, probably relayed by Maslov himself to CG 1500 soon after the survivors were brought aboard—from *Mys Sinyavin* in English said that the first was lost at sea and the second died in the aircraft, no one ashore was ready to accept that sad news as definitive so soon after the ditching. Perhaps it was because of uncertainties about the "third raft," mentioned in some Navy reports and picked up by the Associated Press. Perhaps it was an unwillingness to grant the sea an uncontested victory over Grigsby and Miller, or at least not a victory so soon.

Friday morning, no one was ready to stop looking. SAR flights would continue; CGC *Jarvis* would keep steaming west, too, planning on a rendezvous with *Sinyavin* that would never happen. The base for the search would be Adak. Although more than an hour flight time farther away from the scene than Shemya, Adak had crosswind runways and its routine operations were less sensitive; moreover, it was a Navy facility with a TSC to manage crew succession on station and good P-3 maintenance support. Some Coast Guard C-130 aircraft parts were common with the P-3, engines and engine accessories for example, so Adak was a better site than Shemya for Coast Guard operations, too.

With the assets on hand and given the distance to the SAR coordinates from the Central Aleutians, however, Adak would need reinforcement to support anything like a sustained effort. Reflecting its small targets and weather on station, the Coast Guard's computerized SAR search planning system was prescribing aerial searches with only a mile or two between parallel, "ladder" tracks, some inside investigation areas only five to six hundred miles square. Tight track spacing and small areas meant more aircraft and crews were essential. Adak's on-top fuel requirement gave a P-3 only forty thousand pounds to burn (literally) before it had to be back overhead the airfield. The restriction meant that P-3s could remain on station in the SAR area not much more than four hours before climbing for home, unless they had certain access to Shemya's fuel farm. In view of the weather, no plane commander could gamble on getting into Shemya.

The pace of the continuing search and rescue effort, however, was not set by geography or aircraft availability. It was fixed by the weather. The weather already had played a key role in the drama. It imperiled the success of the ditching, threatened the lives of the men in the rafts and extinguished three of them, locked the parajumpers aboard Rescue 804 and 805 (the two Air Force H-3 helicopters) out of the action entirely, complicated *Sinyavin*'s courageous small boat rescue of the ten, and delayed *Jarvis*'s arrival on station by forcing it through forty- and fifty-foot seas. Now in a small act of apparent mercy, it would open a window on Friday morning through which additional aircraft and crews could reinforce Adak. That forbearance would be short-lived. Early Friday afternoon, the weather window was to slam shut, effectively closing down the SAR operation entirely just twenty-four hours after it began.

Finding of Fact. Victor Bravo 760, a P-3 launched from Moffett Field, California, arrived in Naval Station Adak at 0259, October 27th, to bolster search and rescue aircraft assets.

Victor Bravo 760 was a Patrol Squadron 46 aircraft. Patrol Squadron 46, the "Gray Knights," was a sister to Patrol Squadron 9, one of the five (four and two-thirds, really) squadrons present on a rolling basis at the home station all the time.

VB 760 left Moffett Field around 10:00 P.M. Thursday night, California time; slow for a Ready Alert launch but fast for anything else. It is likely that the wing's operations officer elected to wait until the situation in the north became somewhat clearer before committing the first of what could easily be several more crews to the effort. The delay was not due to Third Fleet–Seventh Fleet politics, which occasionally ensnared the movement of operational forces between the eastern and western Pacific across an imaginary, midocean "chop" line, where operational control was "chopped," passed, from one commander to the other.

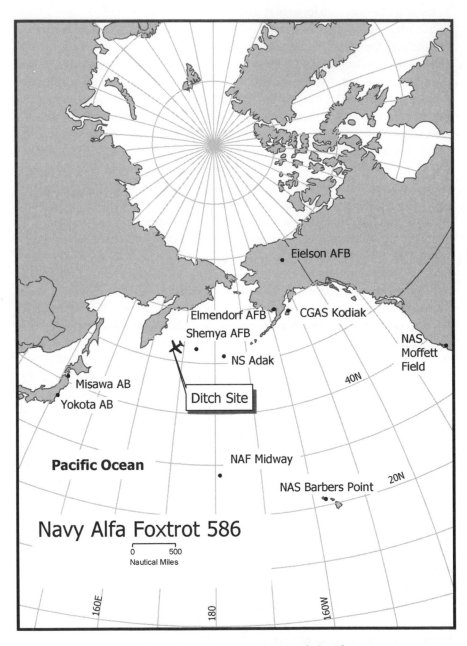

Eielson AFB

Elmendorf AFB   CGAS Kodiak
Shemya AFB   NAS
                    NS Adak   Moffett
                                 Field
Misawa AB   40N
Yokota AB
            Ditch Site

Pacific Ocean   NAF Midway
                            20N
                NAS Barbers Point

Navy Alfa Foxtrot 586

0   500
Nautical Miles

160E   180   160W

U.S. stations and bases in the North Pacific

Adak belonged to the commander of the U.S. Third Fleet, just as Moffett Field did. As far as the fleet commander, a three star admiral on Pearl Harbor's sleepy Ford Island, was concerned, moving aircraft and crews between the stations was just like shifting change from one pocket to another.

VB 760 was in the air and on the way to Adak just a few hours after it was clear that there were survivors. Marked by the letters "RC" and a red-plumed armored knight's helmet on the tail, this aircraft would have flown northwest on the same airway jet routes, generally along the great continental arc embracing the Gulf of Alaska, that had guided Jerry Grigsby to Adak days before.

As the just-arrived Patrol Squadron 46 aircrew left the flight line, the Adak detachment's last crew was finishing its preflight inspection. They would launch within the half-hour. The officers from Moffett headed for the club, for a drink and to complain to each other about the winds and turbulence during the approach and landing. That is where John Powers from CG 1600 bumped into them an hour later, rekindling complaints about the weather on final approach. All of them wondered if Bill Porter was going to get in.

Held on the ground by crew rest requirements, the new crew from Moffett Field would not be ready to join the search until early that same evening.

Finding of Fact. Coast Guard 1600 landed at Adak for refueling after having to divert from Shemya because of weather.

Coast Guard 1600, with John Powers in the left seat, was planned to be the relief for 1500 on station, after which the U.S. Navy would presumably fill in until 1500 could be turned around or a third Coast Guard aircraft, CG 1602, was spliced into the rotation. But 1600's failure to get into Shemya because of crosswinds meant that when Coast Guard 1500 left the SAR scene—heading all the way back to Adak, not to nearby Shemya—there would be no U.S. aircraft overhead the ditch site for an hour. *Sinyavin* would be alone until the arrival of Patrol Squadron 9's next flight, manned by the Adak detachment's fourth and last crew. Last, that is, until the Gray Knights finished crew rest and became eligible to fly.

In the meanwhile, Al Delgarbino's crew, the "passengers" aboard CG 1600, was available to relieve the detachment's last available SAR flight crew, which would soon take off as Delta Foxtrot 704. Delgarbino's crew had not logged any time on the long flight from Kodiak, and that fact preserved the fiction that they were fully rested and ready to go to work.

Finding of Fact. At 0324, the second Patrol Squadron 9 Ready Alert aircraft, DF 704, took-off for the S.A.R. scene.

After XF 675, Pat Conway's crew, took off, Mike Harris had emptied the offices and maintenance shops of the detachment to put together an alert crew to take the place of the one just launched. Harris, the squadron's aircraft maintenance officer as well as the detachment's current officer in charge, was scrambling to deal with the crisis. Lt. Anthony Guido and eight others were all he could find. Guido was right at hand. He was standing the detachment duty officer watch, with a new pilot in the squadron, Lt. John Branchflower, with him in the duty office under indoctrination.

Tony Guido had brought PD-2 to Adak from Moffett Field on Tuesday, 24 October, to replace PD-6. Five of the men in the water now had ridden up with him then. The twenty-fourth had been a long day for Guido and the crew. PD-2 was only minutes into its departure climb from Moffett Field Tuesday morning, barely beyond the San Francisco Bay and into airspace over Marin County, when it had to return to correct a now-forgotten problem. The second attempt was more successful, and the plane arrived at Adak just before midnight, after 10.5 hours of flight time. In the face of strong westerlies and forecast poor weather, Guido had stopped on the way at Naval Air Station Whidbey Island, Washington, for more fuel and that had added some time to the trip.

Early Friday morning, less than 48 hours after delivering PD-2 to Adak, Guido was sent to look for it. PD-9, on this flight called DF 704, got away from Adak and sped west during another small, passing hole in the fog and rain, with Tony Guido in the left seat, Lt. John Branchflower in the right, and a made-up crew in the tube. Both of the pilots were 1974 classmates of Ed Caylor's at Annapolis, and "Branch"—an oceanography major, like Caylor—was his new roommate in the Adak bachelor officers quarters. Guido was an experienced, first tour plane commander with his own flight crew, but Branchflower had just checked into Patrol Squadron 9 in late September from an assignment as a training command flight instructor. Branch had never been in the Aleutians before. In common with many on AF 586, his first flight out of Adak would be today. DF 704's flight engineer was Don Tullar, who except for the last minute assignment of Butch Miller to AF 586's crew in his place two days ago, would have been aboard PD-2 on Thursday and in the water now. Their tactical coordinator was Lt. (jg) John Skarzenski, John Ball's bingo partner of Wednesday night.

Less than twenty-five minutes after DF 704 took off from Adak, Air Force Rescue 95825 reported extreme turbulence on the approach into the field, abandoned his attempt to land, and diverted to Cold Bay, more than five hundred miles away.

The most recent information anyone in Alaska had about the men in the water came from CG 1500's last situation report, transmitted while Porter took his crew off station. *Sinyavin* had picked up four survivors from one raft, his report said. The rescue of three or four others was in progress. Two bodies had been recovered. Porter observed that "the Soviets were very cooperative in the rescue effort."

Just over two hours later, with DF 704's navigation lights and blinking red anticollision beacons probably now visible under the overcast to *Sinyavin*'s bridge watch, the ship sent Ed Caylor's report, not identified as such, direct to Adak by radio, in Morse code. A later transmission from the ship provided more details: "F.V. Mys Sinyavin [to] Coast Guard Juneau Alaska. 1322 GMT 27 Oct picked up 13 men at sea. [Three] of them are dead. Brooner. Garcia. Rodriguez. As the American citizen Edwin Flow said Butch Miller died with the airplane and Grigsby was lost at sea because they couldn't pull him on the raft due to bad weather. Continue searching him at sea."

Under the circumstances, DF 704's mission was not completely clear.[1] The replacement crew would arrive on station in the dark—and in fog, rain, and icing—three hours before sunrise. Search for the two missing men would be difficult, if not impossible, until there was enough light on station to see the surface. When the sun came up, they would have an hour to search for a raft, or possibly for two men, afloat in life vests and apart, alone in a vast and turbulent sea. Anyone they flew over would have been adrift in the killing waters for eighteen hours, unlikely to be alive and certainly incapable of signaling to them.

Finding of Fact. At 0525, DF 704 reported on station in the S.A.R. area. They tracked the Mys Sinyavin until daylight, while attempting to communicate on every available frequency. When sufficient daylight was available, they returned to the site of the ditching and searched to the east-southeast for the missing crewmembers until low fuel forced them to return to Shemya.

DF 704 would spend four hours on station trying to be helpful and, sadly, accomplishing nothing. Only Coast Guard aircraft were equipped with the frequency modulated VHF radios that *Sinyavin*'s receivers could hear. For three hours, DF 704's crew flew circles around *Sinyavin*, trying without success to communicate. Working their radios across the high-, very-high-, and ultra-high-frequency bands, they could not raise a response from the ship to any of their calls. The only replies came from curious airliners, transiting six miles above them between the two continents, otherwise oblivious to the drama below.

Once the survivors of AF 586 from both rafts were aboard, *Mys Sinyavin* stayed in the SAR area through the night, searching for more Americans. Finally, seven hours after the rescue, *Sinyavin* gave up the search. Just after 9:00 A.M., DF 704 marked the trawler only a few miles away from the SAR site, but now heading west purposefully at a speed (over)estimated to be fourteen knots.

During the next two days, *Sinyavin* sailed for Petropavlovsk, trailed by a Soviet Navy *Krivak*-class frigate that diligently followed the fisherman all the way to port, for reasons known only to commanders in Moscow and Petropavlovsk.[2] Alfa Foxtrot 586's ditching also provoked serious congestion in what was usually near-vacant airspace. Headquarters, Fifth Air Force at Yokota watched attentively, from over the horizon, as Soviet aircraft collected in the area.

A Tupulov TU-16 Badger was the first Soviet aircraft to respond to the ditching. A few hours after the American Embassy in Moscow asked for the USSR's assistance (and just about the time CG 1500 got on station), one of the subsonic 1950s-era medium bombers was already known at Fifth Air Force headquarters to be heading for the site. The twin turbojet Badger was no more suitable for this low-altitude surveillance mission than was Cliff Carter's much bigger RC-135.

One or more TU-95 Bear bombers soon replaced the shorter-legged Badger, occasionally circling overhead the small, waterborne procession heading for Petropavlovsk, and at least once on Friday taking a long, close look at the mysterious dorsal radome on an Air Force C-130 participating in the search. It, or they, made Juneau nervous. Even with the best of intentions onboard the Bear, the big, four-engine turboprop—with its distinctive glassed-in, bomber's greenhouse nose and sharply swept wings—posed a midair collision risk in the cloudy skies around datum. No Russian aircraft type had communications with any American aircraft on station and no agreed procedures or altitude assignments existed to ensure safe separation.

An Ilyushin IL-14 Crate (the NATO code name for the USSR's Douglas DC-3 clone was especially apt for what was, even then, a flying antique) passed through the area at least once, too, while one of the Bears was in the air. CG 1600 reported seeing it ("twin engine, low wing, DC-3 like appearance") when he was orbiting overhead *Mys Sinyavin* on Friday.

Even while *Sinyavin* steamed west, the Soviets showed continuing interest in the area left behind. Several other Soviet navy vessels congregated briefly around the ditching coordinates, and Soviet air force aircraft continued to spend time in the airspace above (renewing fears of collision with the Americans on station). Their intent was unclear—there were never any communications between U.S. and Soviet military units on station—but no one had any reason to believe this was anything other than assistance in the search for survivors, which Washington had urged them to join. Some Russians would still be at the scene when *Jarvis* finally arrived.

Finding of Fact. At 0532, Adak received word of survivor status: 10 people alive, 3 died in rafts. Grigsby lost at sea, and Miller went down with aircraft.

Caylor's brief muster report, passed to Adak SAR Radio by *Sinyavin*'s radioman in Morse code, was, "Have thirteen members aboard. Three of these are dead. Two others lost prior to pickup. Brooner, Garcia, Rodriguez—dead. Miller died with aircraft. Grigsby lost at sea while trying to board raft." The message was received at the naval station just about the time DF 704 reported on station.

Essentially the same message, minus names, reached the American embassy in Moscow through the Ministry of Foreign Affairs 8:30 Friday night, local time. The names would come to the embassy the following Tuesday in a short telex from Petropavlovsk signed by Ed Caylor and Matt Gibbons: "Caylor, Gibbons, Ball, Forshay, Wagner, Sheppard [*sic*], Hemmer, Flow, Moore, Reynolds all in good condition. Brooner, Garcia, Rodriguez bodies recovered. Grigsby lost at sea. Miller lost with aircraft." By then, who had lived and who had died was generally known everywhere it mattered.

Finding of Fact. At 0738, Coast Guard 1600 departed Adak en route to the S.A.R. area as a relief for DF 704.

Juneau's original plan was that John Powers and his copilot, Lt. Joe Egan, would fly CG 1600 to Shemya from Kodiak late Thursday night, fuel and drop off their extra crew at the air force base, and continue west to relieve Bill Porter in 1500 on station early Friday morning. Later in the day, Delgarbino's crew was to take Porter's aircraft out of Shemya to replace John Powers and company overhead the SAR site. None of that happened. Both Coast Guard aircraft and all three crews ended up in Adak early Friday morning because of the powerful crosswinds overnight at Shemya.

So it was that eleven hours after he left Kodiak the night before, Al Delgarbino in CG 1600 finally took off on his first SAR flight. His mission was to search a small rectangle of ocean 1 degree wide by 30 minutes high, centered slightly southeast of the ditching coordinates, at low altitude. What sounds like a small area spanned 1,050 square miles, and in that space half the size of Delaware the announced object was to find two men. Hours later, John Powers and Joe Egan would take Porter's aircraft and fly a 5.9-hour search mission of their own, flying parallel tracks through another small box. Same mission, same results.

Finding of Fact. At 0928, DF 704 departed the S.A.R. area en route to Shemya. Coast Guard 1600 estimated arrival in the S.A.R. area at 1030, October 27.

Tony Guido landed at Shemya after 7.2 hours in flight with a thoroughly frustrated crew aboard. Their last hour on station had been spent in a futile visual search for Grigsby and Miller. The crew had done everything they could, but accomplished nothing. Their plan was to fuel and return the aircraft quickly to Adak, so that it could be sent out again. Their frustration would increase soon.

The *Sinyavin* was already twenty-five miles west of the ditching site when CG 1600 first spotted it, after marking overhead one of AF 586's PRT-5 beacons on the way to the ship. (The PRT-5s would continue to send their distress signal—SOS three times in Morse code followed by a steady tone, over and over again—by rote, until their batteries died sometime late Saturday or Sunday.) Like DF 704, CG 1600 spent some time in a visual search, and hours orbiting *Sinyavin* while the fishing vessel continued tracking steadily west at eight to ten knots.

Almost three hours after CG 1600 got on station, communications were reestablished with *Sinyavin*, probably when the ship's radio shack was again manned. The first report was a roster of the Americans aboard the trawler, "passed with great language difficulty." At 1:48 P.M., CG 1600 was informed by *Sinyavin* that the ship planned to transfer the Americans to another vessel, apparently to a small combatant ship close aboard. In the transmission, the survivors' condition was described as "poor."

The news quickly triggered a reaction from the State Department. If the crewmembers' condition was too poor to permit them to speak on the ship's radio as the department had been led to believe, State wanted to know early Saturday (Moscow time), how was it possible that they could endure "the rigors involved in transfer of survivors at sea"? The embassy was asked to get more information from the Soviets on the "gravity of survivors' condition."

U.S. aircraft overhead watched carefully to observe the transfer, presumably to the trailing Krivak. It never happened. The U.S. then repeatedly requested that the transfer be made to *Jarvis,* still proceeding to the site at best speed. Captain Arbuzov considered that alternative, but that transfer did not happen either. The trawler's master later explained, "When the danger to their lives come off [*sic*], I was going to meet with the American frigate of the Coast Guard 'Jarvis,' but then it was decided to go to Petropavlovsk-Kamchatsky because the saved men were in need of urgent medical treatment and the time to port was shorter." Ed Caylor and the other survivors of AF 586 remained aboard *Sinyavin.*

In fact, by sunrise (about the time *Sinyavin* broke off the search and turned toward port) Dr. Safronenko apparently had concluded that the Americans, with the possible exception of Hemmer, were out of danger. A rendezvous with CGC *Jarvis* near Attu Island would have been no farther away than was Petropavlovsk. The limited medical facilities aboard the cutter, no doctor, but a chief hospital corpsman running the ship's small sickbay, with a junior assistant, would have been fully adequate to care for the men until they were put ashore at Adak. The bodies would have been moved from an iced hold in *Sinyavin* to bags in *Jarvis*'s walk-in freezer.

The problem was not distance, but weather. If *Sinyavin* had turned east toward *Jarvis,* it would have been steaming with the low, imbedded in a weather system heading in the same direction as was the ship. The three hundred miles to the rendezvous could easily have taken much longer to sail than the same distance to port. Then there would have been the risky transfer in high seas from one ship to the other. Either way, by small boat or *Jarvis*'s HH-52 helicopter, the transfer would have been dangerous, risking the very lives *Mys Sinyavin* had struggled to save.

John Power's Coast Guard aircrew would not fly on Saturday. They would return to Kodiak on Sunday, having flown only one rescue mission since departure from their home station Thursday night.

Finding of Fact. At 1043, SW 608, a Patrol Squadron 9 P-3 returning from Hawaii, landed at Adak.

Once he got the bad news, Lt. Cdr. Jim Dvorak departed Oahu for Adak early Friday morning in such a hurry that he left two men behind. These two, ground pounders who had flown down early in the week with his Crew 12 to Naval Air Station Barbers Point for a three-day visit, would have to find their own way back. Their extra time in Hawaii would be the only benefit anyone would wrench from the loss of AF 586.

Jim Dvorak's crew had left Adak on Wednesday for Oahu, 9.3 hours en route with an operational mission along the midocean track between the two wildly dissimilar islands. Thursday had been devoted to a practice torpedo load and drop on the Navy's Barking Sands weapons range near Kauai, a short 3.8 hour flight. Friday morning was going to be spent on the beach. They would leave for Adak in the afternoon, seven-plus hours at normal cruise speed north-northwest over empty water. A few hours in the sun, rarely seen and never felt on bare skin at Adak in October, were one of the benefits, the "bennies," of a trip to the weapons range.

Very late Thursday, while Crew 6's survivors were still afloat in their rafts below the aircraft circling overhead, the Patrol Wing 2 duty officer at Barbers Point tracked Dvorak down. After the duty officer's call, Dvorak and Lt. Larry Myers, his tactical coordinator, rushed over to the Wing's command center for a briefing. There the two got the news that PD-2 was in the water. They corralled the rest of their crew at the Outrigger Hotel for a few hours rest, and then took off in PD-8 back to Adak just after 4:00 A.M., call sign Sierra Whiskey 608. SW 608 landed at Adak almost seven hours later, after a landing approach that was so turbulent Dvorak had to keep both hands on the control yoke, instructing his flight engineer to adjust engine power almost to touchdown. When Dvorak taxied in, there were only Powers's C-130 and a single Orion parked on the detachment's flight line. It was the P-3 from Patrol Squadron 46 that had arrived hours before.

Finding of Fact. At 1108, DF 704 landed at Shemya. It was unable to continue further S.A.R. operations because of a bad oil leak on the No. 3 engine. No corrective maintenance action could be taken because of the high winds at Shemya.

Delta Foxtrot 704 left the SAR station with enough fuel to get to King Salmon, at the top of the Alaskan Peninsula, if bad weather in the islands forced them that far east, but not enough to reach Anchorage, on the mainland another three hundred miles northeast.

On the way, they managed to put down on the Rock instead. (Branch's daily diary rated Guido's landing on Shemya into fifty knots of wind as "good." He would rate his own performance on that flight as disappointing, without explanation.) Guido, or one of the other officers, immediately phoned the Adak Tactical Support Center with bad news. The TSC watch officer's logbook entry said it all: "11:11 . . . DF 704 on deck—sighted nothing. Aircraft possibly down—bad oil leak No. 3 engine." The confirmation came in another call not long thereafter. "11:50 . . . DF 704 hard down at Shemya, unable to work on aircraft due to high winds." PD-9 was now unflyable and stranded with its crew in the weather system that soon was to ground aviation from one end of the Aleutians to the other.

PD-9 would remain at Shemya for two days, waiting for improved weather, and for a mechanic from Adak with a replacement engine-driven compressor. Meanwhile, Branch, wandering around the barren island to kill time, stumbled across two old Russian graves not far from the water's edge. The discovery could have been an omen: the same day, the crew got the muster of AF 586's dead and missing from a Coast Guardsman on the island.

Finding of Fact. At 1143, Alfa Delta 275, a P-3 from Moffett Field, landed at Adak.

AD 275 was a Patrol Squadron 9 aircraft, one of six still at Moffett Field and the first to Adak after the loss of AF 586 midafternoon the day before. Cdr. Peter Cressy, the squadron executive officer and Bud Powers's planned successor in command, was the senior man aboard.

Of all the supporting cast, Pete Cressy—wolfishly handsome, tirelessly ambitious, and famously lusty—will come out the best from this incident, not simply unscathed but enlarged. He owns the most sensitive political antennae at Moffett Field, perhaps in all of maritime patrol aviation on both coasts, and he will move quickly to contain the damage from loss of an aircraft and some of its crew.

Cressy's is a polarizing personality, stimulating near-fanatical admiration and loyalty from some, and repelling others with his ambition. His critics say that Cressy's tour in command of Patrol Squadron 9 exhausted the undermanned squadron; his admirers say it revitalized it after several failures culminating in the loss of PD-2. Whichever, it will certainly propel him to promotion and his next command, an air wing in Maine. In quick time, Captain Cressy will become Rear Admiral Cressy, Dr. Cressy (a Ph.D. in education), president of two colleges, and finally the sleek, affluent CEO of a big-budget industry association in Washington. There his staff will call him "doctor."

The twenty-seventh of October was long before any of that. Cressy, who will chair the squadron's "aircraft mishap board" and write its report to the Naval Safety Center, had come to talk to the men of the detachment and find out what was going on. That kind of quick, instinctive solidarity after catastrophe often comes at some professional cost in the Navy, where it is difficult for senior line officers, those eligible for command at sea, to escape the taint of failure when a ship or plane is lost for any reason. Two things made his generous gesture risk free.

A consensus would swiftly emerge out of the accident investigations that would lay the failure at the feet of the two men who had paid for it with their lives, Grigsby and Miller. Both were beyond criticism now. Moreover, the aircraft was lost not on Pete Cressy's watch, but on Bud Powers's.[3] Even before the loss of PD-2, things had been tough recently for the Golden Eagles of Patrol Squadron 9.

The squadron had failed an annual special weapons readiness inspection and the annual aircrew standardization exam, too. After the loss of an aircraft and some of its crew, Patrol Squadron 9 had nowhere to go but up. Whether you believed Commander Cressy pulled the squadron up by force of personality or lashed it to a foaming lather and rode it up in 1979 depended on what you thought about the man himself.

Crew 11, weary and still shaken by the sight of squadron mates in the water was surprised, the day after their exhausting mission, to hear their executive officer announce in person that everyone involved would be decorated for his performance. No one had expected that medals would be a topic of discussion.

Six months later, Pete Cressy delivered on his promise. The medals were presented on 30 April 1979, not long after he took command of the squadron. Jerry Grigsby's brilliant airmanship at the very end gave him special status, recognized, possibly ambivalently, by the posthumous award of the Distinguished Flying Cross. Ed Caylor was awarded the Meritorious Service Medal. Matt Gibbons got the Navy Commendation Medal. Eighteen Patrol Squadron 9 men received the Air Medal in connection with the loss of AF 586, the eight who rode AF 586 into the water and the nine aboard XF 675 who helped to save them.[4]

It is difficult to tell just how much these medals meant to the men who got them. Surely not much to the survivors, who had been granted life itself. Today, their medals and those of Crew 11 almost certainly lie nearly forgotten in dresser drawers across America.

In contrast, the Coast Guardsmen aboard CG 1500 alone got no tangible recognition for their effort. Perhaps, in a service dedicated to lifesaving at sea, it was believed that Bill Porter and his crew had done nothing out of the ordinary on 27 and 28 October, but the omission or oversight rankled Bill Porter for years. More than two decades later, Porter, who thought that medals for the acts of his crew would have improved their chances for promotion, was still bitter about the neglect. He was unhappy, too, that his unit's commanding officer had not even bothered to greet the crew when they shut down on the Kodiak flight line after their successful rescue mission.

The Coast Guard's four C-130s based at Kodiak—1500, 1600, 1601, and 1602—flew a total of eleven sorties and 54.5 flight hours atop AF 586, before flight operations were finally suspended on 29 October. Despite their crews' best efforts, none of the missions after Bill Porter's made any difference to the outcome.

Finding of Fact. Between 27 October and 30 October, the weather at Adak, Shemya and in the S.A.R. area became progressively worse. No S.A.R. aircraft were able to launch after 1450, 27 October. Coast Guard Cutter Jarvis did not arrive in the S.A.R. area until late October 28th due to rough seas.

Adak's flight control tower's watch teams kept a flight clearance logbook, an informal record of events during their hours on duty. Section Two was on duty in the tower on Thursday, and the watch supervisor's handwritten notes recorded reports coming in about the emergency and also wary consideration of the deteriorating weather blowing down on them from the northwest.

Adak's main instrument runway, 05-23, is oriented northeast-southwest, aligned along the axis of the prevailing winds from the south-southwest. Even so, as the low closed in on the Central Aleutians, winds, not low ceilings and reduced visibility, were the problem. The flight clearance logbook recorded the progression. From a steady fifteen to twenty knots Thursday morning, the winds strengthened to forty knots with gusts to seventy on Friday midafternoon.

The weather on SAR station on 28 October was daunting: the Associated Press reported sixty knots of wind and seas fifty feet high, presumably the information came from Coast Guard sources. In fact, the seas were likely only half as high. The worst of the weather was now well to the east. Saturday morning along the islands, dawn came accompanied by grounding conditions.

By sunrise on Saturday, Adak's surface winds were forty to fifty knots, with gusts to ninety—just over one hundred miles per hour, well beyond hurricane force—and forecast to remain that way through the day. On Adak, once the winds exceeded fifty knots, ground personnel were no longer permitted to operate the aircraft hangar doors, because the big, steel doors were vulnerable to being blown off their tracks by such strong winds. The danger was not so much that the doors would be jammed ajar, but that they would fall flat, crushing anything—men, aircraft, ground support equipment—caught beneath them.

As the weekend started on Shemya, visibility dropped as low as one-quarter mile in passing snow showers. Occasionally, thunder boomed hollowly out of the clouds even while the snow fell, with a low bass rumble like distant artillery. The problem on Shemya, however, was not visibility or the winds, now out of the west at thirty knots with gusts only to forty-six (powerful but pretty much down Runway 28), or even the lightning flashes almost concealed in the flurries. It was ice on the ground. Shemya's runways and taxiways were glazed with it, making any aircraft movement on the ground perilous even in still air.

The winds on Adak built throughout the morning. At 10:43 A.M., Duty Section One on watch in Adak Tower gave up in the face of high winds, and a forecast calling for more of the same throughout the next fourteen hours. That is when the watch told Anchorage Center and the FAA Flight Service Station at Cold Bay that the airfield was being closed. Section One then shuttered the tower's windows and the watch team abandoned their perch because of high winds.

Finding of Fact. S.A.R. operations were suspended by the North Pacific S.A.R. Coordinator at 1740 on 29 October 1978.

The North Pacific SAR coordinator, at the Coast Guard's 17th District headquarters in Juneau had assumed control of AF 586 SAR operations from his counterpart in Adak late the same evening the airplane went down, at 10:08 P.M. The changeover to the mainland reflected the superior resources and greater expertise in managing such an effort at the district headquarters. Beginning then, Juneau assumed overall responsibility for the general direction of the search.

A series of eight situation reports from Juneau over the next seventy-two hours kept all concerned informed of progress in marshalling search and rescue assets, operations underway and plans for the future. Juneau's morose Situation Report No. 7, transmitted near midday, Sunday, prepared everybody for the inevitable. "Chance of survival of man in water for period of time since aircraft ditched in given weather conditions on station is considered remote," it said. Yielding reluctantly to reality and force majeure, the SAR coordinator in Alaska then went on to recommend to the Third Fleet commander and his own service's superior in San Francisco that the search "be suspended pending further developments."

Over the course of the next few hours, the commander of the U.S. Third Fleet and the commanders in chief of the U.S. Pacific Fleet and of the joint service Pacific Command agreed. "Suspension" was a euphemism; everyone knew that he was talking about ending the search for Grigsby and Miller.

Early Sunday evening, with no search mission flown since midafternoon, Friday, and another twelve hours of grounding weather forecast for Adak and Shemya, Juneau put the recommendation in effect, reluctantly conceded both men's bodies to the sea, and released all participating units to normal operations. Later, the Department of State was requested to inform the Soviet Union that AF 586's SAR effort had been suspended as of 6:40 A.M., Monday, Moscow time. Implementing instructions to the embassy emphasized that this was a "suspension for the time being."

The public explanation came in a press release on Monday, 30 October:

> The Coast Guard has suspended its search for the two missing crewmembers of the Navy P-3 aircraft, which ditched in the North Pacific on Thursday with 15 persons aboard. . . . Ten crewmembers and three bodies were recovered by a Russian fishing trawler in the remote ocean area west of the Aleutian Islands last Friday. . . . Late Saturday afternoon the third of the downed aircraft's three life rafts was located, however, there were no persons in the raft. Fifty-foot seas on Saturday and 22-foot seas on Sunday have decreased the chances that the two missing crewmembers could still survive. Winds gusting to 60 and 70 knots have hampered search aircraft operations throughout the search. . . . The extremely remote possibility that the two men could still be alive in the frigid water and the danger of continued air and surface operations, due to the severe weather, were critical in the decision to suspend the search.

Now Event AK 262 was really over.

Chapter 10

Petropavlovsk and Khabarovsk

During the first half of the twentieth century, Russians endured a revolution, two world wars, three famines (1921–22, 1933, and 1946–47), and twenty-five years of Stalin's terror that murdered hundreds of thousands outright and sent millions more to die in the frozen camps, forests, and mines of Siberia. An accurate accounting of lives lost in all these catastrophes is impossible, but the total could easily approach fifty million.[1] Stalin's successors after 1953 presided over a less lethal but only marginally more successful society. By 1991, the survivors were exhausted, with strength enough only to shrug off the geriatric kleptocracy that lived by stealing the economy's scant output for the exclusive benefit of itself and the 10 or 15 percent of the population who were party members.

But in 1978, long before glasnost, Chernobyl, and Afghanistan, those old thieves, led by Brezhnev, were still firmly in power and the Soviet Union still looked formidable. Even including those few Westerners who saw clearly how ideological cynicism and grotesque economic mismanagement in the USSR had sapped its vitality in the decades since World War II—and they were very few, in Washington or anywhere—most analysts granted that the Soviets' military might gave them superpower status roughly equivalent to that of the United States. And so did everyone one else. Only several years after Gorbachev's assumption of power (he became general secretary in 1985) would events begin to lead everyone to the knowledge that the Soviet Union was a huge Potemkin village, and its Warsaw Pact was a sham.

In October 1978, when AF 586 flew south along the Kamchatka coast, the

USSR was an acknowledged superpower at the head of a military alliance that by some assessments was the military equal of the United States and NATO, and by some important measures (men in uniform, numbers of main battle tanks, and artillery tubes) said to be its superior.[2]

Once *Mys Sinyavin* arrived at the crash coordinates, the U.S. goal was to keep the ship there, searching for survivors until all fifteen men had been found, dead or alive. *Mys Sinyavin* continued the search for Grigsby and Miller for hours after the thirteen were brought aboard (reported to Moscow early Friday morning, local time), but the real follow-on hunt for the two lost men was left to *Mys Belkina* and *Gorodok*. The two vessels remained on station, continuing the search, despite knowing that prior to its departure for port *Sinyavin* had reported the survivors had said the "remaining two crewmen . . . have been killed [*sic*]."

Next (and throughout), Washington wanted the crewmembers transferred from Soviet custody as soon as possible. Pursuit of this objective initially took the form of pressing for a transfer at sea, from *Mys Sinyavin* to CGC *Jarvis,* as soon as the Coast Guard cutter could arrive alongside. By late Friday evening, Moscow time, however, the embassy had concluded correctly that *Sinyavin* was not going to wait for a rendezvous with *Jarvis.* After it became clear that the trawler was proceeding to Petropavlovsk, the Soviet foreign ministry was pelted with embassy requests to clear a U.S. medical evacuation aircraft from Yokota into Petropavlovsk (and later to Khabarovsk when it developed that the men were being flown to that city). For the next five days, until Wednesday night when the effort was finally abandoned, the goal was to get clearance for a U.S. medical evacuation flight into the Soviet Union.

At 8:30 P.M. Friday, Moscow time, some fifteen hours after the first request for assistance had been made, Washington asked the embassy to make "preliminary approaches" to the Ministry of Foreign Affairs to get an American medevac flight cleared into Petropavlovsk from Yokota. The subject, Washington said, had already been "discussed informally" with the Soviet embassy. Preliminary approaches in Moscow were followed up with a formal, written request for flight clearance midday, Saturday, a few hours before *Sinyavin* arrived in Petropavlovsk.

Barely thirty-six hours after plucking them out of the sea, *Mys Sinyavin* was delivering the survivors of Crew 6 to Leviathan's vestibule. *Sinyavin* had saved them from death, pulling them from the water scant hours before the last man in the Mark-12 might have died, but why, each would soon wonder, and for what?

Early Sunday morning, 29 October, as the ten Americans trod under the lights down *Sinyavin*'s gangplank to put foot on Russian soil, each man knew that his status had suddenly changed. No longer was he a survivor of a disaster at sea, aboard ship among fishermen—sympathetic, ordinary sailors—who instinctively understood his experience and respected him for it. Now he was a cold war warrior, alone with nine of his crew and unexpectedly washed up at the enemy's camp.

Their training at Warner Springs had conditioned the crew to anticipate harsh confinement under miserable conditions, and there was nothing in their experience to contradict this expectation. Ignorant of Washington's appeal to Moscow for assistance and of the high-level dialogue between the two governments that had turned *Sinyavin* around and sent it northeast to rescue them, with no indication from their hosts about how long they were to be held and under what conditions, it was easy to imagine that each move was a step on the passage to something worse.

Finding of Fact. During the night of October 28 Mys Sinyavin arrived in Petropavlovsk, USSR. The survivors were taken to the naval hospital, where they received physical examinations and, in their opinions, excellent care.

Sinyavin sailed into port at Petropavlovsk-Kamchatski around midnight, 29 October, local Siberian time, 28 October in Adak across the International Date Line. Its hyphenated name distinguishes this city on the Kamchatka Peninsula's eastern shore from another Petropavlovsk in distant Kazakhstan, but no one can confuse the two. Kamchatka is nothing like arid Kazakhstan in Central Asia.

Three hundred miles across at its greatest breadth, the Kamchatka Peninsula is a cold, calloused thumb of marshes, tundra, and mountains that thrusts down 750 miles between the Bering Sea and the Sea of Okhotsk before it finally dribbles off into the submerged volcanoes that are the Kuril Islands. Like the Aleutians, Kamchatka forms part of the Pacific's Ring of Fire. Fully 22 of the peninsula's 127 volcanoes are thought to be still active, and the ever-present threat of earthquakes has capped the buildings in Petropavlovsk at a maximum of five stories. Five stories of the slab-sided, utilitarian building style ubiquitous throughout the Soviet bloc.

Thanks in part to this drab architecture, the small port city is famously ugly but its setting is majestic. Petropavlovsk-Kamchatski, named in 1740 after founder Vitus Bering's two ships, the *Saint Peter* and *Saint Paul,* hugs on one side the northeast shore of Avachinskaya Bay, a huge, superb natural harbor, and on the other the bases of two imposing volcanoes, Vulkan Koryak (elevation 11,339 feet) and Vulkan Avacha (just over 9,000 feet).[3] Neither is nearly as tall as Klyuchevskaya Volcano, almost 3 miles high and 350 miles away, but in clear weather their sharp cones towering over the squat, waterfront city beneath them are handsome and imposing nonetheless.

Crew 6 had flown far enough down track during its PARPRO mission two days ago to have seen these same peaks sixty miles away, poking up through the clouds above the peninsula's craggy eastern mountain range, from PD-2's cockpit windows. (Grigsby's photos of the volcanoes had gone down to the sea floor in the camera lost with PD-2.) Crewmembers would spend the next forty-eight hours in their shadows.

The city was then the political, economic, and cultural center of the Kamchatka *oblast* (province), the metropolis of a bleak and inhospitable region that boasted scarcely two people per square mile and harsh winters that spanned much of three seasons. In 1978, Petropavlovsk was a fishing town, a center of net and ship repair, of fish processing and canning. It was also an important military center.

The Soviet Union's National Air Defense Forces had a major presence in Kamchatka *oblast* and in Magadan *oblast,* immediately north.[4] Together, these two provinces formed the North Pacific ramparts of a nation that had recently and provocatively taken publicly to calling itself a Pacific power. Air defense fighter bases and radar sites bristled along the coast from Mys Shmidta on the Chukchi Sea, south past Providerniya, Anadyr, and Ust-Kamchatsk to Petropavlovsk. The Soviet Pacific Fleet's headquarters was in Vladivostok, on the Sea of Japan, but Petropavlovsk was one of the fleet's three major home ports, and the one with easiest access to the open sea. Between Petropavlovsk and Vladivostok lay the Sea of Okhotsk, an often ice-covered Soviet lake and a sanctuary for Soviet Pacific Fleet ballistic missile submarines on sea trials.[5]

In light of its strategic importance, and reflecting the Soviet Union's customary xenophobia, Petropavlovsk-Kamchatski was a closed city, like Vladivostok. In addition to the usual restrictions on internal travel imposed on all Soviet citizens, which would have kept many of its own nationals outside of the sensitive area, Moscow had long maintained an absolute prohibition on foreigners in the strategic city. Crew 6, as foreign as anything that could be imagined by Far East Military District headquarters in Vladivostok, would be a temporary exception to this strict injunction.

Sinyavin's speed of advance from the ditching site 370 miles away had almost certainly been carefully adjusted to ensure that it would not arrive pierside until well past sunset, shrouding in autumnal darkness any view of the city and especially of its sensitive navy base complex south of the city center from the American sailors who would soon disembark. As it rounded Mys Mayachny (Beacon Cape), sailed north through the narrow throat into the bay, and entered protected waters, the seas calmed and *Sinyavin* finally began to ride easily during the remaining five miles or so into port. Moore, still nauseous below decks, and the other Americans felt the difference right away. The business of entering port and tying up the trawler at an isolated pier took a while, and by the time the P-3 crew had been assembled on deck, everything was ready.

The scene before them could have come out of a Humphrey Bogart movie. A few pools of weak light illuminated the ground near the bottom of the gangplank. From there to the nearby steep slopes of the volcanic cones rimming the harbor, everything else was obscured in shades of gray. A darkened bus idled pierside at the head of a line of barely visible sedans. Armed guards formed a loose perimeter around the ship and the bus; others stood about ominously in the shadows everywhere on the pier. When the Americans left *Sinyavin* for a brief and peculiar ceremony in what appeared to be a warehouse across from the pier, the sedans disgorged a small troop of men, who strode purposefully aboard the ship as if they were their replacements. Almost certainly this boarding party would closely interrogate the trawler's crew about everything that happened since the pickup from the rafts.

Walking into the warehouse—dim, drab, two long tables illuminated with bare bulbs hanging overhead, uniformed men on its other side, at least one in a photogenic commissar's fur cap—was like returning to the camp at Warner Springs. The ceremony was a formal change of custody. Captain Arbuzov (or his representative, no American knew what he looked like) was turning over ten men and three bodies to the Border Guards and receiving signed receipts in exchange. They were now in the hands of the KGB, which had nearly two days to prepare for them. Standing in the warehouse, Gibbons' reaction to the scene was somber. "Oh, no," he thought, "here we go, handcuff time." Nearby, Forshay steeled himself with the thought that "we're not working for Kinney Shoes. We've got to follow the rules." The rules he had in mind were those they had rehearsed at SERE school. Say little, agree to less, sign nothing, resist everything.

Their minder, here and in Khabarovsk, would be a major wearing the green epaulets of the Border Guards, the KGB's own army. (In a few days the major, Viktor Anyasov, would have relaxed enough to reveal a talent for capitalism. During an unobserved moment aboard their bus, he put ideology aside just long enough to sell some rubles for American dollars, exchanging these paper souvenirs of the Soviet Union for hard currency usable on the black market or in well-stocked stores for party members.)

Ceremony over, the crew was driven uphill to another building some fifteen minutes away and escorted into two-man rooms in an otherwise vacant, upper wing of what proved to be the naval base's hospital. Spotless. Practically empty.

Once the surviving members of the crew were again dry and warm, fed, and rested, all of which was the case before *Sinyavin* pulled into port, only Forshay needed further medical attention (and all he got for his battered back was aspirin). The Russian decision to put them in hospital, first in Petropavlovsk and later in Khabarovsk, must have had more to do with keeping their unexpected American guests isolated until a final decision was made about what to do with this flotsam than with any medical requirement. Hospitals, especially but not exclusively psychiatric hospitals, had a long history as places of confinement in the Soviet Union. Resorting to them for this purpose would have been a natural and easy decision for the KGB, into whose custody Crew 6 was apparently assigned.

U.S. requests for medevac aircraft clearance to the closed city of Petropavlovsk and access to the surviving crewmembers became strident after *Sinyavin* entered port. During the next five days, what started as Bogart shaded over to Brigadoon.

Everything that the Americans saw on the ground—wooden barracks, trucks and cars, x-ray machines and television sets, tape recorders and toothbrushes—looked like something from the past recently withdrawn from a time capsule. Everyone would recall the glass syringe used to take blood samples, grown in memory to the size of a quarter-horsepower drill. Caylor would later describe the experience as akin to being on the set of a 1930s movie.[6]

The crew spent Sunday and Monday getting basic physical exams in pairs, resting and being generally wary and uncooperative, Gibbons especially so. He roamed the hospital and went so far as to insist on being present when the bodies of the three sensor operators were examined. A request of the group to fill out individual biographical questionnaires was refused, without consequences. All other Soviet initiatives to get information seemed half-hearted, almost perfunctory. The crew assigned names to their custodians, drawing on the cast of a familiar cold war–era cartoon for their inspiration: "Rocky," "Bullwinkle," "Boris," and "Natasha."

In a cable late Sunday night from Ambassador Shulman to Ambassador Toon, captioned "Night Action Immediate," Shulman told Toon, "President's instructions are to proceed as energetically as possible to effect return of men soonest. Communicate President's concern and reiterate request in strongest terms for C-141 permission and immediate consular and medical access." When Toon met the next afternoon with Foreign Minister André Gromyko's senior deputy, Georgy Korniyenko, he dutifully delivered the message. Its tone, the embassy reported to Washington, stimulated a "mild complaint" from Korniyenko.[7]

In reply, Korniyenko told the ambassador that the aircrewmen, whose arrival in Petropavlovsk had been delayed until Saturday night (local time) by "heavy storms," were to be flown from Petropavlovsk to Khabarovsk Tuesday evening. There would be no objection, he said, to travel by embassy personnel to Khabarovsk. When Toon's suggestion that the men be flown, instead, to Japan was politely rebuffed, the embassy immediately made plans to send a four-man team to Khabarovsk on the first available Aeroflot flight.

The embassy quickly sent the news by urgent, "night action" message over Toon's signature to the secretaries of state and defense, the Joint Chiefs of Staff, and the commander of the Military Airlift Command (with copies to twenty-two other interested addressees).[8]

As Korniyenko had predicted, the Americans departed Petropavlovsk Tuesday evening on Aeroflot's domestic service. They left from a remote corner of Yelizovo Airport, climbing from their bus directly onto the waiting aircraft, in sight of what appeared to be derelict civil aircraft abandoned around the field. Howard Moore remembers the other passengers—presumably all Soviet citizens, most must have had some government or military connection—staring in goggle-eyed wonder from the back of the crowded Aeroflot Iluyshin 62 transport as the Americans boarded forward, carrying all their flight and survival equipment in their arms, and looking like ET going home. Standing under the dim lights of the transport's cabin and glancing aft across the same cultural divide, the American passengers saw evidence of long neglect. Frayed carpeting, torn cushions, collapsed seat backs, and missing seat belts testified that this aircraft had endured years of hard use. They sat down, with no idea where the tired, scruffy transport was taking them.

Finding of Fact. After two days in Petropavlovsk, the ten survivors and the remains of the three deceased crewmembers were taken to Khabarovsk, U.S.S.R., via commercial airliner. All personnel were required to remain in the hospital until their departure to Niigata, Japan, via Japanese commercial airliner on 2 November 1978.

In daylight and at a distance, the swept-wing Aeroflot IL 62 jet they flew in, painted in the domestic fleet's blue and white livery, would have looked handsome to anyone but an accountant. Its four, tail-mounted engines guaranteed horrendous operating costs for any airline that kept real books. Aeroflot, the USSR's huge flag carrier, like the country itself, could not afford what it was doing but did not know how to do anything else.

Khabarovsk, then the largest city in the eastern third of the Soviet Union, lies at the confluence of the Amur and Ussuri Rivers, just north of the Manchurian border. It is thirty-eight hundred miles, seven time zones, from Moscow and eleven hundred miles from Petropavlovsk. The crew's flight there from Petropavlovsk was nonstop. Two-plus hours in the IL 62, west-southwest across Kamchatka and the Sea of Okhotsk, directly over Sakhalin Island, and finally descending over the mainland straight toward Khabarovsk.

The two cities—Petropavlovsk a seaport amid peat bogs, Khabarovsk an inland crossroads—are very different. Petropavlovsk lies pressed between the bay and the mountains; Khabarovsk stretches out atop three parallel ridges, the source of the poetic, incongruously maritime legend that the city is built on the backs of three whales.

The Americans saw none of this; arrival here was at night, too. Nor was anyone on Crew 6 aware that their destination had a certain special status among historians of the cold war. Khabarovsk was the site of a notorious detention and interrogation camp for UN prisoners during the Korean War, and for captured American electronic warfare aircrews for years after that fighting stopped. Their short stay would be nothing like that.

The Americans were arriving in the city just as its annual cycle, an oscillation between frenzied work during the short summer and near-frozen repose during the long winter, was approaching quiescence. From late spring through early autumn, cargo transport and passenger traffic would have been relatively heavy in and between the city's terminals. The last days of October, however, were already too late to continue resupply of the far North, and a reduction in heavy traffic was the first sign of the near-hibernation to come.

Khabarovsk (from a description in the *San Jose Mercury,* sounding like it was lifted out of a tourist brochure and written on the day the crew arrived there), "is a modern city in the Soviet Orient. Roughly the size of San Jose, it is the center of a territorial [*krai*] government and dates back to 1652. It has an attractive waterfront park and esplanade, and modern factories and apartment blocks housing workers." The *Mercury* went on to note that it "is a major industrial center and is an 'open city,' that is, it is not sealed off to Westerners for security reasons."

Here the Border Guards ran the hospital that was to be their inn for two days. The accommodations were somewhat more comfortable than before, and the food was somewhat better, but the same austerity was visible everywhere to the increasingly restive Americans. In retrospect, Crew 6 was obviously in a holding pattern, watching time go by while Moscow organized itself to deal with them. At the time, no one on the crew knew what to expect. A few hours before being notified they were going to Japan, to be returned to their countrymen, Ed Caylor still thought that their next trip would be to Moscow, for an indefinite stay under uncertain conditions. He was wrong, but Caylor could not have known that the Soviets had evidently decided to return his crew expeditiously, and as early as midday Sunday were just groping for the best way to do that. That is when Isakov, the foreign ministry's deputy director of the USA Division, personally urged his American counterpart to be patient, assuring the embassy's political counselor that "all would turn out well."

If someone in Moscow or in its far eastern military districts ever thought to hold the crew, he apparently quickly lost the internal debate about what to do with these few Americans who had figuratively washed up on the Kamchatka coast. There's no indication of any intent to detain the crew, and scant evidence of any serious effort by the KGB to obtain any military intelligence from them. It is even possible to take at face value Captain Arbuzov's statement that the American crew was taken to Petropavlovsk and not transferred to *Jarvis* for medical reasons, not as an exercise in realpolitik or in an effort by the USSR to keep its options open.

The crew assumed their bunkrooms in both hospitals were bugged. To defeat this eavesdropping, they spoke to each other in affected accents of the Deep South, a sort of vocal code they imagined the Soviets would have difficulty breaking. Their rooms almost certainly were wired. A few of the wandering Americans chanced upon some of their keepers moving a bulky reel-to-reel tape recorder around on the floor below theirs. The device must have been a part of the KGB's surveillance equipment. Some of the "medical personnel" who came to see them, sporting new lab coats and unfamiliar stethoscopes, were obviously intelligence officers. Gibbons, heading to the morgue under escort, passed two surprised men wearing audio headsets on the floor below the crew's rooms. But overall, the intelligence collection effort appeared perfunctory, almost a ritual.

The Soviets took a quick crew photograph on the hospital steps at Khabarovsk, and this high contrast photo of ten somber-faced men facing almost expressionlessly into the sun made it into some American newspapers on November 2. (The picture appeared simultaneously in the *San Jose Mercury,* the *Palo Alto Times,* and the *San Jose Times,* poignantly on the day of Moffett Field's memorial service for the five dead. Only Shepard had objected to the photo. He was fearful of its possible propaganda uses. The group finally agreed among themselves to a short photo session. Everyone was to look military; no one was to smile or gesture.) The Soviets' public relations foray misfired badly, an indication of the fearfulness of those waiting at home. The photo immediately triggered a quick spasm of anxiety among the families. In the three ranks of unsmiling, almost grim faces staring out at the camera, wives and parents imagined the reflection of all kinds of abuse and suffering. One man, his arm partly concealed behind another's, was thought to have suffered an amputation. Other observations were only slightly less hysterical.[9]

Reflecting the same perspective, although more hopeful of an early return, the U.S. Forces Japan headquarters put a C-9 Nightingale medical evacuation aircraft on one-hour alert at Yokota, ready to speed to Khabarovsk as soon as permission was received from the Soviets to evacuate the presumably injured crew.

The consular visit that the embassy had been pressing the Soviets to permit finally happened in the hospital at Khabarovsk. The team members included the naval attaché, Capt. L. Anthony Bracken, the embassy's medical officer, a Dr. Nydell, a consular officer, Carter, and a medic, Briggs. One of the three civilians was a young African American, and he unwittingly provided the team's bona fides to the still-suspicious crewmembers. Once they saw him, crewmembers were reassured, believing that the Soviets would have been very unlikely to have a black, English-speaking agent in their Moscow stable of agent provocateurs. Tony Bracken, who delivered a kit of personal grooming items and embassy souvenirs to each man, is remembered most clearly, perhaps for that reason. Among other things, he wanted confirmation that AF 586's crypto had been properly destroyed. Embassy Moscow reported to the State Department that the team accompanied Patrol Squadron 9's flight crew from the USSR to Japan, and perhaps it did; however, none of the survivors has ever mentioned having American escorts on the JAL flight with them out of Khabarovsk.

The lapse suggests either great fatigue or extraordinary introspection during the flight. Alternatively, the flood of vodka washing over a hastily arranged farewell dinner sponsored by the colonel in command of the Border Guards' hospital may have dampened the Americans' powers of observation. In photographs of the cheery event taken just hours prior to takeoff, the table is set with a white cloth. Clean plates and flatware are evident everywhere, as are carafes of water and bottles of vodka. The only food in the photos is a bowl of apples, being ignored by the hosts and guests alike.

Captain Bracken had briefed Ed Caylor on how the senior man must uphold the honor of the side at such an event. Caylor, who remembers the vodka as "excellent," obediently went drink for drink with his host. He recalls the first four, glass-draining toasts. There were others; the hospital commander was making no secret of his relief to be getting rid of his charges without incident. A photo shows Gibbons and Flow, with their demonstrably empty vodka glasses upside down on their heads, seated next to Moore, getting ready to drain his. Once the vodka ran out, the party switched to grain alcohol. That is when Bracken (who still remembers how the two-hundred-proof medicinal spirits sucked the moisture out of his mouth on contact) decided it was time to leave for the airport. The crew would fly to Japan warmed by Khabarovsk's "excellent" vodka, wearing souvenir Soviet Air Force flight jackets and black fur hats.

The Soviets were eager to see the Americans leave as quickly as possible and had asked the American Embassy to make arrangements to effect their speedy departure. Conveniently, Japan Air Lines served the open city once a week from Niigata, two hours and ten minutes to the south-southeast, across the Sea of Japan, and that is how Crew 6 left the Soviet Union, in a nearly empty JAL DC-9 at 8:00 A.M. They could have gone to Niigata on the weekly Aeroflot flight, but that would have meant delaying the departure one day, until 5:00 A.M. Friday, and no one wanted to wait.

Just after 4:00 P.M. Thursday, Capt. J. W. Hegeman, the chief of the Naval Intelligence Service office in Yokosuka, the home port of the U.S. Seventh Fleet, met the ten survivors of Alfa Foxtrot 586 at Niigata, Japan. He got to them, he said, while they were still at their seats in JAL's DC-9 from Khabarovsk. With Captain Hegeman now escorting them, the survivors changed planes and boarded a Military Airlift Command C-141 transport for the short hop south to Yokota Air Base near Tokyo. (Fifth Air Force had held a C-141 aircraft on three hour alert at Yokota for several days to retrieve the Navy airmen from the USSR, backing up the C-9 medevac waiting for the launch order that never came.) Three welded zinc coffins, containing Brooner, Garcia, and Rodriguez, were transferred smoothly from one plane to the other also. They would be rolled out of the aircraft's cargo door in Japan to meet a Marine Corps honor guard, already draped with the American flags that would cover them on the trip back to California. Once aboard the -141, the men were safe; their ordeal was over. Inside the transport's huge fuselage, Ed Caylor and the others were breathing American air, if not yet standing on American soil. Each man finally let his guard down and relaxed for the first time since John Wagner had restarted PD-2's no. 1 engine one week earlier.

While families waited impatiently at home, the ten survivors would remain at Yokota for two days, time enough for yet another cursory medical examination and for somewhat more extensive intelligence debriefings. In the Navy's eyes, the debriefing had a higher priority than the domestic reunions still to come. Families in the United States would have to wait a few days longer.

Captain Hegeman headed an impromptu team of 14 (eight Navy officers, four senior enlisted men, and two civilians, ponderously dubbed "the P-3 Survivor Recovery Coordinating Element"), which would conduct the intelligence debrief. His team included six who were assigned to intelligence activities in the western Pacific. The other members were drawn from U.S. joint service command's several interested staffs.

Hegeman and his team were to see if and how the Soviets had extracted any secrets during the week the Americans were in their hands. They were also collecting "confirmational intelligence," information from Crew 6's personal observations during five days in the Soviet Union that could verify what the United States thought it already knew from other sources. Had the members of the crew seen anything in Petropavlovsk or Khabarovsk, his team wanted to know, that could affirm, or refute, information gained from other sources? Had they seen anything like this, for example (showing what was obviously a closeup photograph of Soviet Navy ships in port at Petropavlovsk)?[10]

At the end of the two days, Hegeman was fulsome in his praise of the men, even while he was edging himself to center stage. "My firsthand observation, as the man closest to the recovery operation . . . they were superb," Hegeman wrote in a personal message to the wing commander. After reminding Rear Admiral Prindle that he had been "the first Navy man to greet the crew . . . at Niigata and the last to bid them goodbye and a safe trip back to CONUS," Hegeman went on: "They made my job and the job of my debriefing team easy. They anticipated the debriefings and were mentally prepared to provide the details. They were observant and had sound presence of mind and judgment during their ordeal. They wanted to 'unload' as fast as possible. We were overwhelmed with their endurance and in some cases had to put more than one debriefer to a crewman just to absorb the wealth of raw information provided."

"Sound presence of mind" is an apt description.

Once he was thawed out aboard *Sinyavin,* Harold Moore found, to his horror, the copies of the encrypted transmissions he had been recording for Bruce Forshay in a breast pocket of his flight suit. Fearing that the wet, but still legible, sheets with the mysterious encrypted letter groups could reveal something sensitive, Moore spent the next several trips to the ship's head, its communal toilet, carefully discarding damp, wadded fragments of paper into an open hole in the deck that passed for a plumbing fixture.

Shepard, who had been slipped waterlogged briefing notes by some of the enlisted crew while he was aboard *Sinyavin,* carefully got rid of them, too. He also had a magnetic tape reel in a flight suit pocket, recordings of Soviet radar signals copied from the aircraft's electronic support measures intercept equipment operated by Rich Garcia, lifted from the body by Matt Gibbons during his first visit to the morgue. Crewmembers took turns surreptitiously holding the tape cassette flat against the picture tube on the old black-and-white TV set in the hospital lounge at Petropavlovsk, hoping the tube's magnetic field would erase the tape. No one knew if their stratagem worked, but the tape was blank when they replayed it in the United States days later.

Forshay had memorized the configuration of a large search radar antenna their bus had passed on the way to the airport, and he had also made a mental note of the time during dinner at Khabarovsk when every electric light visible in the entire city had suddenly gone dark. Others studied passing radar antennas especially carefully, too.

Even so, it is difficult to picture what Hegeman was referring to when he spoke of a "wealth of raw information provided." Confined to a commercial fishing trawler, then restricted in vacant wings of two military hospitals and transported between them in the dark, it is unlikely that any of the men would have gleaned any especially meaningful "intelligence." Even the indomitable Gibbons, prowling like a hyperactive ferret everywhere he could get into, could not have gleaned an intelligence coup from what little he was able to see. Khabarovsk, moreover, was an open city. It had almost certainly been subjected to street-level surveillance in the past.

The debrief had trailed on for two days, because Hegeman was convinced that the crew could give him a lot of intelligence, and he wanted to be certain that they had given nothing away. Impatiently pressing Hegeman to get on with it, Bud Powers quickly came to the conclusion in Yokota that the interrogation should have been finished in a few hours.

Years later, however, people still believed that Matt Gibbons and "Inu" Shepard, at least, had come home from Russia with the secrets of Petro's submarine base and of Kamchatka's radar order of battle locked in their brains.

Chapter 11

Homecoming

Alfa Foxtrot 586 went down early evening Thursday, California time. During the week that followed the ditching, and while the survivors were in Soviet custody, Bud Powers tried to ensure that the anxious families of the downed crew had what little news was available.

At the beginning, in the hours immediately before the ditching, Powers's information came directly from the HF radio transmissions between AF 586 and Elmendorf being overheard in the patrol wing's operations command center (OpCon), a few minutes drive from his squadron's hangar. The OpCon, a counterpart to Adak's Tactical Support Center, adjoined the offices of the wing's operations staff. The two functions filled an unimpressive single-story, wooden building on the southeast corner of Moffett Field that from the outside resembled nothing so much as an old farm bungalow that had metastasized. The plowed fields that surrounded the OpCon on two sides, air station property leased out to a local truck farmer for onions and tomatoes, were a vestige of the valley's past. At harvest time, the air near the sweeping turn in the road around the approach end of Runways 32 Left and Right was occasionally perfumed with the faint smell of onions, heightening the rustic impression.

Powers raced over to the command center as soon as he got the phone call reporting Crew 6's emergency. He arrived at the OpCon in time to hear most of the radio dialogue himself. He stood there, impotently listening to Matt Gibbons and Bruce Forshay reporting AF 586's evolving emergency to Elmendorf, while

Jerry Grigsby and Ed Caylor wrestled their aircraft first toward Adak and then Shemya. Powers remembers that it was difficult to follow events on station "because [the crew was] talking to Elmendorf Radio, not on a normal Moffett OpCon frequency. . . . The H.F. kept coming in and fading out; so we'd catch part of it and part would be garbled. Then we'd ask Elmendorf to relay the info. So we heard parts of the transmissions, but not all."

Greater clarity would not have made much of a difference. There was not anything that Bud or the command center's watch team could have done to help his flight crew, in extremis forty-four hundred nautical miles away. Someone in Wing Operations might have begun an inventory of Moffett-based crews and aircraft available to send north immediately, if necessary to reinforce the SAR effort. A heads-up call to Patrol Squadron 46 would have put its ready alert crew on notice for a trip to Adak. Someone probably checked the weather and sea state on station and passed the bad news around that AF 586 would be ditching into a wind-churned maelstrom, and someone else in the OpCon certainly would have been plotting AF 586's position on a chart as the aircraft slowly closed on Shemya. The rest of the watch probably put aside whatever they were doing, to stand and listen with rapt attention to the dialogue coming out of the speakers.

Very early in the crisis, looking at AF 586's penciled position creep across the chart, Powers and the veteran watch standers clustered around him must have come to their own glum conclusions about the crew's chances of making it to Shemya. After Gibbons's first Mayday transmission at 4:52 P.M., Pacific Daylight Time, announcing that AF 586 was ditching hundreds of miles west of the island, however, there could have been little doubt at Moffett Field that Event AK 262 was going to end in the water. The pessimism in the command center would not have cleared even though, remarkably, the aircraft remained in the air after that first ditching announcement and even after the second, seven minutes later.

None of the pilots ever spoke by radio to anyone after AF 586 checked out of the air traffic control system with Adak soon after takeoff, to begin the operational portion of its flight. All the subsequent calls from the aircraft and all the descriptions of the emergency came from two naval flight officers, nonpilots, in the cabin, Gibbons and Forshay. Their focus was (quite rightly) on preparing for the ditch and ensuring a successful search and rescue, not on describing in technical detail the fiery disintegration of the no. 1 gearbox. By 5:30 P.M., from the early transmissions he had overheard, Powers knew only that PD-2 was down at sea 250 miles short of Shemya after a no. 1 prop overspeed, nacelle fire, and "total" gearbox failure. Down into huge seas and bitterly cold water.

On the west side of the runways, at the wing's headquarters in Building 19, senior staff officers considering the incomplete information had wondered what had happened to PD-2, and whether or not the Pacific Fleet's force of P-3 aircraft (approximately 130 planes) should be grounded, at least until the cause of the loss became clear. Later, Prindle would consider that course of action again, during a long conversation with his Atlantic Fleet counterpart, Rear Adm. Ralph Hedges.

Over time, while Scone 92, XF 675, CG 1500, and DF 704 were in the air, Powers would have learned there were survivors aboard rafts in the water. Then, he would have found out who those survivors were. Still later (days later, in telephone conversations with Ambassador Toon and Captain Bracken), he would get some news directly from the USSR and pass it on through a quickly improvised telephone-calling tree. All together, however, he had very little information to share with families after the first day. Once his crew arrived in the Soviet Union, Powers would learn more from Tony Bracken directly than from local Navy sources.

Next of kin were quickly told about the accident, but probably not much ahead of the squadron rumor mill, which by 9:00 P.M. Pacific Daylight Time Thursday night had engulfed the squadron's families at Moffett Field in telephone calls from men with the Adak detachment, revealing that one of their planes was in the water. On Friday, the names of the crew became public.

Of the fifteen men on board the aircraft, nine were married. Marital status generally related to age and income. All the officers but Gibbons were married, but only four of the enlisted men were: Shepard, Hemmer, Flow, and Miller. In Navy parlance, their wives were these nine men's "primary next of kin," heirs and identified as such on the Navy Emergency Data Questionnaires that were filed half-forgotten in service records. Among these nine families there were fourteen children. Gary Hemmer had the most, three (Brenda, eleven, DeAnne, nine, and Bradley, five), and his wife was pregnant with their fourth. Jerry Grigsby's nearly twelve-year-old daughter, Mary Ann, was the oldest by a few weeks; Bruce Forshay's sixteen-month-old daughter, Rachel, was the youngest by two months. The unmarried men had all identified a mother or father (and in a few instances both) as their primary next of kin.

The Hemmers had just moved into family housing on Adak one month before the flight. Even so, Barbara Hemmer, Gary's wife, knew all of her husband's shipmates at the TSC. This isolated, self-contained community was too small to keep secrets from itself, and no one could have successfully concealed from her the biggest thing happening on the island, not when everyone at the TSC had suddenly gone to a port and starboard (twelve hours on, twelve off) watch schedule. She probably knew as much about the ditching and rescue as Bud Powers did and got the news at about the same time he did. Thursday afternoon, right after her girls got home from school, Barbara told them the news. Their dad's airplane was down in the water. She did not know what had happened to him after that.

The six wives living in Navy housing on the grounds of the air station or in the civilian communities close by Moffett's gates naturally heard the news next.

One of the wives (Bud thinks it was Barbara Caylor) absorbed the news and then set up camp for two days in his office at the hangar, determined not to miss word of any developments. Paula Powers, too, recalls that Barbara Caylor took the news about the ditching exceptionally hard. Barbara's extreme reaction may have been a reflection of her own troubled state as much as anything else.

Ed and Barbara were married in the Naval Academy chapel June 1976, right after he finished flight training. Two years later, their relationship was under fatal strain. It would not survive the ditching by another year. The two would part in 1979 and never see each other again. In 1980 Ed headed east, out of the Navy and into the airlines. Meanwhile, Barbara had dropped out of law school at Santa Clara and disappeared into the hills of Mendocino County, California.

The squadron sponsorship program, through which newly reported person-nel were paired with old-timers, to help them and their families get acclimated to squadron life, unaccountably failed dismally in the case of Bruce and Carol For-shay. During their first weeks aboard Patrol Squadron 9, the young couple felt iso-lated and ignored. Carol hardly knew the people at her door when Lt. Rory Fisher, his wife, and a second officer appeared there unexpectedly with bad news about her husband, just a few days after Bruce went to Adak.

That is not how the system should have worked. The idea was that the best friends of the crewmembers should carry the news and stay for consolation, but the Forshays had no best friends in the squadron. As Fisher awkwardly delivered his message, Carol heard all her unspoken fears about Bruce's flying career con-firmed. She collapsed on hearing the news that her husband's aircraft had gone down. Her next visitors from the squadron—the second delegation was upgraded to include Pete Cressy and a Navy doctor—came better prepared to deal with an expected emotional tempest. Without any basis for trusting the men in her home, Carol (a licensed practical nurse) quickly concluded that the sedative being offered was for the purpose of keeping her from talking to the press; she chased them out. Like her husband's, Carol's relationship with the squadron never improved from that low point.

The unexplained loss of a fourth P-3 in less than a year put the Navy into a full defensive crouch, hypersensitive to any scrutiny of its maritime patrol opera-tions, much less to any criticism. Later Bruce would be wrongly suspected of crit-ical statements to the press. Twice wrongly: he had said little and the media cov-erage was not damaging. Carol's family connections with Senator Ted Stevens of Alaska counted against the couple, too. Stevens (who knew her father) had writ-ten several letters expressing avuncular concern, and these, too, raised hackles at headquarters.

John Ball would arrive home the next week certain that his wife, Donna, had known almost from the beginning that he had survived. He thought, wrongly, that he had been seen and recognized in the Mark-12 raft by Denny Mette with Crew 11, while XF 675 circled overhead. Pat Conway's crew had seen one man in the Mark-12 and counted eight in the Mark-7, tiny figures bundled in emergency equipment and obscured by speed, distance, and the weather. Identification of any survivor under those conditions was impossible. Conway's postmission "purple" report said only, "Total of at least 9 of the 15 souls on board were definitely sighted. One raft was covered with environmental protection tarp [Ball's Mark-12] and the number of people could not be counted."[1]

The Balls lived in junior officers quarters on the naval air station, a few minutes walk from Cindy and Denny Mette's apartment behind the Navy Exchange store. As soon as the news became public, Cindy and several of the other wives rushed to the Ball's duplex. They would stay with Donna night and day, carving Halloween pumpkins together the first night to kill time and distract her, until she heard that John was safe, healthy, and on the way home. Donna was a rock during his absence, strong and calm even before the news of John's rescue by *Mys Sinyavin* and confident during the days when no news at all came out of the USSR.

Shelly Wagner, at home with Derek and Jay, her sons, knew something was wrong when she looked out of her window late Thursday afternoon and saw Sarah Cressy, the executive officer's wife, coming up the walk toward her door with an officer in Navy uniform. Sarah delivered the news about John and then stayed with her through the night until Shelly fell asleep after sunrise, Friday morning. The next day's news, that John was aboard a Soviet fishing vessel, terrified Shelly. She imagined that her husband would become a cold war POW. Not until she heard that the crew was in Japan did the fear leave her.

That same fear animated many people, not just family members. Senior officers at the wing's headquarters at Moffett Field saw the crew in Petropavlovsk as being "down behind enemy lines." This stark cold war perspective underlay all the pressures on the embassy in Moscow to visit the men and to get them out of the USSR quickly, before some imaginative Soviet officer turned the crew into bargaining chips.

When Carol Flow heard about AF 586's ditching, right after she and Ed junior, nearly three, had dinner Thursday, Scone 92 and XF 675 were still in the air overhead the rafts. A group from the squadron came to the Flows' apartment in Sunnyvale around 8:30 P.M. Pacific Daylight Time to tell her that PD-2 was in the water, that there were survivors—two rafts had been spotted—but that no one knew who had made it out of the aircraft or what shape they were in. One of her visitors—probably not the chaplain or one of the sympathetic flight engineers from Ed's shop, likely the forgotten squadron officer assigned to her "case"—hopefully added the news that a Coast Guard cutter was even then on its way to pick up the crew.

Carol always believed that bad things came in threes. Between December 1977 and September 1978, she remembered, Patrol Wing 5, at Naval Air Station Brunswick, Maine, had lost three aircraft, and right after she was told that her husband's aircraft was down, she had a premonition that there would soon be two more P-3 accidents in the Pacific. In fact, there were.

On 27 June 1979, Patrol Squadron 22 (the Blue Geese, husband Ed's old command) lost QA-6 (Buno. 154596) in the Philippines after catastrophic failures and fires in the no. 3 and 4 engines passing through six thousand feet during climb out from Naval Air Station Cubi Point, on Luzon. The aircraft had been heading out with a full crew and full fuel tanks for an eleven-hour operational mission in the South China Sea. QA-6 turned back to the field with the no. 4 prop gone, no. 3 windmilling, fires in both nacelles on the starboard side now out, and heavy rain showers from a line of squalls separating it from the runway. Fifteen minutes after takeoff, QA-6 hit the water, gear down, in sight of the field and only fourteen hundred yards short of Runway 7. Five of the fifteen aboard died in the crash.[2]

An even more spectacular disaster was still to come. Nine months later, on 19 April 1980, Lt. Allen Glenny took two passes in his P-3 over Pago Pago, American Samoa, to drop members of an Army parachute team. The remote islands were celebrating Flag Day, and the skydivers were one part of the festivities. On his third pass, Glenny flew the airplane, Patrol Squadron 50's SG-3 (Buno. 158213), into a hotel tramcar cable. The steel cable, strung tight across the gorge between Mount Alava and Solo Hill, sliced off most of the plane's vertical stabilizer and all of its rudder. (The amputated stub of the stabilizer is clearly visible in photos of SG-3's last second of flight, printed in the *Samoa News*.) Out of control, SG-3 plowed into the ground at the base of the west wing of the Hotel Rainmaker, notorious now, but perhaps not then, as the worst hotel in the South Pacific. The ensuing fire burned the seventy-eight-room building to the ground but miraculously killed only one guest. All seven aboard SG-3 died.

Ed and Carol had talked about ditching when he was in Patrol Squadron 22, how no one had ever survived a P-3 ditch, and Ed (who had been home overnight the past weekend on an aircraft exchange) had told her about the weather at Adak. So her first question on hearing the news that her husband's plane was in the water was, "What were the sea conditions?" The improbable and wildly inaccurate answer was, "Flat." That said, everyone then went to Karen Miller's place in Orion Park, Navy enlisted men's housing on the air station, to tell Butch's wife the same thing. Carol would stay the night with the Millers, the two wives and four children all crowded together in the small apartment on the air station, the women wondering anxiously what was next. They heard nothing more overnight.

Karen had fought with Butch before he had left for Adak. The fight that Rear Admiral Prindle had speculated about in his endorsement to the investigation had been real. The argument had gotten away from both of them. It ended with neither one talking to the other, fixed in a frozen silence that neither one could dissolve. Butch had left for Adak the next day without a "goodbye" passing between them. When Karen got the news the next morning that Butch had almost certainly gone down in the aircraft, the thought that the last words they had shared had been angry ones haunted her.

While that news was being delivered to Karen, Carol was pulled aside and told that Ed was aboard the rescue vessel, condition unknown but alive. Carol Flow left for her home in town. With Ed alive and Butch dead, the two wives now shared very little, and Carol was suddenly uncomfortable in the other woman's home.

Unlike Carol, who had a job at the Navy Exchange store, Karen did not work. She was not able to, not with three small children at home (the youngest, Jason, was not even two). Without Butch's Navy paycheck, $811 each month including flight pay, things rapidly got very tough. In truth, they had been tough all along. A family of five living in the Santa Clara Valley, even in government quarters, on less than $10,000 a year was used to doing without. But now, with Butch gone, she was no longer eligible to stay in Navy housing and moved out in early November, heading for home. Not in the family's new conversion van. It was repossessed before she left the Bay area to resettle her family in Tulsa, Oklahoma. (Months later, her attorney flew from California to Oklahoma to open Butch's briefcase, to see what was inside. Karen had not been able to bring herself to perform even this act of closure.)

Rich Garcia's father, Guillermo, and Butch Miller's mother, Leta, both lived in the San Francisco Bay area, too, so a squadron representative would have visited them very quickly, not long after the wives were first contacted officially. All other mothers and fathers, primary next of kin of the bachelors, secondary of the married men, lived outside of California. These PNOKs and SNOKs, in the graceless acronyms of the armed forces, would have heard later, from an officer assigned to the nearest Navy activity. In each case a Navy officer delivered the message, often in the company of a chaplain. A pair of stone-faced officers in dress uniform driving through a quiet neighborhood searching mailboxes for one specific address, has become a Hollywood cliché but that is how parents in Oklahoma, Texas, Oregon, Alabama, and Colorado found out officially that their sons had gone down to an uncertain fate.

That is also how Patricia Shepard learned that her husband had been an observer in an aircraft that went down at sea. She was living with their two young sons in St. Cameron, Missouri, near his parents, when a black Navy sedan turned into her street. Pat remembers watching it drive up and down two times, looking for a house number; she sent the kids to a neighborhood playground, closed their door, and hoped the car would go away. The two officers plucked from the naval reserve center in St. Joseph for this duty would be her link to news about Garland. Calls from Senator Eagleton's local office updated her, too.

In a Schenectady suburb, at the Gibbons's home on Grand Avenue, the news came first by phone. Joseph Gibbons and Ann, his wife, had heard about a patrol aircraft accident off Alaska from a radio news broadcast Friday morning. When a commander from the reserve center in Albany called later in the day to ask mysteriously for directions to their home, Joe and Ann "put two and two together." Good news quickly followed the bad. By 9:30 P.M. Eastern Daylight Time they knew their son had been rescued; father Joe and son Jim celebrated by toasting each other and the absent Matt in Jameson's fine Irish whiskey through much of the night. Midmorning on Saturday they learned Matt was in good shape.

In the background, the same story flashed around the Santa Clara Valley's Navy community, whose common core was in the ranks of big aircraft parked on both sides of Moffett Field. Perhaps one-third of the men at Moffett had been, were, or would become Orion flight crewmembers. No civilian in the region was unfamiliar with Moffett Field or unaware of the Navy turboprops that flew very low directly over the Bayshore Freeway on short final approach to landing, so Bay area newspapers, radio and television stations covered the local story attentively. The ditching appeared as a minor item in some national news media; front-page news at the time was 10 percent inflation and fears of an impending recession in the United States and the progress of Egyptian-Israeli peace initiatives in the Middle East. These had just resulted in a shared Nobel Prize for Anwar Sadat and Menachim Begin, the second of the prestigious award's odd couples.

Subsequent reports to families would come through follow-on personal visits, or through a telephone-calling tree hastily set up to keep ahead of whatever might be coming out of the commercial news media tracking the story. Oddly, neither the Pacific Command's nor Juneau's SAR situation report messages were addressed to the squadron at Moffett or to the detachment on Adak, denying Bud Powers this accurate information.[3]

Good news for some families came at the same time as terrible news for others. The first terrible news was confirmation, received via *Mys Sinyavin*, Friday morning that the three youngest men in the rafts had died overnight and that neither Grigsby nor Miller had boarded a raft. Little more could be told to the waiting families during the rest of the day, Friday. *Sinyavin* was on course west toward Kamchatka; the aircraft search for the two missing men continued overhead the site; and CGC *Jarvis* was still en route to the ditching coordinates through heavy seas and gale-force winds.

Midmorning Saturday, Bud Powers relayed to Loreen Grigsby that the Navy had changed her husband's status from "missing" to "dead." In view of conditions at the scene and the passage of time since the ditching, he said to her, the Navy no longer believed that Jerry could still be alive. Forty-five minutes later, Bud delivered the same message to Karen Miller in her quarters on the air station, and to Butch's mother, Leta Aaron.

All three women must have desperately hoped to hear something different, but they could not have truly expected anything else, not so long after the ditch, and not after what Loreen and Karen already had been told the day before. Powers did not have to deliver that message in person. He could have passed on the responsibility to be the messenger with sad news to the casualty assistance officer assigned to each family.

A Western Union telegram on Sunday from the chief of naval personnel confirmed Powers's message. The one delivered to Loreen—on bright yellow paper, captioned "Don't phone. Don't deliver between 10:00 P.M. and 6:00 A.M."—was typical:

> I deeply regret to confirm on behalf of the United States Navy that your husband, Lieutenant Commander Jerry Carson Grigsby, U.S.N., previously reported missing died on 26 October 1978 at sea as a result of an aircraft accident which occurred 200 miles from the Aleutian Island of Shemya. It is with further regret that I must confirm that searches failed to recover your husband's remains. A letter from his commanding officer setting forth the circumstances of death will follow. Your husband died while serving his country. My sincerest sympathy is extended to you in your great loss. . . .
> Vice Admiral Robert B. Baldwin, Chief of Naval Personnel

That Powers had not flinched from his painful duty was one measure of his personal sympathy for the wives of the men under his command. A second was the evening of company and sympathy he and Paula invited the crew wives to at their home Monday night, the day after the telegrams arrived. (Carol Flow did not go. She did not know Powers and was certain that anything she heard from him would be bad news.) Another was the effort he made to meet his men in Japan, after their flight from Khabarovsk. His appearance in Yokota surprised the crew. Caylor remembers being touched by the gesture, and chagrined by the realization that the loss of their aircraft had probably ended Powers's career in the Navy.

Bud's boss at Moffett Field, Rear Adm. Charlie Prindle, would participate in the coming weekend's formal return and welcome ceremony for the crew. He would officially welcome the crew home and then introduce the air station's chaplain, Cdr. Dick McCue, who would lead a prayer and call for a minute of silence for the dead and lost.

Personal relations, the social chemistry, between the Prindles and the Powers had never been good. There was something about the skipper of Patrol Squadron 9 and his wife that did not resonate well in Quarters A, the Prindles' residence on the air station. Perhaps that is why neither the admiral nor his wife, Jane, showed Bud and Paula any of the sympathy or concern that the sudden loss of a flight crew might have been expected to provoke. Neither one called Paula Powers to express sympathy, much less to offer assistance. Bud and Paula took the neglect as a sign that Prindle and his staff were deliberately trying to distance themselves from the failure represented by the loss of an aircraft and crew, the first on the West Coast in recent history. The truth may have been more personal. Early wing drafts of the welcome ceremony schedule had the executive officer, Pete Cressy, not Bud Powers, greeting the returning crew. In a service famously sensitive to protocol, this substitution could not have been an oversight. Years later, Paula Powers would still angrily remember the Wing's lack of support during the incident.[4]

Until World War II, America's armed forces were a culture almost entirely apart from the mainstream civil society. Long periods at sea or in remote frontier garrisons isolated the profession of arms from the larger society that swirled off in the distance, and this isolation encouraged the development of institutions that reflected the unique qualities of life in uniform. One such institution was wives' clubs, which flourished to provide socialization, socializing, and support for married women whose frequent lot was to be left alone for long periods of time. At their best, these clubs satisfied their members' urgent need for companionship in good times and assistance in very bad. At their worst, they were stultifying, hierarchal cliques that gave senior officers' wives a vehicle for their ambitions.

After midcentury, after postwar demobilization had flushed out the millions of uniformed civilians who had fleshed out the country's tiny professional forces, military society began to edge back toward what it had been before that great infusion. The nostalgic movement toward the past lasted only a relatively short time. Before the 1970s, even through the ferment of the 1960s, most Navy wives stayed at home, but after the 1970s, many wives, particularly the younger ones, worked, especially in high-cost-of-living areas, such as surrounded the San Francisco Bay. The change dramatically and permanently altered the scope of wives clubs. It reduced their influence on the lives of wives, and their utility as a social services agency and channel of communications.

Even so, in the late 1970s, all but the smallest Navy commands had two wives clubs, one for the wives of officers and one for those of enlisted men. Patrol Squadron 9 did, too. When the men were at home, these clubs were purely social; when the men were deployed, the clubs played a much more important role: helping their members manage being alone or single parents for months on end. The more savvy older women helped the younger (some still in their teens) cope with separation. As the wives of the squadron's commanding and executive officers, it fell by Navy custom to Paula Powers and Sarah Cressy to manage the dispensation of aid, comfort, and information to the families of crewmembers while deployed. Both took these responsibilities seriously, and evidently did them well.

Bud and Paula nursed the crew's families through two phases. The first phase was shock at the fact of the accident and grief over the loss of life. The second was concern about the health and safety of the survivors in Russian hands. The families' fear was that the men would be imprisoned and interrogated, and then become small, forgotten pieces on the cold war game board. This second phase lasted until Moffett got the word that the crew was in Japan.

Under a carefully scripted plan drafted by Prindle's aide, Lt. Perry Martini, the survivors were to return to Moffett Field from Yokota, Japan, midmorning, Saturday, 4 November. The quick, ten-minute repatriation ceremony at home included all the essentials: an armed honor guard, the Navy band from San Francisco, senior wing and air station officers to greet the crew, a Navy chaplain, and a mini–press conference.[5] In the minute before the crewmembers were to be reunited with their families, Ed Caylor was to "make prepared statements as approved by . . . the Commander, Naval Forces Japan Public Affairs Office." After what he had been through, Caylor was not going to be trusted to wing it, even for one minute. Ed was a very reluctant spokesman. Bud had to talk him into saying anything.

The survivors, however, insisted that their dead crewmates return to Moffett Field in the same aircraft that was bringing them home, and this insistence changed the character of the planned ceremony significantly. The mood of happy welcome was to be commingled with one of mournful regret.

Air Force 59406, a Military Airlift Command C-141, landed at Moffett Field at 10:29, Saturday morning, nine hours and forty-five minutes out of Yokota. The landing was exactly on time, but only because the aircraft had been deliberately held in the air for twenty minutes to ensure it would not arrive early and disrupt the schedule.

Bud Powers had sat with Ed Caylor on the long flight home. They and the other members of the returning Navy flight crew were in the pallet of passenger seats clipped onto the floor of the big transport, just above the three coffins in the cargo hold below. Four Zero Six back-taxied down the runway and turned off to park in front of the welcoming crowd on the tarmac at the station's operations building. The Air Force visitor dwarfed the many P-3s of Patrol Squadron 31 parked in a double line outside of Hangar 1, just to its north.

The crowd assembled to greet the -141 included several very different groups. The largest was the assembled blue and gold ranks of the officers and men of Patrol Squadron 9, those not with the detachment in Adak, salted at the formation's margins with uniformed well wishers from the wing and air station, and the Navy Band. Nearby was a smaller and more colorfully dressed contingent, mostly female, holding bouquets and concealing pounding hearts, the family members of the survivors. Among that number were Barbara Caylor, Carol Forshay, Shelly Wagner, Donna Ball, and Claire Gibbons, bachelor Matt's sister. Some grinning parents hovered there, also, relieved their sons were alive after all or their daughters were not widowed.

The last and smallest group was family members, too: the families of the men who had not survived AF 586's ordeal. They had come to witness the grim procession of three flag-draped coffins roll off the aircraft. The Brooner, Garcia, and Rodriguez families were assembled there. At the request of the Garcias, full military honors, including a ceremonial rifle salute, were rendered as the coffins moved across the tarmac and into three waiting hearses.

By 11:00 A.M. it was all over. Crew 6, what remained of it, was home again. A P-3 from Patrol Squadron 47 left immediately after the ceremony to take Master Chief Shepard and PO 1st Class Hemmer back to Adak, Alaska. Even before it left the ground, the coffins containing Petty Officer Brooner's and Airmen Rodriguez's and Garcia's remains were being driven to the Navy's regional medical center, Oak Knoll. The return trip to Adak was Hemmer's last flight in a P-3. He would never agree to board one again.

The next Monday, everyone but Howard Moore (who immediately left for home in Alabama and convalescent leave) went back to work. The first order of business was the investigation into the accident. In Moscow, that same Monday, the embassy sent its monthly travel report to the State Department. This routine report catalogued requests to the Ministry of Foreign Affairs made during October for travel outside of the immediate capital area by American embassy personnel. The picture the report described was bleak. "Embassy travelers ran into a stone wall of [Ministry of Foreign Affairs] resistance during the month of October. . . . The basic developments of the month reinforce the conclusion that travel to any but the most common tourist spots in the Soviet Union is actively discouraged by Soviet authorities." The embassy recommended that Washington "retaliate" appropriately, presumably by denying travel requests by Soviet diplomats in the United States.

The tit-for-tat calculus allowed for one exception. Embassy Moscow recommended that the Soviets' refusal of permission for travel to Petropavlovsk (an acknowledged closed area) not be counted against them, in view of the Ministry of Foreign Affair's "generally cooperative attitude" during the rescue.

Finding of Fact. The remains of Lieutenant Commander Jerry Carson Grigsby, USN, and Petty Officer Second Class Harold Richard Miller, USN, were not recovered and were considered lost at sea.

Moffett Field's chapel is not one of the original buildings on what was called Naval Air Station Sunnyvale, when the station was put into active service in April 1933, near the end of the brief era when rigid airships were still thought to have an important role in scouting for the fleet. These structures included Hangar 1, a cluster of handsome senior officers' quarters on "the Circle," several office buildings cum barracks lining three sides of the station's central esplanade, and a large helium storage tank. Back then, Naval Air Station Sunnyvale stood in near-complete isolation amid the rich farm fields and orchards that surrounded it. A place of worship on the property was considered essential for the moral development of the men (as was the brig in the basement of the enlisted men's barracks), and so a small chapel was located inside a building adjoining the barracks.

Navy Seabees built the station's stand-alone chapel during the early 1940s, one part of the wartime expansion of support facilities on the airfield. A facelift twenty years later matched the chapel's utilitarian exterior to the station's overall design motif: cream-colored stucco capped with a red, clay-tile roof. The pretty, vaguely Spanish mission–style building conceals an ecumenical innovation, a revolving altar suitable on one side for the celebration of Catholic mass and on the other side for Protestant services. When the light is just right, the chapel's stained glass windows cast a soothing, Technicolor glow across the small transept.

On 2 November, a few days after Adak had offered its own communal farewell and two days before AF 586's survivors would arrive home, a memorial service was held in the Moffett chapel for the five who had lost their lives in the ditching. The short service was conducted by all three station chaplains. Because Bud Powers was in Japan with the crew, Pete Cressy spoke on behalf of the squadron. When he finished, the congregation rose to sing Hymn 196, accompanied by music from the chapel's small organ. It was a naval prayer set to music and a favorite of the congregation:

> Eternal Father, strong to save,
> Whose arm hath bound the restless wave,
> Who bidd'st the mighty ocean deep
> Its own appointed limits keep.
> Oh hear us when we cry to thee
> For those in peril on the sea.

At this point everyone present paused, then earnestly sang the final verse, for the special comfort of airmen:

> Lord, Guide and guard the men who fly
> Through the great spaces of the sky.
> Be with them always in the air,
> In darkening storms or sunlight fair.
> Oh hear us when we lift our prayer
> For those in peril in the air.

Thinking about her loss later, Jerry Grigsby's mother explained that her son had been saved from drowning at the age of twelve. She drew strength from the fact that twenty-four years later, he had been able to save the lives of ten others. He had been spared death in childhood specifically to perform that great sacrifice, she believed, and the belief clearly gave comfort and meaning to her loss.

In 1983, the Navy dedicated a new basic water survival training center, a part of the Naval Aviation Schools Command at Pensacola, Florida. Fledgling pilots and flight officers would get their first exposure to survival training in this pool and gym complex on the palm-shaded grounds of the Navy's historic first naval air station, its "Annapolis of the air." The center, Building No. 3828, was named after Jerry Grigsby, a memorial to him and a reminder to students of what is at risk in flight over water. The plaque reads:

> Jerry Grigsby Survival Training Center
> Dedicated 28 October 1983
> In honor of Lieutenant Commander Jerry C. Grigsby, USN
> Who gave his life 26 October 1978 in the Northern Pacific
> helping his crew survive

Finding of Fact. The remains of Petty Officer Third Class James D. Brooner, USN, Airman Richard Martin Garcia, USN, and Airman Randall Paul Rodriguez, USN, were recovered. Cause of death was officially stated as exposure to low environmental temperature combined with seawater immersion.

PO Jim Brooner was buried Friday, 10 November. The squadron sent an aircraft up to Eugene, Oregon, with his crewmates for the funeral. Interment was in Bend, and so aircraft and crew then flew east from one to the other, to be there at the end. Matt Gibbons took charge once again, and spoke at length at the rite. Ed Caylor, now ill and exhausted, who had actually been in the raft with Jim during the last twelve hours of his life, said very little. Jim Brooner's death, he thought, had not been peaceful or painless, and he wanted to spare Jim's family the anguish of knowing any more than they did.

Airman Rich Garcia was buried with full military honors in Pine Bluff, Arkansas, where his mother, Frances, was living. Airman Randy Rodriguez returned to Colorado for interment, brought home for the last time by his parents, Delores and Paul. On November 8, the squadron sent an aircraft east to Denver and Little Rock, carrying Gibbons, Forshay, and its other representatives to the two funerals.

On 8 December Rich Garcia's parents wrote two gracious letters to Bud Powers. The first commended the performance of Lt. (jg) Dave Weeks, a former Coast Guard pilot who had been assigned by Powers to assist the Garcias while they coped with the loss of their son and dealt with the inescapable bureaucratic details that attended it. A second letter mentioned PO Michael Brooks, who, together with Dave Weeks, escorted their son's body to Arkansas, for the funeral. Mike Brooks was the radar operator on Crew 7, and so a natural choice for this assignment.

On the first Navy payday after Crew 6's celebrated return from the Soviet

Union, the Disbursing Department provided its own special "welcome home." None of the enlisted crewmembers got a paycheck, and the checks of officer members of the crew were sharply reduced.[6]

Disbursing's math was simple and its logic was unassailable. All members of the crew had received advance per diem payments of a few dollars a day for the weeks they expected to be gone, but they had returned home one month early. Moreover, no-cost food and lodging had been available to the crew for the week while they were in the rafts, aboard *Sinyavin*, in the Soviet Union and Japan, and aboard the C-141 that flew them back from Yokota to Moffett Field. Wrongly paid allowances to cover these unrealized costs, naturally, were deducted from the next regular paycheck.

Chapter 12

Postmortem

Much changed in Patrol Squadron 9's corner of its hangar at Moffett Field between the fall of 1978 and the summer of 1979. Through the continuous process of renewal common to all Navy commands, during those eight months perhaps a dozen officers and fifty, or more, enlisted men checked out of the squadron at the end of their tours of duty, taking with them the experience they had gained over the past two or three years. Some went to other assignments; others left the Navy and became civilians again. A like number of new men reported aboard. Most of them were young kids in their first full-time job, right out of high school, right out of Navy schools. Many were away from home for the first time, too. Even some old-timers, the salty senior petty officers who normally would be expected to provide leadership and instruction on the hangar deck, were new to the mission and the aircraft when they checked in.[1]

The skipper, Bud Powers, left Moffett Field for the Pentagon and his next assignment as head of the Navy staff's nuclear division. Pete Cressy "fleeted up" to CO, meaning that Cressy made the scheduled move, and replaced Powers at the helm of the Golden Eagles. Cdr. Carter Nute reported aboard to become the squadron's executive officer, its second in command, replacing Cressy. At the change of command ceremony that marked her husband's departure, Paula Powers was unexpectedly called to the dais to receive an award from Admiral Pringle for her services to the squadron and its families during the trial. For a moment, memories from October and November came flooding back and she thought about refusing it, but she did not.

Crew 6 was reconstituted around its tacco, Matt Gibbons. Renumbered and renamed as "Lethal Eleven" (for its presumed sub-hunting skills), on its 1979 deployment to the western Pacific the crew would participate in life-saving operations for boat people fleeing Vietnam, belying its moniker.[2]

Ed Caylor, who took over Crew 7 in December, filed for divorce from his wife in January. Out of earshot of the news media, she had greeted his return from the USSR two months earlier with the stunning complaint that its timing had conflicted with her exam schedule at school. But that frigid welcome was not the reason for the break; it was Barbara's suspected drug abuse that had alienated and impoverished him. Their marriage, solemnized by the same Chaplain Dick McCue who had presided at the 2 November memorial services for Grigsby and Miller, lasted barely three years.

Some things, however, had not changed; they were irreversible. The Grigsbys (Loreen and her two daughters) and the Millers (Karen, her two daughters, and her son) were without a husband and father. Phyllis Davis, Paul and Delores Rodriguez, and Guillermo Garcia and Frances Laly all continued to mourn the sudden loss of their young sons.

With memorial services done, accident reports moving up the chain of command, and a new commanding officer in place, Patrol Squadron 9 got on with what it had to do.

On 2 April, the survivors of old Crew 6 flew to Eielson AFB in Fairbanks for a three-day "rescue seminar" hosted by the 24th SRS. In company with Carter's and Feldkamp's crews, they toured each other's aircraft, drank and talked about the rescue, and, in sober moments, pondered their mortality in a way unfamiliar to most young men. For the unique occasion, Det. 1, on Shemya, was reduced to a single alert aircraft and crew, freeing Carter and Feldkamp to join in the celebration of life.

Later in April, three months before the Misawa Air Base deployment began, a squadron liaison team flew west to introduce the Golden Eagles to their new operational boss, Commo. Jerry MacKay.[3] MacKay, the commander of Task Force 72, the Seventh Fleet's patrol and reconnaissance force, had his headquarters at Kami Seya, Japan, near Atsugi.

Jerry MacKay's command included deployed squadrons at Misawa and Naha, Japan, and Cubi Point in the Philippines. These three supported occasional detachments throughout the Western Pacific and on faraway Diego Garcia in the Indian Ocean. Diego Garcia, in turn, ran an aircraft in and out of Bandar Abbas, Iran, for surveillance of the North Arabian Sea and support of the aircraft carrier battle group often on "Camel Station," the wryly named counterpart to the "Yankee" and "Dixie" carrier stations of the air war in Vietnam.

MacKay, a trim native Canadian with watery blue eyes, was known for his brusque, no-nonsense approach to business. The visiting team must have expected a crisp hello and a quick pass to the chief of staff. Even so, his curt greeting was a shock. MacKay told Cressy that the squadron's reputation had preceded it.

He did not want it working for him in the western Pacific. True to form, Cressy quickly replied that Patrol Squadron 9 would perform better than any squadron MacKay had ever seen.

The commodore's cold welcome did not change the schedule. Absent a catastrophe, the carefully pieced together calendar for twelve squadrons was not going to be disrupted by MacKay's doubts about the next one heading west to join him. It put Patrol Squadron 9 on notice, however. More than most, the Golden Eagles would have to prove themselves.

Just before the squadron took off for Japan, Buno. 159892, lost at sea, was finally replaced by another aircraft, Buno. 159505, bringing the squadron back up to its complement of nine aircraft. During the first few days of July 1979, Patrol Squadron 9's aircraft began the two-day trip from Moffett Field to the Air Force base at Misawa, Japan, where the full squadron—approximately 350 officers and men, twelve crews, and nine aircraft—would be deployed for the next six months. They would stay in Misawa through its predictably heavy winter snows and return home in early January 1980.

Squadron flight crews crossing the Pacific staged through the Midway Islands, at the far western end of the Hawaiian island chain, fully eleven hundred miles from Pearl Harbor. Naval Air Facility Midway, the scene of the American triumph in June 1942, included three small islets. The largest was Sand Island, half the size of Shemya and only thirteen feet above the Pacific at its highest point. Eastern, the second largest, was just big enough for an abandoned World War II airfield. Between them lay tiny Spit Island, a punctuation point expressed as dry land, too small for any use. The three were embraced by a single, roughly circular coral reef. They lay, almost touching, in the southern half of the reef's small lagoon, somnolent in the hot sun.

A landing approach in a P-3 to Sand Island's runway on a moonless night—faint lights outlining a slender rectangle afloat in stygian darkness, nothing to give you scale or perspective—was like descending into an astronomical black hole, like ditching with your landing gear down.

Midway was more than just a stepping stone across the world's largest ocean. It also secretly hosted the terminus of the Navy's mid-Pacific SOSUS acoustic arrays. The Navy's austere establishment on Midway gingerly shared its space with the island's dominant life-form, the blue- and black-footed gooney birds that nested in huge numbers everywhere during the breeding season. At the right time of year, the birds' unique mating ritual, a percussive clacking of big beaks that sounded like a crazed flamenco dancer's castanets followed by an almost bovine exhalation, could be heard everywhere above the sound of the surf. Months later, sharks would fill the lagoon, snacking enthusiastically on the young albatross fledglings who spun in while learning how to fly.[4]

Sand Island was too compact and its ecology too delicate for cars. The residents rode bicycles, styled "horses," exclusively, navigating carefully around the gooney bird nests spaced a few feet apart, on their way from place to place.

Inevitably and rightly, the place had the look and feel of a leftover from an old war, a tropical backwater covered with guano. Patrol aircrews were glad to land there, and then glad to refuel and leave.

Caylor took Crew 7, now his crew, over, with John Branchflower in the right seat as copilot. Moffett to Midway was nine hours. Out of Midway, it was another eight or so flight hours to Japan. Over the course of several days in July, everything the squadron owned would be flown fifty-eight hundred nautical miles to Aomori Prefecture, Japan, at the north end of Honshu, either in its own aircraft or in a Military Airlift Command transport. (The return flow would bring Patrol Squadron 47 back to California after six months in the western Pacific.) If the move were done correctly, the exchange of squadrons would be seamless. The Golden Eagles would be flying their first operational patrols out of their new home even as some squadron gear was still being unpacked and stowed.

Patrol Squadron 9's first aircraft arrived in Japan about the time that the Pacific Fleet commander finished reviewing Lieutenant Commander Dvorak's report of his investigation into the loss of PD-2. The manual of the Navy judge advocate general prescribes a three-part format for formal investigations. The investigating officer is to report findings of fact, drawn from sworn testimony, to present his opinions based on these facts, and to make recommendations. Only after that is done is his work complete. Dvorak finished his investigation on 12 December and delivered his report to Bud Powers the same day. Beginning then, and for many months to follow, the aircraft investigation moved slowly up the chain of command. At each stop, the reviewing officer would add his endorsement (comments on everything said before) and send it on.

No crewmember had survived to explain why LE-8 flew into a mountain on Hiero, why LJ-4 hit the water near the Azores, or why LC-7 came apart in the air over western Maine. There was no last-minute radio transmission from any of these aircraft that hinted at what might have gone wrong during the final minutes of flight, and nothing was later found at any site that led investigators toward a definitive conclusion. No cockpit recorders to reveal anything said or audible in the cockpit and any flight or engine parameters during the last moments leading up to impact. None of the questions that accident investigators asked themselves, while they pondered the sudden and mysterious loss of aircraft, had any obvious answers.

PD-2 was different. Most of the crew had survived, including two of three pilots and one of the two flight engineers. Their testimony, coupled with the observations of the other five living crewmembers, made it possible to assemble an answer to the fundamental question—what had happened—even though the two key players were gone.

Jim Dvorak first focused his investigation on the cause of the overspeed. He had a logical place to begin his inquiry: it was almost certain that loss of hydraulic fluid had led to loss of control of the prop, and just two weeks before PD-2 went to Adak, its no. 1 and 2 propeller controls had been filled with

MIL-H-83282 fluid during routine servicing. Because the new hydraulic fluid had been put into the no. 1 prop so recently, the fluid itself became the subject of intense scrutiny. Perhaps, by attacking internal seals or otherwise, it had caused leaks that led to the loss of control.

MIL-H-83282 was quickly exonerated by the investigation. Even though the new fluid was known to have a slightly more powerful detergent action than the old (which resulted in a "de-sludging" action that could contaminate filters), there was no evidence that fluid properties had caused the failure.

With 159892 sunk in twenty-four hundred fathoms of salt water, obviously no inspection of the assembly was possible, but Hamilton Standard representatives concluded, based on statements from Ed Caylor, John Wagner, and Ed Flow, and their own knowledge of the system, that there were four possible causes for the initial prop malfunction.

First, a "ring" seal could have failed, allowing fluid to leak *out* of the prop. The fact that certain cockpit warning lights did not illuminate undercut that hypothesis. Second, certain other seals could have failed, resulting in a fluid leak and loss of pressure *inside* of the prop. The sudden loss of control was inconsistent with this hypothesis, however. Third, some foreign object could have found its way into the prop during overhaul, and that object could have damaged a seal, leading to an internal leak. Finally, and, based on symptoms and historic experience, most likely in the eyes of the manufacturer's experts, the soft metal bearing (called the "Babbit transfer bearing") that supported the prop shaft could have peeled apart under high pressure, leading to a massive internal leak. This would have resulted in a quick loss of control fluid, followed by an overspeed as centrifugal twisting moment spun the blades flat toward high rpm.

Their conclusion was that the prior failure of one or more adjacent neoprene O-ring seals—penny parts in a quarter-million-dollar prop—set the stage for failure of the bearing. The problem was not entirely new. Other prop controls had failed this way before, although no other failures had resulted in the loss of an aircraft. The solution was smaller-diameter O-rings. Approved parts were already in the Navy's logistic pipeline.

Bud Powers lost his battle with Charlie Prindle for an immediate, fleet-wide program to change the suspect O-ring seals. Such a program would have required cycling nearly one thousand gearboxes through overhaul facilities in California and Florida. The Naval Air Systems Command's "urgent" program to make the change was not finished until December 1980, more than two years after PD-2 went down. Prindle's gamble—that is what it was—paid off. No other P-3 was lost for this reason before his slower remedial program was finished.[5]

But why had a prop overspeed forced a ditching?

The fact that the prescribed emergency procedure had not been fully executed, against the backdrop of all the other data Lt. Cdr. Jim Dvorak had compiled during the six weeks he studied the loss of AF 586, led to his unambiguous conclusion, presented as "Opinion 7." In clear and unemotional language,

Dvorak said that his contemporary, Jerry Grigsby, had made a fatal error: "The ultimate cause of the ditch was catastrophic failure of the reduction gearbox, which resulted in multiple engine fires and eventually became uncontrollable, and extreme vibrations of the No. 1 engine and propeller assembly. The failure of the gearbox was a direct result of the 'Propeller Fails-to-Feather' procedures not being completed, in that oil was not restored to the gearbox after engine shut-down utilizing the E-handle."

An internal failure in the propeller control had drained hydraulic pressure from the blade pitch change mechanism, permitting the overspeed. The over-speed, alone, was survivable. The subsequent catastrophic failure of the gearbox was not, however, and that had happened because the gearbox was allowed to run dry. Dvorak opined that this pilot error—failure to restore lubricating oil—committed just minutes after no. 1 was restarted, had doomed AF 586 and cost Grigsby and four others their lives. "The judgment decision not to restore oil to the reduction gearbox after the fails to feather," he wrote, "must be considered the primary cause of the gearbox failure which resulted in the ditch."

In their separate, sequential reviews early in 1979 of the JAG investigation of the accident, Rear Admiral Prindle and Vice Adm. Robert Coogan, commander, Naval Air Force, U.S. Pacific Fleet, both focused on this fact. Both came to the same conclusion about the ditching. The cause was pilot error, a failure to com-plete the "prop fails-to-feather" emergency checklist.

Unlike Prindle, a maritime patrol pilot who had both administrative and operational roles in the Navy's bifurcated chain of command, Vice Admiral Coogan was neither a former patrol plane pilot nor an operator. He was responsi-ble for the support and efficient management of the Pacific Fleet's carriers, avia-tion squadrons, and air stations. It was left to the operational commanders to tell the ships and aircraft squadrons of the Pacific Fleet where to go and what to do when they got there. Coogan was in the loop because PD-2 "belonged" to him. He, or more properly his command, was the custodian of the aircraft that was lost, and he would have to account for its removal from the Navy aircraft inventory.

Differences in perspective aside, Coogan's conclusion was essentially identi-cal to Prindle's: "Commander Naval Air Force, U.S. Pacific Fleet specifically con-curs . . . that the gear box failure was a direct result of the plane commander's fail-ure to follow the prescribed 'fails-to-feather' procedure. Had the oil tank shut off valve circuit breaker been deactivated by re-inserting the E-handle and pulling the circuit breaker immediately after engine shutdown, the aircraft would only have been subjected to a three engine ferry operation to Shemya with a wind-milling pitch-locked propeller."

The manufacturers' technical representatives thought so, too. If Grigsby had enough fuel, one of them told Dvorak in November, he could have flown his air-craft all the way to Moffett Field on three engines in the condition it was in.

Others were not so sure.

Ed Caylor—who saw from the right seat that nothing Grigsby, Flow, and he had done in the cockpit during 90 minutes of troubleshooting and emergency procedures seemed to work—suspected years later that, with the oil tank valve open, the windmilling prop would have "scavenged," mechanically sucked, the remaining six or seven gallons of lubricating oil out of the tank eventually. If so, that would have simply delayed the first of the nacelle fires that eventually would push AF 586 into the water. Others he had consulted in the years since the accident thought so, too.

Later versions of the flight manual would seem to lend some support to that view. Pilots and flight engineers are now warned, when operating with a pitch-locked propeller, "Extended operation with a decoupled windmilling propeller after an unsuccessful attempt to feather will ultimately result in oil depletion for that engine and reduction gearbox. . . . Failure of the reduction gearbox due to oil starvation can result in a fire and/or propeller separation from the aircraft."

If Caylor and his confidants were right, with the circuit breaker reset and oil flowing to the gearbox, PD-2 might have flown gamely on until far away from *Sinyavin* or any other rescue vessel and then, well short of land, gone into the water to its fate. In the vacant seas near Attu, the crew's only hope for survival would have been CGC *Jarvis*. In view of the weather, *Jarvis* would still not have made it to the rafts in time. It is probable that under this new scenario, PD-2 ditching Thursday late afternoon and 100–150 miles farther east, everyone in the rafts (perhaps excepting Gibbons) would have died of exposure waiting for the cutter to appear.

At the end, Crew 6's survival came down to several things.

First, the glacial coolness of the crew in the tube. Reflecting Matt Gibbons's leadership, the young tactical crew remained tightly disciplined throughout the protracted emergency, systematically dealing with mission security and then turning to preparing for their own survival. Their professionalism swept their two passengers, one of whom had no aviation experience, along with it. When PD-2 hit the water and the lights went out, every man aboard moved quickly to execute his responsibilities. Despite the astonishing speed with which the aircraft sank, no one alive failed to escape.

Second, there was the structural integrity of PD-2 when forward motion on the surface of the sea stopped. This depended almost entirely on Jerry Grigsby's skill as an aviator. If he had misread the swells or mishandled the splashdown, PD-2 would have shattered on water entry and sunk immediately (as did JB 022, off Cubi Point), drowning everyone who had managed to survive the impact. Grigsby's skill made the ditching survivable. His expertise in "water landings" gave them all a minute, or two or three, to escape the sinking aircraft.

Nevertheless, the investigation disclosed that six areas on the aircraft, which could have been expected to remain intact, failed on impact, threatening the lives of Forshay, Hemmer, and Reynolds. (The circumstances and cause of Miller's death remained a mystery. Some thought he had been crushed by the galley refrigerator, torn free from its attachment to the deck.) On 16 November, even before Dvorak had completed his investigation, Lockheed submitted a proposal to the Navy for "Structural Improvements to Increase Ditching Capability."[6] The approved program focused on strengthening interior galley and lavatory fittings in the aft fuselage, where Miller had died and Ball and Reynolds had nearly been trapped in the sinking aircraft.

Third, the successful launch of the life rafts played a part in the crew's survival. PD-2 went down so quickly that the crew was hard-pressed to get out of the aircraft alive before it sank. Of the survival equipment prescribed for ditching (three 2.5-gallon drinking-water breakers, two first aid kits, the emergency sonobuoy, and three rafts), only the minimum, essential gear was carried out of the emergency hatches: two of the three rafts. Conditions in the Mark-7 almost certainly resulted in the early deaths of the three sensor operators. Had Reynolds, Garcia, and Rodriguez been in the marginally better protected Mark-12, instead of the swamped Mark-7, it is possible the three would have been picked up alive by *Sinyavin*.

And finally, there was the timely arrival of a rescue vessel. As soon as each man stepped through an overwing escape hatch and jumped into the water, a clock began to tick. Under the conditions off Shemya, anyone not in a raft after several hours would almost certainly be dead of exposure. In a raft, thanks to its protection and the enveloping QD-1 suits, survival time was extended to between ten and eighteen to twenty-four hours, with those in the Mark-12 at the longer end of the scale.

Juneau, recognizing the urgency of getting a ship to the site, immediately interrogated the AMVER database for nearby candidates and directed Adak and Honolulu to transmit the usual urgent appeals for assistance over emergency frequencies. That unsuccessful effort went so far as to include a radio exchange with the chief of the Soviet Bering Sea Expedition, afloat in the trawler *Tajikistan,* seeking his help in communicating with naval auxiliary vessels thought to be in the area.[7] Success finally came with the State Department's appeal to the Foreign Ministry in Moscow, prompted by information from Scone 92.

Had *Sinyavin* been ten to fifteen miles closer to the SAR datum when she came about to head northeast, it is possible that all thirteen of the crew would have survived. Ten or fifteen miles farther away, perhaps only three of the four in the Mark-12 would have survived.

A chain of events made the survival of the ten possible, beginning with AF 586's success in finding the trawler and ditching fairly close aboard. The next link was CG 1500's appearance on station, which freed XF 675 to look for a surface ship. Then came Scone 92's call to Washington, reporting that a ship (*Sinyavin*) was only hours sailing time away from the rafts. Washington's plea for assistance and Moscow's quick agreement to divert ships for SAR followed. CG 1500's guidance saved *Sinyavin* from what could have been a long or even fruitless search for two small rafts under storm conditions. Finally, the courage and seamanship of *Sinyavin*'s small boat crew was the last link in the successful rescue.

Even a single failure in the chain of events would have cost the last ten crewmen their lives.

Epilogue

In October 1979, almost one year after Alfa Foxtrot 586 went down and just days ahead of a statute of limitations deadline, Loreen Grigsby joined Karen Miller and Guillermo Garcia in their lawsuits against Lockheed, Allison, and Hamilton Standard. A Redwood City, California, attorney, Philip Silvestri, filed the suits on behalf of Grigsby, Miller, Garcia, and the women's five children. Silvestri was a local lawyer, a graduate of the University of San Francisco and of the university's school of law.

From Redwood City, Moffett Field was just a short drive south on the Bayshore Freeway. During any one of the area's crystalline days and from almost any vantage point in the small city where Silvestri practiced, a keen eye could have seen Navy P-3s departing north from Moffett or, less commonly, landing south over San Francisco Bay, just by glancing up. The familiar turboprops would have stood out clearly from the swept-wing, jet transport traffic swarming around the busy civil airports at San Francisco, Oakland, and San José that surrounded the naval air station.

Two bereaved widows and five fatherless children. A father without his son. A front-page story of loss that everyone around the Bay still remembered. A recent history of five fatal P-3 crashes spanning more than half the globe, from the Canary Islands to the Philippines (the flaming disaster at Pago Pago was still six months in the future). Prosperous corporate defendants. The cases must have seemed naturals, even though the damages that could be awarded would be very small.

The law governing such cases was the Death on the High Seas Act (DOHSA), passed by Congress in 1920 to make it possible for sailors' immediate families to recover damages if their breadwinners died in international waters. Although DOHSA provided heirs with means of obtaining relief for lost support, it was hardly generous. In 1979, as it had in 1920, the law sharply limited claims to actual financial loss, that is, the future income of the wage earner. In the AF 586 suits, DOHSA's miserly arithmetic would begin with Grigsby's, Miller's, and Garcia's pay and allowances in October 1978 and calculate future earnings over the course of what would have been their normal working lives. The burden of proof, naturally, was on the families to present evidence of defects that caused the crash.

In response to Silvestri's filings, the corporate defendants would rely on the powerful "military contractors defense." This legal doctrine was based on the premise that military aircraft specifications should not be subject to legal review because the government may rightfully value combat efficiency more highly than safety and consequently approve designs that traded the latter for the former. The military contractors defense provided that the P-3's contractors would not be liable for design defects, if they could demonstrate that their government customer had provided precise specifications for the P-3, that the airplane conformed to these specifications, and that the Navy had been informed of any hazards in operating aircraft systems that otherwise might have been unknown to it.

That is how things stood through 1980 and into 1981, as the legal actions inched slowly forward while lawyers on both sides exchanged correspondence: one side looking to the slim comforts of the Death on the High Seas Act, the other brandishing the familiar military contractors defense.

It is difficult to predict the outcome had the lawsuits made it to federal district court, but executives at Hamilton Standard and United Technologies (Hamilton Standard's corporate parent) must have known that they were vulnerable. The loss of PD-2 was not an act of God. It began with a mechanical failure in the prop that had been experienced before and studied carefully enough to have resulted in redesign of a deficient part critically important to the control of propeller rpm.

Robert Masden and George Nesky, Hamilton Standard's technical representatives, had not given Jim Dvorak a sworn statement about the likely nature of the failure inside of AF 586's no. 1 nacelle, but they had spoken candidly to him. The rapid loss of prop control and the resulting overspeed were symptomatic, the two said, of the failure of the Babbit transfer bearing in the propeller control. Masden and Nesky believed that this bearing failure had caused PD-2's no. 1 prop overspeed. The failure, they had explained to Dvorak while he took careful notes, had "considerable historical precedent," meaning that it had happened a number of times in the past. So often, in fact, that a fix had been approved for use, the smaller diameter O-rings that Powers and Prindle had heatedly argued about months earlier.

Those new O-rings were not installed in PD-2.

Matt Gibbons had a complete copy of Jim Dvorak's investigation, which he had gotten as a "souvenir" from Pat Conway. Gibbons's copy included the full text of Masden's and Nesky's unsworn statement. (The heavily edited version of the investigation the three contractors had was much less revealing and less damning.) Confronted unexpectedly with Gibbons's version during a deposition conference in late spring 1981, the defense yielded. Allison's counsel led the defendants to their decision to offer an out-of-court settlement.

But what DOHSA gave it also took away. The fact that AF 586 sank in international waters deprived the three families of an opportunity for financial recovery more representative of their losses. Together, they were able to collect only several hundred thousand dollars, a sum probably below the deductible in Hamilton Standard's liability insurance policy. An amount so trivial as not to warrant even a footnote in anyone's annual report.

Notes

Introduction

1. The value of Aleutian Islands real estate was appraised even more harshly centuries later, in the mid-1900s, when the United States first began planning to use the island of Amchitka as a site for nuclear-weapons testing. Underground tests were actually conducted on the island three times between 1965 and 1971. The last test, "Cannikin," on 6 November 1971, was a shot equal to five million tons of TNT and recorded 7.0 on the Richter scale. Cannikin was reportedly the largest underground nuclear weapons test in history. Amchitka would be used briefly in the early 1990s as the site for a Navy high-frequency, over-the-horizon radar.

2. Another native animal first described by Georg Steller, Steller's Sea Cow, was even less lucky. Fate was cruel to this defenseless, cold-water cousin of the manatee. Although the sea cow's hide had no special use, its thick subcutaneous fat tasted good, kept well, burned cleanly in oil lamps, and even had a medicinal purpose, as a laxative. In less than thirty years after expedition landfall, Steller's Sea Cows were extinct on Bering Island, their only habitat. Only use of the blubber as an aphrodisiac could have sped the slaughter any faster. Richard Ellis, *Aquagenesis* (New York: Viking, 2001).

   Americans entered the sea otter trade in 1787–90, when the ship *Columbia* loaded skins in the Pacific Northwest, took them to Canton, and then returned home to Boston, completing the first American circumnavigation of the globe. A voyage of nearly forty-two thousand miles in thirty-four months, aboard a vessel just eighty-three feet long. K. Jack Bauer, *A Maritime History of the United States* (Columbia: University of South Carolina Press, 1988). Sea otter skins were one of the few native American products (ginseng root was another) that found a ready market in China. In the next century, the skins would play a central role in the fabulous China trade. Robert A. Kilmarx, ed., *America's Maritime Legacy* (Boulder, Colo.: Westview Press, 1979).

3. Other Native American populations suffered the same experience. One century after contact with Europeans, aboriginal populations everywhere were only 10–15 percent of their original number. Imported disease was the principal cause of these demographic collapses. Nobel David Cook, *Born to Die* (Cambridge: Cambridge University Press, 1998).

4. The hasty, mismanaged American evacuation of the approximately nine hundred natives from the Pribiloffs and seven Aleutian villages in June and July 1942 caused great suffering. The removals were underway before resettlement sites—ultimately in abandoned, derelict camps and canneries in southeastern Alaska—were selected. In mid-September 1942, occupied Attu's few residents (fewer than fifty) were removed to Otaru, Japan as POWs. All returned three years later to villages pillaged by bored GIs. Dean Kohlhoff, *When the Wind Was a River: Aleut Evacuation in World War II* (Seattle: University of Washington Press, 1995).

Chapter 1. Crew Six

1. "I have been told by a native of this forsaken land," one temporary island resident wrote in the mid-1960s, that Adak "is gradually making progress in the general direction of the Arctic Circle due entirely to the unbelievable strength of the winds." Karl Beeman, quoted in James Bamford, *Body of Secrets* (New York: Doubleday, 2001). Beeman, an NSA employee, got lost on the island during a hike alone. Searchers found his body days later.
2. "AK 262" identified the second flight out of Adak (AK) on the twenty-sixth day of the month.
3. For a history of the early PARPRO program, see William E. Burrows, *By Any Means Necessary* (New York: Farrar, Straus & Giroux, 2001).
4. And unscripted incidents (such as the EP-3 midair collision with a Chinese fighter off the coast of Hainan in 2001), which could seriously upset international relations, were always possible.
5. The P-2 Neptune, the P-3's land-based predecessor, suffered from a similar middle-age weight gain. Most airplanes do. That problem was solved in the P-2E and later models with the addition of small Westinghouse J-34 auxiliary jet engines. Thereafter, four-engine flight in the P-2 was described as with "two turnin' and two burnin'." The J-34s devoured fuel and were normally used for take off and landing only. The J-34 was Westinghouse's only successful turbojet engine.
6. The first two P-6Ms, serial numbers 138821 and 138822, were destroyed in crashes in 1955 and 1956, respectively. Bits and pieces of a P-6 are displayed at the Glenn L. Martin Aviation Museum, Middle River, Maryland. No complete aircraft is exhibited anywhere. An intact P-5M, No. 135533, is on display at the National Naval Aviation Museum, in Pensacola, Florida.
7. USS *Macon* was the last of the Navy's large, rigid airships, after USS *Shenandoah*, USS *Los Angeles*, and USS *Akron*. (Another big ship, the unnamed ZR-2, exploded in 1921 during trials in England, where it had been built under Navy contract.) The *Macon* was put into service in 1931 and crashed into the Pacific off Point Sur, California, in 1935. Two other ships had been lost under similar circumstances in violent weather: *Shenandoah* in 1925 over Ohio and *Akron* in 1933 off New Jersey. The German-built *Los Angeles* managed to stay in the air and remain in service for eight years, amassing more than four thousand flight hours, before it was decommissioned. None of the others logged more than eighteen hundred hours. Rear Adm. William Moffett, the Navy's senior airship advocate, was among the seventy-three who died in the *Akron* disaster, likely of hypothermia in the cold waters off Barnegat Bay, New Jersey. He gave his name to Moffett Field and to

Mount Moffett on Adak. D. H. Robinson and C. L. Keller, *Up Ship* (Annapolis: Naval Institute Press, 1982).

Navy airships suffered from delicacy in bad weather and from a lack of enthusiasm in senior officer circles, but their real problem was poor timing. The C&O Canal, the Pony Express, and commercial turboprop transport aircraft went into service just as a much better technology appeared on the horizon: the B&O Railroad, the Western Union telegraph, and the Boeing 707. So did airships. In their case, the superior technology was fixed wing aircraft in general and two maritime patrol seaplanes in particular, PBY Catalinas and PBM Mariners.

8. Progress through the ranks was so slow that the Royal Navy forbad duels between officers of different ranks, fearing that deliberately provoking an encounter with a senior could become a promotion strategy for an impatient and reckless junior officer. James E. Valle, *Rocks and Shoals* (Annapolis: Naval Institute Press, 1980).

9. The nuclear-powered aircraft carrier, USS *Theodore Roosevelt,* would steam in the Arabian Sea in late 2001, launching combat missions day and night against the Taliban in Afghanistan with a crew whose median age was nineteen. "Out of High School and into a Combat Zone," Carol Morello, *Washington Post,* 6 December 2001. The *Roosevelt* would spend 160 consecutive days at sea during the cruise, a Navy record.

10. The Navy could not recruit enough naval flight officers to fill nonpilot aircrew officer requirements until their career path included the opportunity to compete for squadron command and subsequent promotion. Such an opportunity, naturally, came at the expense of pilots. The first NFO took command of a maritime patrol squadron in the early 1970s, Patrol Squadron 5, in Jacksonville, Florida.

11. Crypto hardware captured in the fall of Vietnam likely followed the same route. So rich and sensitive was this new information (and that flowing from rooftop listening stations in Washington and New York City and on Long Island) that in 1968 the KGB established a new directorate, the sixteenth, dedicated to signals intelligence. Christopher Andrew and Vasili Mitrokhin, *The Sword and the Shield* (New York: Basic Books, 1999).

12. If true, this was not the first time that military intelligence would be misused in Moscow. Stalin ignored clear proof from many sources of the Germans' plans to invade the Soviet Union in June 1941. Reportedly Soviet intelligence services during World War II made little use of the information they were receiving from Kim Philby and the other spies of "the Magnificent Five" because of rivalry and suspicion. Miranda Carter, *Anthony Blunt* (New York: Farrar, Straus & Giroux, 2001).

Chapter 2. Papa Delta Two

1. P-3s had a planned 29.5 year service life. In January 1987, the Navy issued a request for proposals to industry for a P-3C derivative, the P-3G (later P-7), to replace its aging fleet of -Bs and -Cs. The new program had its start as LRAACA, the long-range air antisubmarine warfare capable aircraft (an acronym pronounced as a hawking sound, deep in the throat). Lockheed was selected in October 1988 as the winner of an expanded competition; one that eventually had also considered modified commercial transport aircraft from Boeing and McDonnell Douglas. A contract for 125 P-7 aircraft—$58 million each—was signed with Lockheed in January 1989 but terminated in 1990 because of

cost overruns and schedule delays, leaving the P-3 in front-line service. Life extension programs have since extended the P-3's life to about 2007.

The new replacement aircraft program for the evergreen P-3 is called Multi-mission Maritime Aircraft. Boeing, Lockheed Martin, Raytheon, Northrup Grumman, Gulfstream, and the UK's BAE Systems have expressed interest. Lockheed Martin executives in Marietta, Georgia, with nothing to propose but a modernized P-3 are fearful that the Navy will inevitably be drawn to a newer turbojet airframe. Such a decision would end seven decades during which their company dominated the global market for land-based maritime patrol aircraft, and an era that began in 1941, when the Navy bought the first twenty PBO-1 Hudson coastal patrol aircraft, derivatives of Lockheed's Model 14 Super Electra airliner. Unless program funds are accelerated, under the current schedule the first squadrons of MMAs will not get to the fleet until several years after the P-3 inventory first falls below operational requirements.

2. The Comet's introduction into service was no less scarred than would be the Electra's a few years later. Three early Comets suffered catastrophic structural failures in 1953 and 1954 with passengers aboard. Their fuselages had survived only a few thousand flight hours at the cabin pressurization levels required for high-altitude cruise. The losses grounded the world's first commercial jet aircraft. When a redesigned and smaller Comet 4 finally went into service in 1958, the new Boeing 707 trampled it. Only sixty-nine Comet 4s were built. *Smithsonian,* June 2002. Comet accident reports are quoted on the web at http://surf.to/comet. The Nimrod's manufacturer reportedly intends to propose the MRA4 version of its aircraft to the U.S. Navy as a P-3 replacement in the MMA program.

3. Overload operations could be conducted up to the aircraft's maximum structural takeoff weight limit of 139,760 pounds.

Chapter 3. On Station

1. *Arctic Rose* was built as a Gulf of Mexico shrimper and later modified to fish in Alaskan waters. Many think the ship was too small for the job. On the night it was lost, the crew was fishing for flathead sole. Only the body of the ship's captain, David Rundall, was found at the time. An expert witness opined during one Coast Guard hearing that the ship had sunk in "chaotic" seas with waves as high as twenty-one feet. The Coast Guard found the wreckage of the *Arctic Rose* in mid–July, fifteen weeks after it had disappeared, on the Bering Sea floor two hundred miles northwest of St. Paul Island. The mystery of the cause of the sinking was heightened by the discovery that *Arctic Rose* was sitting almost upright on the sea floor, 428 feet down, suggesting that the ship had not capsized prior to suddenly going down. Extensive reporting on the incident is in the online archive of the *Seattle Times,* at www.archives.seattletimes.nwsource.com.

2. See Patrick Dillon, *Lost at Sea* (New York: Dial, 1998). A gripping story told wonderfully well.

3. "Jezebel" might have been named after the powerful, pagan queen of Israel in the Old Testament. The origins of the nickname are obscure. Not so for a companion ASW system, "Julie," used for explosive echo ranging until active sonar buoys supplanted the complex tactic. Julie was named after an exotic dancer at Washington's Bayou Club in

the 1950s, whose obvious charms were said to make "passive boys (buoys) active." Julie was a tactical dead end; Jezebel was not.

4. The Liberian tanker would turn out to be MV *Mikasa*. Looking for help later that afternoon, the U.S. Coast Guard would raise *Mikasa* on the radio. In response, the ship would report its position (52°30' N, 172°30' W), and continue heading west-southwest for Pohang, South Korea, at a reported 13.5 knots. The position, four degrees *east* of Adak, was an obvious error.

5. The full story, as told by the pilot, is in Jeff Harrison, "They Said It Would Never Happen," *Foundation Magazine,* Spring 1997, 15–20.

Chapter 4. Emergency

1. FNGs stood for Fuckin' New Guys. The acronym was meant to be descriptive, not critical. The all-purpose F-word lent no particular meaning to the phrase. FNGs were sometimes, less profanely, also called "nuggets." Unless otherwise annotated, all times are Adak local time, one hour later than local time at the ditching coordinates.

2. Even midsummer serves up challenging flying weather on Shemya. July averages twenty-seven days during which the ceiling is two hundred feet or below and visibility is half a mile or less. Denizens boasted that Shemya's fog was thick enough to cut into slabs and mail off island as a souvenir.

3. The EP-3's diversion to Hainan—instead of ditching—after a midair with a Chinese F-8 fighter on 1 April 2001 says less about the two crews than about how the world had changed in twenty-three years. The crew flew home from China after eleven days. Their EP-3, PR-32 (Buno. 156511), was dismantled by Lockheed Martin engineers on site in June, and finally returned in pieces to Marietta, Georgia, aboard a chartered, Russian-built Antonov 124 transport that left Hainan for Dobbins AFB on 3 July 2001.

4. The Naval Air Systems Command, then in Arlington, Virginia, and now in Lexington Park, Maryland, wrote the procurement specification for the suit and established QD-1 inspection and maintenance procedures.

5. Radio transmissions are quoted verbatim from contemporary audiotapes. In some cases call signs and repetition have been removed to improve readability.

6. "Five by five" means loud and clear.

7. "Mayday" (probably from the French *m'aidez,* "help me") signaled to any listener that the aircraft was in grave and imminent danger of loss of life and needed immediate assistance.

8. On 1 and 2 December 1941, Tokyo instructed certain important diplomatic and consular posts, including the embassy in Washington, to destroy "purple" encryption machines and most of their codes and ciphers, and to burn other important classified documents. The Navy staff in Washington informed commanders in the Pacific of these intercepts the next day, rightly understood to be revealing of a crisis in relations, and coupled the news with instructions to U.S. Navy facilities in Japan, China, and Guam, to do the same with their own codes.

9. Reflecting its more advanced technology, Cobra Ball's crypto holdings were even more modest than those of the P-3s. A single, programmable board slotted into the Ball's KG-35 crypto unit provided on-line encryption for all communications leaving the aircraft.

10. "Charlie" means correct, affirmative. From Morse code practice, where the single letter
    C signified confirmation.
11. In February 1979, after interviewing Caylor and Flow personally, the wing commander
    reported his conclusion that "the combination of [the fourth] fire, increased propeller
    wobble, increased aircraft control difficulties, and the sighting of a ship in the immedi-
    ate vicinity caused the plane commander to ditch the aircraft when and where he did."
    All other reports say the fourth fire blew itself out almost immediately, before AF 586 hit
    the water.

    Ten years earlier, on 1 April 1968, Patrol Squadron 26's Crew 1 was flying in Buno.
    153445 over the Gulf of Siam, not far from Phu Quoc Island on an Operation Market
    Time surface surveillance mission. They were part of the around-the-clock search for
    infiltrators trying to sneak arms and men into South Vietnam. They overflew a Cambo-
    dian Navy LCM, a former U.S. Navy World War II medium landing craft now in Khmer
    hands by way of the French, and it fired on them. The LCM's .50-caliber machine-gun
    rounds, slugs as big as your thumb and moving at nearly three thousand feet per second,
    took out the P-3B's no. 4 engine, holed the wing, and started a fire.

    Flying too low to bail out, Lt. (jg) Stu McLellan, the backup plane commander on
    the commanding officer's crew, headed his airplane for Phu Quoc and the thirty-five-
    hundred-foot runway he knew was near An Toi, off the island's southern tip, while he
    thought about ditching. Approaching the runway five or six minutes later, McLellan
    rolled into a left 270-degree turn and made it through 180 degrees before—no more
    than a minute away from touchdown—the starboard wing burned through and the air-
    plane fell into the gulf, immediately killing its crew of twelve. McLellan's aircraft was the
    second Patrol Squadron 26 had lost out of Utapao, Thailand, in two months. The cause
    of the first loss, Crew 8 in Buno. 153440 on 6 February, was never conclusively estab-
    lished, but it is possible it was also shot down, perhaps by the same Cambodian LCM. I
    am indebted to Scott Wilson, Patrol Squadron 26's Crew 12 plane commander, for this
    information. Wilson's crew found the wreckage of Crew 8's aircraft the same day and
    was relieved on station by the luckless Crew 1 two months later, hours before they were
    shot down. (Jerry Grigsby's intuition was better than Stu McLellan's; he had put his air-
    craft into the water just before its wing came off. At the survivors' 4 November press con-
    ference, Ed Caylor told media representatives that he thought Grigsby ditched PD-2 just
    thirty seconds before they lost control.) During the same few months in 1968, three
    highly modified OP-2 Neptunes based at Nakom Phanom, Thailand, and belonging to
    Navy Observation Squadron 67, were shot down while dropping sensors from low alti-
    tude on the Ho Chi Minh Trail, taking most of their three crews with them.

Chapter 5. Ditching

1. A lengthy "ditching bibliography" is at www.equipped.com/ditchbib.htm. Its focus,
   however, is on general aviation and commercial transport aircraft.
2. The valve, located aft beneath the floorboards on the port side, normally cycles automatically to maintain cabin pressurization as required. Closing it would prevent seawater from flooding into the opening after touchdown, presumably slowing the rate at
   which an otherwise intact fuselage would fill and sink.

3. Sea states are described as States 1 (mirror calm) through 9 (sea white with driving spray, waves greater than eighty feet).

4. If Grigsby really did fly at several knots below stall speed, as Caylor later remembered, their final approach to the water would have been at approximately 100 knots, and impact at around 60 knots, or 69 miles per hour. AF 586's stall speed at the time would have been 106 knots.

5. Estimates of water depth vary enormously. At this point, Gibbons says eighteen inches deep, to the bottoms of the crew seats, and Forshay says knee-high, two feet. All ten accounts agree that the aircraft filled very rapidly and during the latter stages of the escape, the overwing hatches were underwater, requiring the remaining crewmembers to swim out to the surface. Even before then, the rolling of the aircraft had alternately submerged and exposed the hatches.

6. Howard Moore's account is drawn entirely from memory; he was never interviewed for the record during Lt. Cdr. Jim Dvorak's fact-finding investigation.

7. One AN/PRT-5 emergency radio was in each raft's survival kit, but this is a beacon, too, transmitting a constant emergency signal on 243.0 MHz and 8,364 KHz. The PRT-5 cannot transmit voice and has no receiver.

8. Ball and Moore would later fly out of Naval Station Keflavik, Iceland, together, during the squadron's 1980 deployment to the Atlantic Fleet. Their Crew 4 would wear Cub Scout hats and "Den 4" patches sewn on their shoulders, and warm clothes under their flight suits.

9. Shepard's and Hemmer's ditching stations assigned both men to the Mark-12 raft.

10. It was gone during the Adak deployment, leaving only a moustache behind.

Chapter 6. Search

1. On his second look around the Mark-7, Ed Caylor decided that Gary Hemmer, the only "ground pounder" aboard the aircraft, was in the worst shape of the nine in the raft. Caylor was probably correct. Hemmer would have never passed a flight physical. Among other things, he was on a prescription for three hundred milligrams a day of Phenytoin, an anticonvulsant. Attempts to pass this medical information to *Mys Sinyavin* by radio were evidently not successful. It is not clear if a relay attempt through the Soviet trawler *Tajikistan,* in the Bering Sea, succeeded. A consular officer from Embassy Moscow finally delivered the medicine to Hemmer in Khabarovsk. Gary Hemmer survived AF 586's ditching by nearly twenty years. He died 22 June 1998 in Denver, Colorado, five years after he retired from the Navy as a master chief petty officer with thirty years of service.

2. The FAA's current Technical Standard Order (TSO C70a) governing aircraft life rafts requires 3.6ft^2 per person of "usable sitting area" on deck. "Rubber Ducky III," the raft in which Steven Callahan survived almost eleven weeks alone in the Atlantic in 1982, was a circular Avon six-man raft, about five feet six inches in diameter. He judged it adequate only for two. Steven Callahan, *Adrift* (Boston: Houghton Mifflin, 1986).

3. Not all. Wagner remained dry in his.

4. The now nearly forgotten draft lottery affected different lives in different ways. Caylor's draft number was lower still, 26. It was not a factor in his decision to go to the Naval

Academy, but it was an incentive to keep his grades up. The year before Conway's birth date drew 32, William Jefferson Clinton's came up 311, and he promptly lost all interest in the ROTC at the University of Arkansas. David Halberstam, *War in a Time of Peace* (New York: Scribner's, 2001). Gibbons's lottery number was higher still, 324. He had stood no chance of being drafted.

5. Load complete, Crew 12 flew their practice torpedo drops on the weapons range Wednesday. There was no such range at Adak. They were off duty Thursday afternoon.

6. Cobra Ball missions actually carried two crews. The pilots and navigators in the front end of the RC-135S were one. The tactical commander, electronic warfare officers, and technicians in the back end were the other. The two were scheduled and deployed together. Like Crew 6 in AF 586, however, Scone 92's tactical crew was not a single unit. On 26 October, the men in the back of Scone 92 were drawn from six different 24th SRS flight crews.

7. Winkleman's first message actually said there was a P-3 "down" and gave latitude/longitude coordinates, which the flight crew took to be merely a traffic advisory about a friendly aircraft far to the south. When this message was clarified to be a report of a ditching, Carter and Feldkamp immediately terminated their mission and turned south, toward the ditch site, on their own initiative. Minutes later, at 3:22, Scone 92 received Winkleman's direction to do just that. Wayne Winklemann was in a high-visibility job. Its incumbents routinely were selected for promotion to colonel. His quick decision to abort an operational Cobra Ball mission for the SAR could have been criticized because there was already a Navy P-3 heading for the site, but it was not.

8. This time comes from the TSC log. The OPREP-3 message's date-time group is actually fourteen minutes later.

9. "Gibson girl" because of the radio's hourglass shape.

10. A heaving line might have saved Grigsby, but only if the raft could have supported another man. Years later, the Naval Air Systems Command's manual on survival equipment annotated its discussion of the Mark-7 life raft (then renamed "LRU-13") with the note that "newly procured LRU-13 liferaft assemblies will be configured with heaving line assemblies. Earlier configurations without heaving lines will be considered serviceable."

11. As soon as *Jarvis* left the fuel pier, the Kodiak-based buoy tender CGC *Ironwood* moved alongside to top off with diesel oil, in case it was also ordered to the SAR scene. The long trip west for the much smaller (180 feet) and slower (fourteen knots) *Ironwood* would have been futile and perhaps dangerous. Fortunately, it was not ordered to sea. The tough wooden ship was decommissioned in 2000, after fifty-seven years in service.

12. AMVER, is the Automated Vessel Reporting system. Sail plans, weather, or other reports filed by cooperating ships allow the U.S. Coast Guard to identify vessels near a ship or aircraft in distress, so they can be diverted to provide assistance. Participation is voluntary. In 1978, the system was managed at Governors Island, in New York Harbor, but run on a CDC 3300 mainframe computer located at the Transportation Computer Center, at Department of Transportation/Coast Guard headquarters, in Washington, D.C.

13. *Sinyavin* had not filed a sail plan with the Coast Guard (most Soviet vessels did not), so its position was not continuously updated by AMVER. *Sinyavin* appeared in the system's

"static plot" database only because it was reporting the weather. On the course (225°) and at the speed (eight knots) AMVER held for *Sinyavin,* its position at time of ditch would have been close enough to AF 586 for timely rescue, but someone would have had to manually update the old position to see that.

14. Between mid-December 1897 and late February 1898, then-Lieutenant Jarvis famously led a three-man relief expedition from the U.S. Revenue Cutter *Bear* overland on foot fifteen hundred miles, driving nearly 450 reindeer before them, food to save hundreds of whalers stranded in the Arctic near Point Barrow, Alaska. Six vessels were caught fast in the ice. Two other ships had also stranded their crews. Rescue of all finally came in August 1898. One assessment is that Jarvis's contribution was less the food than discipline, without which the motley band at Point Barrow would have disintegrated into rabble. John Bockstoce, *Whales, Ice and Men* (Seattle: University of Washington Press, 1986). See also "Report of the Cruise of U.S. Revenue-cutter Bear and the Overland Expedition for Relief of the Whalers in the Arctic Ocean," Treasury Department Doc. 2101 (Washington, D.C.: GPO, 1899).

15. Tony Tuliano, then a damage control man in the cutter's engineering department and riding below the waterline, remembers bone-rattling shudders and the seas shaking the cutter hard as it plowed through them toward the site.

16. All of the Ball's sensors and observation windows are on the starboard side of the aircraft.

17. The message was sent under the classified originator address of the Joint Chiefs of Staff chairman.

18. "Gaslight" is visual contact on the incandescent heat plume of a Soviet ICBM reentry vehicle.

19. Three weeks later, Capt. D. K. Cho, the new master of MV *Hanwoo,* would tell Juneau that his predecessor was fired ("dismissed from the mastership of *Hanwoo*") because of his failure to respond positively. Too late (for Cho's predecessor), it would be discovered that the ditching coordinates he had been passed were in error by five degrees of latitude, fully three hundred miles. Some of the crew wives, Shelly Wagner was one, were told Thursday night that a Korean vessel was on the way to rescue their husbands. They were deflated Friday morning when they found out this had not happened.

20. This is similar to the geometry of the Williamson Turn, known to sailors worldwide for its use in maneuvering a ship to come down the reciprocal of its current track, often used in searching for men overboard.

21. Mike Harris would later comment that continual requests from Yokota for information over the primary SAR radio frequency had been "detrimental to the effort." The Soviets would make a somewhat similar complaint on Sunday, 29 October, telling an American embassy officer, "The fact that U.S. aircraft were always on [*Sinyavin*'s] radio channel did not help communications between the ship and port."

22. When Petty Officer Horning went aft to act as drop master, Porter replaced him in the C-130 flight engineer's seat with one of the crew scanners, Seaman Dan Mallot. Young Mallot had never filled a cockpit seat before, so Porter kept the instructions simple. He pointed out the pilot's altimeter on the panel and told Mallot to tap him gently on the shoulder if the big hand went below two hundred feet.

23. On 21 March 1991, two Patrol Squadron 50 P-3s had a midair collision in a training area offshore San Diego, California. Twenty-seven died instantly in the collision of Bunos. 159325 and 158930.

24. A C-130 with H-3 helicopters was also available at Kadena AB on Okinawa, but the Kadena Rescue Coordination Center was understandably reluctant to launch its SAR team on what would have been a twenty-hour, fifteen-hundred-mile repositioning flight across the North Pacific.

25. As 65825 headed east toward the mainland, Adak's winds were twenty to thirty knots, with gusts nearly twice that strong. The aircraft would participate in later searches for Grigsby and Miller with a squadronmate, 65824. When the 71st Air Rescue and Recovery Squadron at Elmendorf finally closed its books on this mission on 29 October, squadron aircraft had flown thirteen sorties and almost fifty-six flight hours.

26. *Sinyavin* would be laid up in 1996, after twenty-five years at sea. Captain Arbuzov would then move ashore and become the director of fleet security for Pilenga, a Russian-Japanese fishing joint venture with offices in Yuzhno on Sakhalin Island.

27. Ron Price's statement has *Sinyavin* originally steaming 240°T, *away* from the site when XF 675 arrives overhead, however, the above account is consistent with the quoted contemporary description of events by A. Lavrov, chief of navigation safety and communications of the Far Eastern Fish Association. Moreover, Cliff Carter's hand-written log of the flight says that *Sinyavin* was already heading *for* the crash site "with all marker lights and search light [illuminated]" when XF 675 marked on top.

28. The story is told and this dialogue is taken from Bill Porter, "Manislov [*sic*], This Is Bill," *Alaska Magazine*, December 1979, online at http://www.upnavy.com/upg_mishap.html.

29. In early 1942, three U.S. Navy enlisted aircrew men survived thirty-four days in a raft in the Pacific, living on rainwater and very little else. Starting only with the contents of their pockets, by the thirty-third day they had lost even their clothing. Robert Trumbull, *The Raft* (New York: Henry Holt, 1942). Callahan began his eleven-week trial in Rubber Ducky III with only three pounds of food and eight pints of water. He lived on distilled water and sun-dried dorado jerky and lost one-third his weight.

    The large library of literature about survival at sea in temperate or tropical climates is not matched by a similar body of work about survival afloat on cold water. The explanation is found in the fact that one cannot survive as long in the cold. What can be endured for days or weeks on warm water cannot be survived even for hours in extreme cold. One classic tale of survival on the cold ocean is that of Sir Ernest Shackleton and the crew of the *Endurance*. On 24 April 1916, during his second Antarctic expedition and five months after his ship was destroyed by pack ice, Shackleton set sail with a crew of five in a small boat from near Elephant Island (in the South Shetlands group) to South Georgia Island, eight hundred miles away across the Scotia Sea. They were in the *James Caird*, the largest of *Endurance*'s three surviving boats and named after one of Shackleton's financial backers. The six would make the autumn crossing in a wooden boat that was not even thirty-three feet long and boasted just over two feet of freeboard. Granted *James Caird* was decked over, but only at both ends; it was uncovered amidships. In this small lifeboat, Shackleton's party would sail and row east for two weeks, successfully seeking help for the twenty-two men stranded on Elephant Island by the loss of *Endeavor* and for themselves. F. A. Worsley, *Shackleton's Boat Journey* (New York: Norton,

1977). Expedition photographs are in Frank Hurley, *South with Endurance: Shackleton's Antarctic Expedition, 1914–1917* (New York: Simon & Schuster, 2001).

30. Rascher was not among the twenty-three German doctors and medical administrators tried by the allies during December 1946–August 1947 for committing atrocities. This truly evil man—he had conducted terrible experiments in high-altitude physiology, also—escaped trial and execution, but not justice. Rascher and his wife had deceived Reichsfuehrer SS Heinrich Himmler into believing that she had given birth in her late forties to three children, later discovered to have been adopted kidnapees from orphanages. Himmler's revenge for the deception was to imprison the two in Dachau and Ravensbrueck, where both died. William Shirer, *The Rise and Fall of the Third Reich* (New York: Simon & Schuster, 1960). The availability of Rascher's database, in a document called "the Alexander Report," has raised profound ethical questions for researchers. ("The Treatment of Shock from Prolonged Exposure to Cold, Especially in Water," Leo T. Alexander, Major, M.C., AUS. Combined Intelligence Objectives Subcommittee, Item 24, July 1945.) For the most part, these have been answered by rejecting its use or general publication.

31. Temperature (thermo-) regulation is done by the hypothalamus, in the central core of the forebrain and atop the brain stem. In reaction to extreme cold, the hypothalamus initiates vasoconstriction, elevates the metabolic rate, and triggers shivering. It also helps regulate blood pressure and the rate and force of heartbeat. At around 29 degrees C, the hypothalamus can no longer regulate.

Chapter 7. Washington and Moscow

1. Shulman, an academic, served Secretary Cyrus Vance as a special advisor for Soviet Affairs, with the rank of ambassador, from 1977 to 1980. Not until the eighth message had passed between the State Department and the embassy was the aircraft correctly identified as belonging to the Navy.

2. In the 1950s, "CB" painted on the vertical stabilizer identified Patrol Squadron 9 aircraft.

3. This was the first of at least four such expressions of gratitude from the American side. Two others were sent by President Carter and Secretary of Defense Harold Brown to their counterparts, Brezhnev and Marshall D. F. Ustinov, after the successful completion of the humanitarian mission. Carter's message to Brezhnev mentioned his own navy service, implying a special understanding of the heroism of the Soviet rescue crew. The Coast Guard's 17th District commandant, Rear Adm. Robert Duin, also sent a telegram of thanks to Moscow.

Chapter 8. Rescue

1. By the 1970s, extended confinement in a small box had become a survival training cliché. USAF reconnaissance aircrewmen decades before the war in Vietnam were closed up in wall lockers at Forbes AFB for thirty-six hours, while their "captors" pounded on the outsides, screaming insults and orders.

2. Caylor and others could not get a winter jacket for the 1978 Adak detachment. They were not able to get one the next year, either, when Patrol Squadron 9 was deployed to

Misawa, Japan, and aircrews were regularly flying over the cold, Western Pacific Kuroshio and Oyashio currents. Shepard had one with him aboard AF 586 but did not wear it out the hatch. He thought that it would be too bulky beneath the QD-1 and survival and flotation vests.

3. The QD-1 suit mittens were not much better. The squadron's Rescue Report said of them, "The mittens provided little protection and easily filled with water and allowed no mobility."

4. *Izvestiya* indicated in a 31 October article datelined Vladivostok that three other sailors were also aboard the whaleboat, Y. Trofimov, R. Kilibayev, and V. Matveyev. None of the five in the small boat got any other recognition for their heroism. Soviet press coverage of the rescue was factual and restrained. In the capital, *Pravda, Sovyetskaya Rossiya,* and evening and morning TV news programs covered the story, also. On 7 November, *Pravda* published a mawkish commemorative poem by Yevgeny Yevtushenko, "attempting," in the embassy's words, "to extend the humanitarian aspect of the P-3 rescue to international affairs generally."

5. The shiver reflex seems to be shut off by a high level of calcium in cold muscle cells. Shivering stops at a loss of about 10 degrees F in core temperature. By this time, oxygen consumption has dropped to about 70 percent of normal, signaling a roughly proportional decline in metabolic rate.

6. Squadron Operations at Kodiak briefly explored the possibility of getting the airfield on the south end of Amchitka opened temporarily for CG 1500 (Porter would have to fly past the island on his way to Adak), but it proved to be impossible to get Amchitka's runway lights on in time.

7. The request was in the form of a joint Department of State–Department of Defense message.

8. They were all wearing the standard-issue "Jacket, Flying, Man's, Intermediate, Type G-1," the same type of jacket that Grigsby had put on that morning. Almost every crewmember in XF 675, CG 1500, and DF 704 was wearing a similar jacket.

9. Some at Moffett Field who knew "Inu" Shepard from his tour in Patrol Squadron 40 were especially concerned that he might be forced to reveal all he knew to the Russians. Shepard was thought to have a photographic memory, and believed to have remembered everything he had ever seen about U.S. Navy antisubmarine tactics, equipment, and intelligence during his long career.

10. A normal reaction to hypothermia is increased urine production, a signal that the kidneys are trying to cope with the body core fluid overload associated with constriction of blood vessels in arms and legs. The survivors in the Mark-12 resisted the urge to urinate, fearful that the waste water would carry precious body heat away with it.

11. P-3s now carry a neoprene "quick donning anti-exposure coverall" in place of the old QD-1. Used together with cold weather underwear, an insulated coverall, and a life vest, the resulting new CWU-62P "apparel assembly" is designed to provide flotation without a raft and at least six hours protection from hypothermia, the old specification. Mittens and gloves are attached to the ends of the suit's sleeves, and the hood is stored in a thigh pocket.

12. The concept and the quotation come from Sheldon Watts, *Epidemics and History* (New Haven, Conn.: Yale University Press, 1997). The opposite view is in Mike Dash, *Batavia's*

Graveyard (New York: Crown, 2002). "Studies of shipwreck survivors have shown," Dash writes (in connection with the grounding in 1629 of the Dutch East Indiaman *Batavia* on Morning Reef, off western Australia), "that men who do have hope outlive those who may be physically as strong or stronger but give way to despair. A stubborn determination to make land, perhaps see a wife or family again, has helped many sailors survive long periods in open boats."

13. The importance of "the will to live" is a very durable idea. In the mid-1990s for example, TWA's B-747 flight handbook was instructing its international flight crews "the most important requirement in survival is mental attitude, the will to live." The handbook then went on to concede that "exposure to the elements is the greatest problem in survival."

14. Gary Hemmer reported that he thought the Mark-7 sank while the *Sinyavin*'s boat crew was trying to bring it aboard. The others believed it was brought aboard with them, but they were mistaken. Neither raft was available for inspection as part of the investigation. In 2001, Arbuzov sounded apologetic that conditions had prevented them from recovering the rafts.

15. See Peter Stark, "As Freezing Persons Recollect the Snow . . . the Cold Hard Facts of Freezing to Death," *Outside Magazine,* January 1997, online at http://www.outsidemag.com/magazine/0197/9701fefreez.html, for a description of the process on land. Also included in Peter Stark, *Last Breath, Cautionary Tales from the Limits of Human Endurance* (New York: Ballantine, 2001). See also www.sarbc.org/hypo.html, a site of the Search and Rescue Society of British Columbia.

16. Shepard was so concerned about Hemmer's dazed condition and all the man knew about the capabilities of SOSUS, the Navy's acoustic ocean surveillance system, that he tried to remain close to him, to ensure against any unconscious, mumbled disclosures to the Russians.

17. He received aspirin but no other medication. In time the bruise went away, and Forshay easily passed Navy physicals for the next twenty years. He retired from active duty in the Naval Reserve in 1998.

Chapter 9. The Search Continues

1. Their postmission "purple" report spoke of looking for the "one crewmember [Grigsby] which [*sic*] was lost at sea." Detachment personnel on Adak had already decided among themselves that Miller was dead, but Grigsby's fate was less certain.

2. The *Krivak*s were a class of small combatant ships operated by the navy and by the border guards. Two unidentified Soviet Navy vessels would also appear and remain within a few miles of the abandoned Mark-12 through Saturday night, 28 October, despite weather that was then reported as "500 to 1,000 overcast, seas 30 feet, winds 310°/40 knots, white caps, visibility 1–2 miles." Gibbons was surprised to see how well the trailing *Krivak* was riding the seas.

3. Bud Powers, on the radio in the Patrol Wings Pacific command center and listening to everything during the crisis, would slowly get past the natural thought that with an aircraft in his squadron lost at sea his career was over, and move on with the last few months in squadron command. Powers would soon fly to Japan with Crew 6's medical

records, to greet them there on arrival from the Soviet Union. He would be denied the use of a squadron aircraft for the trip by the wing commander, and fly in a commercial airliner instead. Powers, a 1960 graduate of the Naval Academy, would later be selected for captain and retire in that grade in May 1987.

4. The DFC is traditionally awarded for "heroism or extraordinary achievement while participating in aerial flight." Gibbons was proposed for the Coast Guard's Gold Life Saving Medal, for his successful pursuit of the Mark-12 raft. The award was denied because one of the lives saved by his courageous action was his own.

Chapter 10. Petropavlovsk and Khabarovsk

1. This figure includes as many as twenty-five million civilian and military deaths during World War II alone. Mortality estimates are in Catherine Merridale, *Night of Stone, Death and Memory in Twentieth-Century Russia* (New York: Viking, 2001).

2. When AF 586 went down, the Soviet invasion of Afghanistan was still fourteen months away. Nine hard years would pass before the last Soviet soldier in Afghanistan, Gen. Boris Gromov, hiked across the Friendship Bridge back into the Uzbek SSR. Gromov's retreat confirmed the Red Army's first military failure in forty-five years, the first since its defeat of two German armies at Stalingrad. But not until the evaporation of East Germany and the Red Army's further humiliation in Chechnya would the West get a clear look at the wizard behind the curtain, and suddenly realize how badly it had overestimated its adversary's vitality, practically until the day of the collapse. Surprise at the collapse was near universal. An example is Caspar Weinberger, whose seven years as secretary of defense under President Ronald Reagan should have made him one of the best-informed people in Washington, if not in the world. Weinberger's first biography, *Fighting for Peace* (Norwalk, Conn.: Easton Press, 1990), reveals he was entirely unaware of the possibility of the Soviet Union's imminent implosion.

3. The next year Bering discovered the Aleutians and the Commander (Komondorski) Islands on the way to North America. He died in December 1741 of scurvy. In 1991, on the 250th anniversary of his death, the site of Bering's grave was discovered, aptly, on Bering Island.

4. The Voyska Protivovozdushnoy Oborony Strany, more commonly PVO Strany. Air defense was one of five separate services in Moscow's military structure.

5. Also a busy fishing grounds, but less a secure "lake" than it was thought to be. Beginning in 1971–72, the submarine USS *Halibut* repeatedly entered the Sea of O' covertly to tap the Soviet underwater communications cable between the submarine base at Petropavlovsk and fleet headquarters in Vladivostok. Sherry Sontag and Christopher Drew, *Blind Man's Bluff* (New York: Public Affairs, 1998).

6. U.S. engineers had the same time warp sensation when inspecting Lieutenant Victor Belenko's MIG-25 Foxbat, after he defected to Japan with it on 6 September 1976. Belenko's front-line air defense interceptor had a welded steel (no titanium) fuselage and its fire control radar used vacuum tube (not solid state) technology, both twenty years behind the U.S. state of the art. In twenty-five years, the world would change so much that a self-indulgent tourist could charter a demonstration flight "to the edge of space" in a Foxbat for $12,595.

7. During Brezhnev's last decade in power, Georgy Markovich Korniyenko was the foreign ministry's chief "Americanist," next to Foreign Minister Andrei Gromyko himself and to Anatoly Dobrynin, Moscow's "ambassador-for-life" in Washington. (Dobrynin was the Soviet ambassador through the terms of six presidents, Kennedy through Reagan.) Korniyenko's personal involvement is one indication of the high level of attention AF 586 received in the Soviet government.

8. Embassy cables go out over the signature of the ambassador automatically. Toon's personal participation in this incident, however, is confirmed by the message exchanges with Shulman and by Bud Powers's telephone conversations with the ambassador directly during the period Powers's crew was held in the USSR.

9. The families' anguish was unfortunate and unnecessary. The embassy's team at Khabarovsk had already reported that all ten men were "basically in very good condition," and its report was in Washington, in wing headquarters at Moffett Field and on Adak early Wednesday morning.

10. The photos were purchased from merchant seamen or fishermen, whose ships had access to the port. The U.S. Navy paid well for the many photographs it bought from these sources.

Chapter 11. Homecoming

1. The same "purple" was the source of the erroneous information that there were three rafts in the water, and that Scone 92 (called Gull 92 in the report by mistake) had "attempted location of surface vessels to assist with pickup." Headquarters, Fifth Air Force also referred to Cliff Carter's RC-135 as Gull 92.

2. The loss of this aircraft, call sign Juliet Bravo 022, is a story in its own right (a very short story, the flight lasted only fourteen minutes and twenty-seven seconds). JB 022's no. 4 propeller and gearbox were not recovered, so the cause of the initial failure was never established conclusively. Audio and most data channels of the flight recorder operated normally, however, so accident investigators were able to reconstruct the other events during the flight in great detail, including a stall and a momentary 11,400-feet-per-minute rate of descent during the first quarter turn of a spin before recovery was effected. JB 022 stalled again on short final approach as it slowed below minimum control speed, at 38 feet altitude, and then the right wing tip hit the water. The aircraft splashed down at 127 knots (146 mph) weighing more than sixty-two tons. The impact tore the wings from the fuselage, and broke it into three pieces. The five deaths were from drowning. Lt. Bob Verschure, the plane commander and one of the survivors, had 1,270 pilot hours in the P-3.

3. The lack of information to the squadron from Department of Defense comm. channels is striking. Very few, a handful, of the literally hundreds of messages about AF 586 that flew between interested commands included Patrol Squadron 9 or its Adak detachment in their address.

4. This account is taken from the Powers's recollections. Others, officers on the Wing staff, remember Admiral and Mrs. Prindle's roles very differently, describing him as extremely supportive of the squadron and instructing his staff to be as helpful as possible.

5. Media interest in the men was intense, albeit fleeting. Crew 6's audience included AP,

UPI, ABC, CBS, NBC, television and radio, and all four daily newspapers in the San Francisco area, with the result that the press conference stretched to half an hour. Even though they were treated with deference, the crew found the experience trying enough that shortly thereafter they refused a request by a national morning news show's producers to fly to New York to appear on their network TV broadcast. The refusal disappointed the Pacific Fleet's public affairs officer, who welcomed the opportunity for Navy visibility on network television.

6. Perhaps anticipating this result, Howard Moore had annotated his travel reimbursement voucher before he submitted it. "Living conditions," he observed on 6 December, "in a liferaft with four people while being buffeted by high waves and most inclement weather is [sic] most unacceptable. Per diem while in Russian territory unknown, notwithstanding the caviar and vodka served." His good-humored appeal for special consideration got him nothing.

Chapter 12. Postmortem

1. Patrol Squadron 9's two most senior enlisted men in the maintenance department came to it from attack squadrons, with no prior service in a maritime patrol squadron and with no experience in the P-3 aircraft.

2. The flights out of Cubi Point were styled as the "First Annual Joan Baez Boat People Hunt," honoring the singer-activist, who reportedly flew aboard one of them. Matt Gibbons swapped ditching stories with the survivors of the Patrol Squadron 22 accident when he passed through the Philippines.

3. The title "commodore" was an honorific. MacKay was a senior captain at the time. A few years later he would be promoted to rear admiral and move to Moffett Field to command the Pacific Fleet's patrol squadrons.

4. For a sympathetic natural history of the albatross, see Carl Safina, *Eye of the Albatross: Visions of Hope and Survival* (New York: Henry Holt, 2002). One in ten of the fledgling albatross chicks Safina saw learning to fly over Tern Island (770 miles southeast of Midway) was eaten by tiger sharks waiting in the lagoon below.

5. The failure did happen again, ironically the very next time it was with Bud Powers in the left seat and Howard Moore as the in-flight observer in the tube. They landed on three engines.

6. Engineering Change Proposal (ECP) 936, which defined the work package on new production aircraft, was approved on 23 October 1980 and introduced in November 1981 with Buno. 161336, the ninety-first aircraft to come off the assembly line after PD-2. Three years later, in August, a similar program was approved for aircraft out of production and going through overhaul at the rework facility at Alameda, California, where Jerry Grigsby had been assigned almost fifteen years before. The first modification of an aircraft in service, however, was not actually done until May 1987.

7. U.S. communications with the official addressed him as "Soviet Fleet Commander Alexeev," but Alexeev himself used the lesser title of "expedition chief." Alexeev's message of condolence to the 17th Coast Guard District Commander late on 31 October said that *Sinyavin* and an otherwise unidentified second vessel, *Belkina,* "did all in their power" to save American lives.

Bibliography

Books

Andrew, Christopher, and Vasili Mitrokhin. *The Sword and the Shield.* New York: Basic Books, 1999.

Bamford, James. *Body of Secrets.* New York: Doubleday, 2001.

Bauer, K. Jack. *A Maritime History of the United States.* Columbia: University of South Carolina Press, 1988.

Bockstoce, John. *Whales, Ice and Men.* Seattle: University of Washington Press, 1986.

Burrows, William E. *By Any Means Necessary.* New York: Farrar, Straus & Giroux, 2001.

Callahan, Steven. *Adrift.* Boston: Houghton Mifflin, 1986.

Carter, Miranda. *Anthony Blunt.* New York: Farrar, Straus & Giroux, 2001.

Cook, Nobel David. *Born to Die.* Cambridge: Cambridge University Press, 1998.

Dillon, Patrick. *Lost at Sea.* New York: Dial, 1998.

Ellis, Richard. *Aquagenesis.* New York: Viking, 2001.

Halberstam, David. *War in a Time of Peace.* New York: Scribner's, 2001.

Hurley, Frank. *South with Endurance: Shackleton's Antarctic Expedition, 1914–1917.* New York: Simon & Schuster, 2001.

Kilmarx, Robert A., ed. *America's Maritime Legacy.* Boulder, Colo.: Westview Press, 1979.

Kohlhoff, Dean. *When the Wind Was a River: Aleut Evacuation in World War II.* Seattle: University of Washington Press, 1995.

Merridale, Catherine. *Night of Stone: Death and Memory in Twentieth-Century Russia.* New York: Viking, 2001.

Robinson, D. H., and C. L. Keller. *Up Ship.* Annapolis: Naval Institute Press, 1982.

Safina, Carl. *Eye of the Albatross: Visions of Hope and Survival.* New York: Henry Holt, 2002.

Shirer, William. *The Rise and Fall of the Third Reich.* New York: Simon & Schuster, 1960.

Sontag, Sherry, and Christopher Drew. *Blind Man's Bluff.* New York: Public Affairs, 1998.

Stark, Peter. *Last Breath, Cautionary Tales from the Limits of Human Endurance.* New York: Ballantine, 2001.

Trumbull, Robert. *The Raft.* New York: Henry Holt, 1942.

Valle, James E. *Rocks and Shoals.* Annapolis: Naval Institute Press, 1980.

Watts, Sheldon. *Epidemics and History.* New Haven, Conn.: Yale University Press, 1997.

Weinberger, Caspar. *Fighting for Peace.* Norwalk, Conn.: Easton Press, 1990.
Worsley, F. A. *Shackleton's Boat Journey.* New York: Norton, 1977.

Articles

Harrison, Jeff. "They Said It Would Never Happen." *Foundation Magazine,* Spring 1997,
    15–20.
Porter, Bill. "Manislov [*sic*], This Is Bill." *Alaska Magazine,* December 1979. Online at
    http://www.upnavy.com/upg_mishap.html.
Stark, Peter. "As Freezing Persons Recollect the Snow . . . the Cold Hard Facts of Freezing to
    Death." *Outside Magazine,* January 1997. Online at http://www.outsidemag.com/maga-
    zine/0197/9701fefreez.html.

About the Author

Andrew Jampoler lives in the Lost Corner of Loudoun County, Virginia, with his wife, Susan, a professional geographer, and two golden retrievers. They have married children in Pennsylvania and Iowa.

His last flight as a P-3 Orion patrol plane commander from Naval Station Adak, Alaska, was in December 1976, twenty-one months before Alfa Foxtrot 586 went down. While in the Navy, Jampoler commanded Patrol Squadron 19 and Naval Air Station Moffett Field, California, and logged more than three thousand pilot hours in P-3A and P-3C aircraft. More recently, he was a senior sales and marketing executive with American and German companies.

Jampoler is a graduate of Columbia College and the School of International and Public Affairs, both of Columbia University, in New York City, and of the Foreign Service Institute's School of Language Study.

Adak is his first book. He is now at work on a book recounting the true story of a Navy small boat expedition down the River Jordan and across the Dead Sea in 1848.